Yale Historical Publications, Miscellany, 100

Between Science and Religion

The Reaction to Scientific Naturalism in Late Victorian England

Frank Miller Turner

New Haven and London, Yale University Press

Designed by John O. C. McCrillis
and set in Baskerville type.
Printed in the United States of America by
Alpine Press, South Braintree, Massachusetts.

Published in Great Britain, Europe, Africa, and Asia
by Yale University Press, Ltd., London.
Distributed in Latin America by Kaiman & Polon, Inc.,
New York City; and in Australia and New Zealand by Book & Film
Services, Artarmon, N.S.W., Australia.

For Peggy

Contents

Preface

A chief feature of European intellectual life since the Enlightenment has been the search for alternatives to Christianity as a determinant of personal and social values. Quite often that pursuit has in one way or another involved appeals to the theories or methods of physical science. This was particularly true during the second half of the nineteenth century, when the religion of science found articulate spokesmen throughout the Western world. This study deals with six late nineteenth-century Englishmen who abandoned the Christian faith but then found it impossible to accept in its stead the scientific naturalism that proved so attractive to many of their contemporaries.

Why these six particular figures—Henry Sidgwick, Alfred Russel Wallace, Frederic Myers, George Romanes, Samuel Butler, and James Ward—if, as noted in chapter 1, others might have been treated? In the first place, they stand outside two other reactions to naturalistic thought about which considerable information is already available—those of liberal Christians and British Hegelians. By examining writers outside these two areas, it seemed that a new dimension might be added to present understanding of late Victorian intellectual life. Second, this group provides a reasonably complete cross-section of the English intellectual community since it includes two academic philosophers, two scientists, and two men of letters. Moreover, their productive lives extend roughly from 1860 to 1914, with Wallace coming a few years earlier and Ward living a few years later. The productive years of other men who might have been included, such as James Hinton, Oliver Lodge, or Havelock Ellis, fall somewhat before 1860 or after World War I. Finally, each man chosen left a body of work and manuscripts sufficient to permit a reasonably intimate examination of his religious and moral thought. Only for James Ward are meaningful manuscript sources lacking.

Professor Franklin L. Baumer guided this study through its dissertation stage with never-failing sympathy and good humor tempered with critical rigor. I am more than happy to acknowledge his suggestion to consider these men as dwelling between the contemporary versions of science and religion; hence the title of the study. Professor Sydney Ahlstrom read and commented on several early drafts. Martin Griffin, Ronald Jager, and R. Laurence Moore offered much useful criticism. At Yale University Press Edward Tripp gave me warm encouragement and Judy Metro saved me from many an unfortunate slip of pen and turn of phrase. I should also like to acknowledge a long-standing debt of gratitude to Professors Bruce McCully, Harold Fowler, and Richard Sherman of The College of William and Mary, who did not directly contribute to this book but who introduced me while an undergraduate to the pleasures of history.

I should like to express my appreciation for the generous financial support underwriting research and manuscript preparation provided by the Danforth Foundation of St. Louis, Missouri, the Yale University Council of Comparative and European Studies, and the Yale History Department. As a dissertation this study received the John Addison Porter Prize of Yale University.

For allowing me to examine manuscripts I should like to thank the Bristol University Library; the British Museum; the Imperial College of Science and Technology, London; the Linnean Society, London; the Royal Botanical Library at Kew; the Society for Psychical Research, London; the Trinity College Library, Cambridge; the University Library, Cambridge; the University of Edinburgh Library; and the Chapin Library, Williams College, Williamstown, Massachusetts. I should also like to thank the following persons for permitting me to quote from unpublished manuscripts for which they retain copyright privileges: Miss S. C. Campbell; Mr. Brian Hill and Sir Geoffrey Keynes, literary executors of Samuel Butler; Mrs. E. Q. Nicholson; Mr. Giles Romanes; Mr. C. Sidgwick; Mr. John Wallace; and Mr. Richard Wallace. Professor Alan Gauld and the late Professor C. D. Broad were most helpful in aiding me to locate manuscripts.

My deepest and most pleasant debt of thanks I owe to my wife, who will now happily be able to find other books to read.

As usual, the errors of omission and commission remain my own.

F. M. T.

New Haven, Connecticut
April 1973

Between Science and Religion

1

Between Science and Religion

"A narrowly conceived science," Gordon Allport once observed, "can never do business with a narrowly conceived religion."[1] He might have added as a corollary that men who construe both religion and science broadly can rarely do business with men who conceive either one narrowly. The figures whose lives and thought will be explored in the following pages encountered this latter impasse. During the years of the Victorian crisis of faith they found the Christianity in which they had been reared too limited for their intellects and the scientific naturalism that bid for their allegiance too restrictive for the range of their ideals and aspirations. Consequently, in terms of their contemporary intellectual and social environment, they came to dwell between the science that beckoned them and the religion they had forsaken.

At first sight these men appear a rather mixed lot. Two of them, Henry Sidgwick and James Ward, were Cambridge philosophers. The former specialized in ethics and political philosophy; the latter in psychology and metaphysics. Alfred Russel Wallace and George John Romanes were scientists. Wallace was the co-discoverer of evolution by natural selection. Romanes pursued the study of physiology and comparative psychology. Frederic W. H. Myers and Samuel Butler were men of letters. Myers wrote poetry and critical essays and explored psychology and psychical research. Like Ward, he had studied with Henry Sidgwick. Samuel Butler was the author of several books, among them *Erewhon* and *The Way of All Flesh*. He became noted for his quarrel with Charles Darwin and for his peculiar capacity to exasperate most of his contemporaries.

What allows Sidgwick, Wallace, Myers, Romanes, Butler, and Ward to constitute a group within the context of Victorian intellectual history is their common discovery that

1. Gordon Allport, *The Individual and His Religion: A Psychological Interpretation* (New York: Macmillan Co., 1950), p. vi.

> just as the old orthodoxy of religion was too narrow to contain
> men's knowledge, so now the new orthodoxy of materialistic
> science is too narrow to contain their feelings and aspirations;
> and consequently . . . just as the fabric of religious orthodoxy
> used to be strained in order to admit the discoveries of geology
> or astronomy, so now also the obvious deductions of material-
> istic science are strained or overpassed in order to give sanction
> to feelings and aspirations which it is found impossible to
> ignore.[2]

These men generally accepted the concepts and theories of science.
At one time or another each had contributed to the naturalistic
synthesis or had been trained in scientific procedures and philosophy
or had been profoundly affected by its ideas. Yet they could not
accept the proposition that all valid human experiences and ideals
could be expressed through or subsumed under existing scientific
categories and laws. This opposition to scientific naturalism did not
represent a rearguard defense of Christianity. These writers had
fully relinquished the Christian concepts of God, the Incarnation,
redemptive salvation, miracles, and scriptural revelation. Nonetheless, they could not forsake the questions and experiences that these
and other Christian doctrines had in one manner or another interpreted.

As early as 1852 James Martineau, the most distinguished of
nineteenth-century English Unitarians, had described the intellectual
paradox that would spawn this dual protest against the dogmas of
both contemporary Christianity and science.

> There is . . . a certain secret affinity of feeling between a
> Religion which exaggerates the functions and overstrains the
> validity of an external authority, and a Science which deals only
> with objective facts, perceived or imagined. The point of sym-
> pathy is found in a common distrust of everything internal, even
> of the very faculties (as soon as they are contemplated as such)
> by which the external is apprehended and received. And be-
> tween this sort of faith and the mathematics there is another
> analogy, which may explain so curious a mutual understanding.
> Both rest upon *hypotheses,* which it is beyond their province to

2. F. W. H. Myers, Introduction, to *Phantasms of the Living,* by E. Gurney, F. W. H. Myers, and F. Podmore (London: Trubner & Co., 1886), 1 : liv–v.

look into, but after the assumption of which, all room for opinion is shut out by a rigid necessity. *Once get* your infallible book, and (supposing the meaning unambiguous) it settles every matter on which it pronounces; and once allow the first principles and definitions in geometry to express truths and realities, and you can deny nothing afterwards.[3]

Just as the piety and bibliolatry of Evangelicalism had bred the honest doubter in matters of religion, so also the narrow confines of the dogmatic science of T. H. Huxley, John Tyndall, and Herbert Spencer nurtured a new variety of honest doubter who questioned the all-sufficiency of contemporary scientific concepts, theories, and categories to describe and interpret every facet of life.

Frederic Myers suggested the temper of this new doubt in 1893 when he remarked, "There are still those who, while accepting to the full the methods and results of Science, will not yet surrender the ancient hopes of our race." [4] Most of those ancient hopes involved the nature of man and his place in the universe. They included various beliefs whereby men had conceived of themselves as possessing uniquely human characteristics, such as moral personalities, creative minds, the capacity to lead rational lives, a potential for transcendental knowledge, immortality, and a destiny that partook of a divine or transcendental purpose. The unbelievers in this study sought to preserve such ancient hopes outside the context of Christianity and within a broadly construed scientific framework or at least an intellectual framework that was not wholly incompatible with scientific knowledge.

Those ancient hopes in one way or another supplied the spiritual needs of these men. The word *spiritual* is one of the most difficult and important terms in late nineteenth-century thought. Usually its meaning excluded Christian doctrine and ceremony but preserved in a non-Christian context the questions, issues, and problems of human life previously addressed by that faith. H. V. Routh has given perhaps the best expression of what *spiritual* suggested to men in the second half of the century.

3. James Martineau, *Studies in Christianity* (Boston: American Unitarian Association, 1900), p. 395.

4. Myers, *Science and a Future Life with Other Essays* (London: Macmillan & Co., 1893), p. 192.

> It implies, in the first place, that the speaker has cultivated a system of principles, an edifice of ideas, an ideology, which gives shape and direction to his plexus and nexus of thought. This framework, partly inherited, is cherished because it is congenial to the individual's aspirations; it helps him contemplate humanity as a force capable of growth even to perfection; it suggests forms in which his own vitality can find imaginative self-expression.[5]

To maintain such a mental edifice, each figure in this study felt compelled to recognize dimensions of human life often neglected in naturalistic literature. In relation to the prevailing reductionist naturalism, they embraced what might best be termed "extranaturalism." [6] In effect they said to the leaders of scientific naturalism, as Hamlet once said to his companion: "There are more things in heaven and earth, Horatio, / Than are dreamt of in your philosophy" (act 1, scene 5). Yet in voicing similar sentiments, they were no more defending the Christian faith than was the troubled Danish prince.

Nevertheless, in seeking what Henry Sidgwick termed "a final reconcilement of spiritual needs with intellectual principles," each man eventually pursued a variety of religious life defined by William James as a belief "that there is an unseen order, and that our supreme good lies in harmoniously adjusting ourselves thereto." They embraced that belief, however, only after convincing themselves that they could not meaningfully guide their lives with reference solely to the visible world. Their religious life consisted of what Gordon Allport has characterized as a "ceaseless struggle to assimilate the scientific frame of thought within an expanded religious frame." The struggle arose from a determination to overcome the apparent incommensurability between their spiritual aspirations and the doctrines of science.

> A person with a mature religious sentiment characteristically attempts this course, and though he seldom succeeds perfectly, he continues to affirm the ultimate possibility of so doing. Under no circumstances will he side-step or disparage the scien-

5. H. V. Routh, *Towards the Twentieth Century: Essays in the Spiritual History of the Nineteenth* (New York: Macmillan Co., 1937), p. 4.

6. The term "extranaturalism" is borrowed from John Dewey but does not denote the same meaning that he ascribed to it. See John Dewey, "Antinaturalism in Extremis," in *Naturalism and the Human Spirit*, ed. Yervant H. Krikorian (New York: Columbia University Press, 1944), p. 2.

tific mode of doubting, but under no circumstances will he allow it to curtail the range of his curiosity or aspiration.

Ward, Romanes, Butler, Sidgwick, Wallace, and Myers simply refused to exchange the alleged certainty of science for the emotional and intellectual disappointment of abandoning what Whitehead would later term the "perplexing fundamental questions" usually associated with metaphysics and religion.[7] They would not tolerate the curtailment of curiosity and the limitation of moral horizon that acceptance of scientific naturalism seemed to require.

Though neither Christians nor scientists on the whole approved of the ideas of Myers, Butler, Wallace, and the rest, the latter were not wanting for compatriots at home or abroad. They were part of the English contingent in the widespread late nineteenth-century protest against the pretensions of science to dominate thought and culture. Within Britain, authors such as Edmund Gurney, Edward Carpenter, Walter Leaf, Oliver Lodge, George Bernard Shaw, and F. C. S. Schiller generally approved their endeavor. In America William James proved a kindred spirit. In France Ravaisson, Boutroux, and Bergson spoke from a similar point of view, as did Lotze in Germany and many continental writers who probed the non-rational side of human nature and the unconscious.[8]

Near the turn of the century, Havelock Ellis, another like-minded author, composed a dialogue in which one of his characters, after reviewing the rise of science in the nineteenth century, epitomized the thought of these non-Christian opponents of scientific naturalism.

Enormous as the mission of science must then have appeared, it was of course foolish to worship science; it would have been as

7. H. Sidgwick to Roden Noel, February or March 1862, in A. and E. Sidgwick, *Henry Sidgwick: A Memoir* (London: Macmillan & Co., 1906), p. 75; William James, *The Varieties of Religious Experience* (New York: Random House, Modern Library, 1929), p. 53; Allport, *The Individual and His Religion*, p. 116; ibid.; A. N. Whitehead, *Adventures of Ideas* (New York: New American Library, Mentor Books, 1962), p. 130.

8. Antonio Aliotta, *The Idealistic Reaction against Science* (London: Macmillan & Co., 1914); Alfred Fouillée, *Le Mouvement Idéaliste et la Réaction contre la Science Positive* (Paris: Ancienne Librairie Gemer Braillière et Cie, 1896), pp. 5–68; J. A. Gunn, *Modern French Philosophy, 1851–1921* (London: Allen and Unwin, 1922); Harald Höffding, *A History of Modern Philosophy*, trans. B. E. Meyer (London: Macmillan & Co., 1915), 2 : 508–24; H. Stuart Hughes, *Consciousness and Society: The Reorientation of European Social Thought, 1890–1930* (New York: Random House, Vintage Books, 1958), pp. 33–66; D. Parodi, *Du Positivisme à l'idéalisme* (Paris: Librairie Philosophique J. Vrin, 1930), pp. 88–103.

reasonable to worship the bipedal attitude which, by liberating men's upper limbs, led to the development of our hands, the primary instruments of science. Science was merely mechanical aptitude, the aptitude to make and to measure. It was a condition of human civilization, and one of its most essential conditions. But it was no more than that, and in itself could never furnish any guide to life.[9]

This was the very protest that Sidgwick, Wallace, Myers, Romanes, Butler, and Ward lodged against the scientific writers who sought to remold English culture in their own image.

The complaint focused on three major considerations. In the first place, these men questioned the integrity of the naturalistic interpretation of man and nature. They argued that men of science and their nonprofessional advocates generally refused to investigate external phenomena that might suggest the inadequacy of present scientific theory or the existence of a spirit realm. They also believed that scientific writers too often dismissed certain subjective elements of human experience that implied a nonphysical nature in man or in the universe. In this respect, they belong to the tradition of European thought that Professor Mandelbaum has termed "metaphysical idealism," for they contended "that within natural human experience one can find the clue to an understanding of the ultimate nature of reality, and this clue is revealed through those traits which distinguish man as a spiritual being." [10] Sidgwick, Myers, and Wallace thought psychical occurrences might provide objective empirical evidence of a spiritual realm and of the existence of mind or personality in disassociation from a physical body. Romanes, Butler, and Ward believed a thorough introspective examination of the human mind provided evidence that mechanistic nature was only an appearance or a mode of an underlying nonmechanical reality.

Second, along with critical writers throughout Europe they challenged the philosophical foundations of scientific naturalism. Sidgwick denied that science was actually pursued according to an empirical epistemology. Butler contended that reason itself was rooted in nonrational impulses. James Ward accused the exponents of

9. Havelock Ellis, *The Nineteenth Century: A Dialogue in Utopia* (London: Grant Richards, 1900), p. 48.

10. Maurice Mandelbaum, *History, Man, & Reason: A Study in Nineteenth-Century Thought* (Baltimore: Johns Hopkins Press, 1971), p. 6.

naturalism of confusing concepts with reality. All of them denied the capacity of scientific thought to provide philosophical justification for the first principles of scientific investigation. If scientists could not provide an adequate philosophy for their own procedures, how could they provide an adequate philosophy for other men?

Finally, and most important, these men contended that the theories and methods of scientific naturalism failed to deal logically, rationally, or adequately with certain inevitable human questions, such as "What ought I to do?" Sidgwick discovered that he could not construct on strictly naturalistic premises a system of ethics providing for rational decisions. Myers found naturalism totally impotent before the specter of death. Wallace perceived that science might provide principles for improving technology but not values to direct the use of that technology. These were very telling criticisms for, if correct, they disclosed the failure of scientific naturalism to fulfill the much-vaunted promise of its adherents to provide a complete guide to life. This promise justified the claim of men of science to lead and to redirect the culture of late Victorian England.

2

Victorian Scientific Naturalism

"Science touched the imagination by its tangible results," declared G. M. Young of early Victorian England.[1] Over the course of Queen Victoria's reign, those tangible results multiplied rapidly and extensively. The average Englishman came to enjoy better food, softer clothing, and a warmer home. Although his landscape might have become less lovely and the air he breathed less pure, he could live longer and dwell in greater security from the vicissitudes of nature than any man before him. The seventeenth-century Baconian vision of science come to the aid of man's estate reflected itself in so many facets of daily life that by the year of the queen's golden jubilee, T. H. Huxley could boast without exaggeration of a "new Nature created by science" manifested in "every mechanical artifice, every chemically pure substance employed in manufacture, every abnormally fertile race of plants, or rapidly growing and fattening breed of animals."[2]

Huxley and many of his contemporaries considered the quality of life so fully transformed as to require an almost complete reorientation in the thought and expectations of men and society. The New Nature itself, rather than God, heaven, or human nature, now furnished the chief points of reference for the organization and direction of life. "[T]his new Nature begotten by science upon fact," continued Huxley, had come to constitute

> the foundation of our wealth and the condition of our safety from submergence by another flood of barbarous hordes; it is the bond which unites into a solid political whole, regions larger than any empire of antiquity; it secures us from the recurrence of pestilences and famines of former times; it is the

1. G. M. Young, *Victorian England: Portrait of an Age,* 2nd ed. (New York: Oxford University Press, 1964), p. 7. See also Walter Houghton, *The Victorian Frame of Mind, 1830–1870* (New Haven: Yale University Press, 1957), pp. 33–45.

2. T. H. Huxley, *Collected Essays* (New York: D. Appleton & Co., 1894), 1 : 51.

source of endless comforts and conveniences, which are not mere luxuries, but conduce to physical and moral well-being.[3]

Huxley and others believed the New Nature and the scientific theories associated with it sufficient for the expression, explanation, and guidance of human life. A wholly secular culture seemed altogether possible.

Nevertheless, Huxley realized that before the complete physical and moral benefits of the New Nature could be enjoyed, two tasks must be accomplished. First, the ordinary Englishman must be persuaded to look toward rational, scientific, and secular ideas to solve his problems and to interpret his experiences rather than toward Christian, metaphysical, or other prescientific modes of thought. Second, scientifically trained and scientifically oriented men must supplant clergymen and Christian laymen as educators and leaders of English culture.[4] The champions of the New Nature set out to publicize the advantages of embracing scientific and secular ideas and of acknowledging the cultural preeminence of men of science. That the tomb of Newton in Westminster Abbey stands surrounded by the graves and monuments of Victorian scientists illustrates not only the achievements of the latter but also the success of the nineteenth-century publicists in establishing a favorable image of science in the public mind.

Not since the genius of the seventeenth-century virtuosi stirred learned imaginations had so many eloquent voices praised the cause of science. The leadership of this effort to educate and to persuade the public consisted of Huxley himself, professor of biology at the Royal School of Mines and chief apologist for Charles Darwin; John Tyndall, a physicist and successor to Faraday as superintendent of the Royal Institution; Herbert Spencer, the philosopher par excellence of evolution; W. K. Clifford, an outspoken mathematician at University College, London; and Sir Francis Galton, cousin of Charles Darwin, a eugenicist, a statistician, and an advocate of professionalism in science. Another coterie related to this core

3. Ibid.
4. John Tyndall, *Fragments of Science*, 6th ed. (New York: D. Appleton & Co., 1892), 2 : 1–8, 40–45; Francis Galton, *English Men of Science: Their Nature and Nurture* (New York: D. Appleton & Co., 1875); John Morley, *The Struggle for National Education* (London: Chapman & Hall, 1873); and the anonymous article "The National Importance of Research," *Westminster Review* 99 (1873) : 343–66.

leadership but more closely associated with English Positivism included Frederic Harrison, a lawyer and leading English Positivist; John Morley, a freethinker and the editor of *Fortnightly Review,* in which most of these men published; and G. H. Lewes, Positivist, historian, and psychologist. Anthropologists, such as Edward Tylor and John Lubbock, extended the theories of science into the study of society. Biologist E. Ray Lankester and physician Henry Maudsley wrote and spoke on behalf of naturalistic ideas. Among essayists and men of letters who advocated the cause of science, Leslie Stephen was the outstanding author. He was joined by lesser literary figures, such as Grant Allen and Edward Clodd. The list could be greatly expanded.

These men rarely stood in complete agreement with one another. None of them embraced all the specific ideas and theories associated with the movement in the public mind. On more than one occasion they indulged in the luxury of internecine quarrels. Huxley was an avowed enemy of Positivism; Spencer was a Lamarckian. Few scientific writers were so enamored with the determinism of the nebular hypothesis as was Tyndall. The movement for scientific publicism was thus far from monolithic; it was not even coterminous with Victorian science. However, these authors knew and visited one another, enjoyed mutual friends, cited one another in their books and articles, and sparred with mutual enemies. A composite of their leading ideas may risk presenting a caricature of the thought of any single figure but will nevertheless suggest the image that even the sophisticated reading public gleaned from their works. For what impressed contemporaries far more than their differences was the unity of their conviction that "in the struggle of life with the facts of existence, Science is a bringer of aid; in the struggle of the soul with the mystery of existence, Science is a bringer of light." [5]

Settling upon a label for a movement united more by common sentiment than by specific ideas or goals was a problem that plagued the participants as well as the historian. John Morley recalled that during the early days of the *Fortnightly Review,* "People quarreled for a short season whether we should be labelled Comtist, Positivist,

5. G. H. Lewes, "On the Dread and Dislike of Science," *Fortnightly Review* 29 (1878) : 805. See also J. Vernon Jensen, "The X Club: Fraternity of Victorian Scientists," *British Journal for the History of Science* 5 (1970–71) : 63–72. Consult the Bibliographical Essay for some of the numerous books and articles on these men and the institutions with which they were associated.

Naturalist. They were conscious of a certain concurrence in the writers, though it was not easy to define." [6] While no single word or phrase will exactly describe the cluster of men and ideas associated with Huxley's New Nature or perhaps avoid creating another of what Lovejoy termed "trouble-breeding and usually thought-obscuring terms," *Victorian scientific naturalism* appears more inclusive than any other phrase.[7] *Positivism* cannot serve because of Huxley's vehement antipathy to the sect and because in England Positivism was simply one part of the larger effort to advance science in the public forum. *Scientism* was coined during the period but seems to have had little vogue until the twentieth century. *Rationalism* fails to suggest the crucial role of science in addition to critical reasoning. *Free thought* is simply too imprecise. By the close of the nineteenth century, the words *naturalism* or *naturalistic* appear to be the terms employed most frequently to denote the movement associated with contemporary scientific men and ideas. By 1902 "Naturalism" had received an entry (discarded in 1970) in the *Encyclopaedia Britannica.*[8]

Though the nature of its thought stemmed from the seventeenth-century scientific revolution and represented a further extension of the "touch of cold philosophy," the movement was distinctly Victorian in that it arose and flourished in circumstances unique to the period 1850 to 1900. By that era the reality of the New Nature had fully emerged so as to grant plausibility to a wholly secular life. Moreover, the midcentury public-health campaign, the effort after

6. John Viscount Morley, *Works of Lord Morley* (London: Macmillan & Co., 1921), 1 : 81.

7. Arthur O. Lovejoy, *The Great Chain of Being: A Study in the History of an Idea* (New York: Harper Torchbooks, 1960), p. 6.

8. See Sydney Eisen, "Huxley and the Positivists," *Victorian Studies* 7 (1964) : 337–58; "Scientism," *Oxford English Dictionary* (Oxford: The Clarendon Press, 1933), 9 : 223; A. W. Benn, *A History of English Rationalism in the Nineteenth Century* (London: Longmans, Green & Co., 1906), 1 : 1–58; J. M. Robertson, *A History of Freethought* (New York: G. P. Putnam's Sons, 1930); A. J. Balfour, *The Foundations of Belief* (London: Longmans, Green & Co., 1895); H. W. Blunt, "Philosophy and Naturalism," *Proceedings of the Aristotelian Society* 3, no. 2, (1896) : 43–51; C. Lloyd Morgan, "Naturalism," *Monist* 6 (1895) : 76–90; Andrew Seth, " 'Naturalism' in Recent Discussions," *The Philosophical Review* 5 (1896) : 576–84; W. R. Sorley, *On the Ethics of Naturalism* (Edinburgh and London: W. Blackwood & Sons, 1885), pp. 16–21, 277; James Ward, *Naturalism and Agnosticism*, 2 vols. (London: A. and C. Black, 1899); and *Encyclopaedia Britannica*, 11th ed., s.v. "Naturalism." Balfour's book and the responses it evoked were primarily responsible for giving currency to *naturalism* as the term under which scientific writing and philosophy became subsumed.

the repeal of the Corn Laws to make farming more efficient, and later the necessity of meeting the threat of German industrial competition intimately related science to the affairs of business and everyday life. Furthermore, during the second half of the century numerous men of science, partly because of the earlier debates over geology and partly because of the necessity of finding employment, relinquished, if they did not openly renounce, the time-honored belief that the scientist's occupation complemented that of the clergy by discovering the glory of God in nature.[9] From the 1850s onward scientists consciously moved toward greater professionalism involving social and intellectual emancipation from theology and financial independence from aristocratic patronage. Finally, this period marked what would appear to be the last era when the essential theories of science could be understood by the layman without training in advanced mathematics. Such a comprehension on the part of laymen was essential for the popularization of new scientific theories around which they were encouraged to organize their lives.

The movement was scientifically naturalistic in that it derived its repudiation of supernaturalism and its new interpretations of man, nature, and society from the theories, methods, and categories of empirical science rather than from rational analysis.[10] Beatrice Webb described the "religion of science," which for a time attracted her, as "an implicit faith that by the methods of physical science, and by these methods alone, could be solved all the problems arising out of the relation of man to man and of man towards the universe." [11]

9. See C. C. Gillispie, *Genesis and Geology: A Study in the Relations of Scientific Thought, Natural Theology, and Social Opinion in Great Britain, 1790–1850* (New York: Harper Torchbooks, 1959); Robert Young, "The Impact of Darwin on Conventional Thought," in *The Victorian Crisis of Faith*, ed. A. Symondson (London: Society for Promoting Christian Knowledge, 1970), pp. 13–35; George Basalla, William Coleman, and Robert H. Kargon, eds., *Victorian Science: A Self-portrait from the Presidential Addresses to the British Association for the Advancement of Science* (Garden City, N.Y.: Doubleday & Co., 1970).

10. Noel Annan, "The Strands of Unbelief," and J. Bronowski, "Unbelief and Science," in *Ideas and Beliefs of the Victorians*, ed. H. Grisewood (New York: E. P. Dutton & Co., 1966), pp. 150–56, 164–72.

11. Beatrice Webb, *My Apprenticeship* (London: Longmans, Green & Co., 1926), p. 83. Mrs. Webb's chapter on the religious turmoil of her late adolescence is exceptionally revealing since much of it is taken from her diary. Her rejection of both Christianity and the religion of science closely resembles the figures examined in this study.

In this regard Victorian scientific naturalism represented the English version of a general cult of science that swept across Europe during the second half of the century and that was associated with the names of Renan, Taine, Bernard, Buchner, and Haeckel as well as with various forms of scientific materialism and scientific socialism.[12]

The intimate relation of Victorian scientific naturalism to contemporary science renders the movement not only datable but also distinctly dated. Its exponents aligned themselves with the specific physical theories of the third quarter of the century and uncritically accepted the current concept of scientific law. The new physics of Rutherford and Einstein rendered their picture of nature obsolete. Twentieth-century philosophy of science redefined the nature of scientific laws. Consequently, the specific concepts of Victorian scientific naturalism became largely outmoded and no longer proved a source of present or enduring wisdom. As one historian has commented, "None of the nineteenth-century scientific publicists is of any great importance as a philosopher." [13]

Nevertheless, between 1850 and 1900 the advocates of scientific naturalism exercised a considerable influence in Britain. Any thinking man or woman found himself compelled to consider what they said. Beatrice Webb, remembering her youthful friendships with Spencer, Huxley, Tyndall, and Galton, wrote:

> [W]ho will deny that the men of science were the leading British intellectuals of that period; that it was they who stood out as men of genius with international reputations; that it was

12. D. G. Charlton, *Positivist Thought in France during the Second Empire* (Oxford: The Clarendon Press, 1959); Friedrich Albert Lange, *The History of Materialism and Criticism of Its Present Importance*, trans. Ernest Chester Thomas (London: Routledge & K. Paul, 1957); Maurice Mandelbaum, *History, Man, & Reason: A Study in Nineteenth-Century Thought* (Baltimore: Johns Hopkins Press, 1971), pp. 10–28; George Mosse, *The Culture of Western Europe: The Nineteenth and Twentieth Centuries* (New York: Rand McNally & Co., 1961), pp. 197–212; John Herman Randall, Jr., *The Making of the Modern Mind*, rev. ed. (New York: Houghton Mifflin Co., 1954), p. 458–576.

13. John Passmore, *A Hundred Years of Philosophy* (London: Penguin Books, 1968), p. 48. For a series of discussions of the modifications in scientific theory that undermined the nineteenth-century scientific world view, see Herbert Dingle, ed., *A Century of Science, 1851–1951* (London: Hutchinson's Scientific and Technical Publications, 1951) and J. Bronowski, *The Common Sense of Science* (London: William Heinemann, Ltd., 1951), pp. 97–119. For a more broad-ranging discussion of the problem of epistemology in light of twentieth-century science, see Stephen Toulmin, *Human Understanding* (Oxford: The Clarendon Press, 1972).

they who were the self-confident militants of the period; that it
was they who were routing the theologians, confounding the
mystics, imposing their theories on philosophers, their inven-
tions on capitalists, and their discoveries on medical men; whilst
they were at the same time snubbing the artists, ignoring the
poets, and even casting doubts on the capacity of the politi-
cians? [14]

As the dissolution of the Christian faith led many intelligent people
to seek alternative means of organizing their lives, the achievements
of science and the surface plausibility of the views of the scientific
publicists rendered confidence in the methods and results of science
a convincing substitute for the discarded religion.

However naïve the mid- and late-Victorian optimism about science
may now appear, it then seemed productive of entirely constructive
ends. As Charles Kingsley once reminded an audience, "[S]cience has
as yet done nothing but good. Will any one tell me what harm it has
ever done?" [15] Moreover, scientific naturalism could flourish because
the most vocal intellectual opposition stemmed from writers who
criticized it while defending Christian or scriptural positions weak-
ened by the higher criticism or scientfic theory.[16] Effective criticism
had to originate in dissatisfaction with scientific naturalism as an
alternative non-Christian and self-sufficient world view.

James Ward, a Cambridge psychologist, philosopher, and former
Christian, contributed the most significant and systematic discussion
of scientific naturalism as a would-be complete interpretation of man
and nature. In the Gifford Lectures, delivered at Aberdeen between
1896 and 1898, Ward explained:

14. Webb, *My Apprenticeship,* pp. 130–31. See also Henry Holland, *Recollections of
Past Life,* 2nd ed. (London: Longmans, Green & Co., 1872), p. 311, and George Bernard
Shaw, Preface to "Back to Methuselah" in *Complete Plays with Prefaces* (New York:
Dodd, Mead & Company, 1963), 2 : ix–xc.

15. Charles Kingsley, *Health and Education* (London: W. Ibister & Co., 1874), p. 292.

16. For a series of essays by two sensible and intelligent Christians who opposed
scientific naturalism, see John Tulloch, *Modern Theories in Philosophy and Religion*
(Edinburgh and London: W. Blackwood & Sons, 1884), and R. H. Hutton, *Aspects of
Religious and Scientific Thought,* ed. Elizabeth Roscoe (London: Macmillan & Co.,
1899). Two enlightening essays on the varied Christian response to science are Noel
Annan, "Science, Religion, and the Critical Mind: Introduction," and Basil Willey,
"Darwin and Clerical Orthodoxy," in *1859: Entering an Age of Crisis,* ed. P. Appleman,
W. A. Madden, and M. Wolff (Bloomington, Ind.: Indiana University Press, 1959),
pp. 31–62.

This naturalistic philosophy consists in the union of three fundamental theories: (1) the theory that nature is ultimately resolvable into a single vast mechanism; (2) the theory of evolution as the working of this mechanism; and (3) the theory of psychophysical parallelism or conscious automatism, according to which theory mental phenomena occasionally accompany but never determine the movements and interactions of the material world.

Naturalistic writers employed these three theories to formulate what they considered a complete *Weltanschauung* that "separates Nature from God, subordinates Spirit to Matter, and sets up unchangeable law as supreme." [17]

In 1902 in the *Encyclopaedia Britannica* article on "Naturalism," Ward distinguished between "objective" and "subjective" naturalism. The latter consisted of a mechanical explanation of mind; the former, a mechanical explanation of physical nature. Since the time of Hume and Hartley, subjective naturalism had merged with objective naturalism to produce associationist psychology. This illicit combination formed the keystone of current naturalism. Ward declared, "As long as association of ideas (or sensory residue) is held to explain judgment and conscience, so long may naturalism stand." [18] Once spontaneity had been purged from the mind, there was no difficulty in extending the check to spontaneity throughout all nature.

Though in both the lectures and the article Ward set mechanistic naturalism in opposition to spiritual or idealistic interpretations of the universe, he did not regard naturalism as materialistic. In this regard he displayed considerably more perception than did the Christian critics of naturalism. Ward regarded the chief characteristic of naturalistic metaphysics to be a neutral monism that *tended* toward materialism when employed to deal with any specific problem.

[W]hen the question arises, how best to systematize experience as a whole, it is contended we must begin from the physical side. Here we have precise conceptions, quantitative exactness and thoroughgoing continuity; every thought that has ever stirred

17. Ward, *Naturalism and Agnosticism*, 1 : 186; ibid.
18. *Encyclopaedia Britannica,* 11th ed., s.v. "Naturalism" by Ward.

the hearts of men, not less than every breeze that has ever rippled the face of the deep, has meant a perfectly definite redistribution of matter and motion. To the mechanical principles of this redistribution an ultimate analysis brings us down; and—beginning from these—the nebular hypothesis and the theory of natural selection will enable us to explain all subsequent synthesis. Life and mind now clearly take a secondary place; the cosmical mechanism determines *them,* while they are powerless to modify it. The spiritual becomes the 'epiphenomenal,' a merely incidental phosphorescence, so to say, that regularly accompanies physical processes of a certain type and complexity.

This neutrally monistic, mechanical interpretation of the universe had produced "cosmological naturalism." He concluded that the psychological naturalism of associationism and the cosmological naturalism of mechanism had over the course of the nineteenth century merged to form "absolute naturalism," which totally denigrated life and mind.[19]

Ward's definitive treatment of scientific naturalism pointed up two important features that permitted a non-Christian critique of the whole system. First, Ward very carefully refused to equate scientific naturalism with science itself. Rather, he considered naturalism to be "a philosophy of . . . being which is especially plausible to, and hence is widely prevalent among, scientific men." [20] Ward was quite correct in drawing this distinction. The naturalistic publicists sought to expand the influence of scientific ideas for the purpose of secularizing society rather than for the goal of advancing science internally. Secularization was their goal; science, their weapon. Ward realized that one of the chief solvents of the naturalistic philosophy might well come from the internal development of science itself. New discoveries and new theories might lead men of science away from the narrow reductionism that had characterized the popular theories of the third quarter of the century. If this were the case, contemporary scientific naturalism might very well be rejected on empirical and scientific grounds.

19. Ibid. Ward, Sorley, and Blunt stood in firm agreement that the subordination of the active mind to mechanical nature was the heart of naturalism.
20. Ward, *Naturalism and Agnosticism,* 1 : 39.

Second, Ward recognized that naturalism represented an alternative to Christianity rather than an attack upon it. The scientific publicists viewed contemporary scientific methods and ideas as capable of gratifying what G. H. Lewes termed "the great desire of this age" for "a Doctrine which may serve to condense our knowledge, guide our researches, and shape our lives, so that Conduct may really be the consequence of Belief." [21] Ward and others argued that naturalism would fulfill that desire only at the cost of life itself. If it could be demonstrated that naturalism could guide men's lives only by ignoring whole areas of human experience, by dismissing inescapable human questions, and by applying inapplicable scientific categories to other areas and questions, naturalism might be rejected as incapable of meeting the stated goals of its advocates. Such a rejection would in no manner necessarily constitute a defense of Christianity. However, during the 1860s and 1870s, the halcyon years of scientific naturalism, such criticism had been most difficult because the advocates of naturalism defined the nature of truth and the means to its discovery so as to exclude the validity and reality of any experience or question not amenable to their own methods.

The Truth According to Scientific Naturalism

In 1866 Huxley delivered to a group of workingmen a lecture entitled "On Improving Natural Knowledge." In his usual manner he outlined the most recent scientific triumphs and enthusiastically pointed to the benefits derived from scientific knowledge by all men in all stations of life. In a crescendo of exuberance, he told his audience:

> If these ideas be destined, as I believe they are, to be more and more firmly established as the world grows older; if that spirit be fated, as I believe it is, *to extend itself into all departments of human thought, and to become co-extensive with the range of knowledge;* if, as our race approaches its maturity, it discovers, as I believe it will, that *there is but one kind of knowledge and but one method of acquiring it;* then we, who are still children, may justly feel it our highest duty to recognise the advisableness of improving natural knowledge, and so to aid ourselves and

21. G. H. Lewes, *Problems of Life and Mind, First Series* (London: Trubner & Co., 1874), 1 : 2.

our successors in our course toward the noble goal which lies
before mankind.[22]

In this address Huxley voiced the general convictions of adherents to
scientific naturalism. He appealed to the traditional view of science
as playing a normative role in ascertaining truth and to the widespread belief in the unity of truth.[23] However, Huxley broke with
both traditions in the breadth of validity he ascribed to science and
in his assertion that the scientific method was the only means of
acquiring true knowledge.

What Huxley, Spencer, Clifford, and other naturalistic writers
said about the nature of truth was not original. The roots of their
opinions lay in the empirical philosophy of the English Enlightenment and in the works of Comte and J. S. Mill. Epistemologically
the spokesmen of scientific naturalism were positivists. To the jest-
ing Pilate's question, "What is Truth?", they responded that truth
is always description of the phenomena of the external world and
of the mind and description of the laws of succession and coexistences
of those phenomena. With this concept of truth they sought to
sustain their own scientific positions and simultaneously to preempt
those of potential opponents. Naturalistic truth included no information about the nature of the underlying reality (if there were such
a reality) of phenomena. Naturalistic writers usually classed speculations upon this latter question as metaphysics that pertained to a
prescientific pattern of thought.

The publicists of scientific naturalism claimed to possess neither
old truth nor new truth, neither absolute truth nor relative truth,
but rather the only truth accessible to men and the only truth sufficient and necessary for men dwelling in the New Nature. G. H.
Lewes spoke for most of his fellow champions of the New Nature
when he defined this truth as "the correspondence between the order
of ideas and the order of phenomena, so that the one becomes a
reflection of the other—the movement of Thought following the
movement of Things." [24] Only when internal human thought came

22. Huxley, *Collected Essays*, 1 : 41 (FMT's emphasis).

23. Walter Cannon, "The Normative Role of Science in Early Victorian Thought,"
Journal of the History of Ideas 25 (1964) : 487–502, and "Scientists and Broad Churchmen: An Early Victorian Intellectual Network," *Journal of British Studies* 4 (1964) :
65–88.

24. G. H. Lewes, *History of Philosophy from Thales to Comte*, 4th ed. (London:
Longmans, Green & Co., 1871), 1 : xxxi. See also Passmore, *A Hundred Years of
Philosophy*, pp. 13–47.

to reflect the external movement of things or phenomena could human actions approximately correspond to the actual nature of the perceivable world and become genuinely meaningful and effective. In this process the human mind contributed little more than its capacity to receive external impressions from the senses and to arrange them according to the laws of association.

Lewes argued that there were essentially two modes of approaching empirical evidence so as to achieve a proper correspondence between thought and things. The first was the subjective method; the second, the objective method. According to the former the direction of truth was determined by thought; according to the latter it was controlled by things. Both methods employed inference, but the subjective method employed unverifiable inference.

Lewes associated the subjective method with religion, intuitionism, metaphysics, and prescientific thought. Each of these committed the fundamental error of attempting "to explain the scheme of the visible from the invisible, [to] deduce the knowable from the unknowable." The subjective method could not lead to truth because it lacked the chief virtue of the objective method—"vigilant Verification." The absence of verification meant that the subjective method confounded "concepts with percepts, ideas with objects, conjectures with realities" and tried to make things conform to thought.[25] Experience proved that this method encouraged men to reach for chimeras. No evangelical Christian feared the snare of the inner man more than did the adherents of naturalistic truth.

The objective method, on the other hand, accepted no inference that could not be verified by observable empirical facts and correspondence with the known laws of nature. This method prevented an investigator from confusing ideas with objects or his own hypothetical concepts with reality. The objective method assured the proper coordination between the materials of experience and the ideas of the mind. It assured that the latter would always correspond to the former. Such knowledge permitted men to act with certainty and prevented them from pursuing phantoms that arose from subjective illusions.

In subscribing to this particular standpoint, the advocates of scientific naturalism chose among alternative views of the scientific method. Various studies of the last twenty-five years have revealed

25. Lewes, *History of Philosophy*, 2 : 212; ibid., 1 : xxxix; ibid., 1 : xl. See also Lewes, *Problems of Life and Mind, First Series*, 1 : 1–87.

one crucial fact about Victorian science—namely, that there was little agreement among the scientists themselves as to what exactly constituted the method of science. For example, much of the serious objection to natural selection concentrated on whether Darwin's method had been genuinely "scientific." Consequently, the adherents of naturalism never spoke for the entire scientific community. In describing their own view of truth, they had chosen empiricism over idealism, objectivity over any mode of subjectivity, and most significantly the logic of Mill over that of Whewell.[26]

It is questionable how much attention the naturalistic writers paid to the more technical aspects of Mill's laws of induction. It is even less sure that the scientists among them ever consciously employed Mill's *System of Logic* to guide their own research. Mill's system could explain scientific laws after they had been discovered, but it could not account for the mode of discovery itself. The naturalistic publicists, having embraced an essentially descriptive view of science, encountered considerable difficulty in coming to grips with the role of hypothesis in scientific investigaton. For this reason in 1900 Sidgwick could speak of "the actual impossibility of finding a satisfactory scientific explanation of the development of scientific knowledge."[27]

Nevertheless, two of Mill's theories were of utmost importance for the naturalistic view of knowledge. First, the spokesmen for naturalism accepted Mill's idea that man could have knowledge of phenomena alone. Second, they accepted Mill's definition of causation as being the law of the invariable succession of phenomena. The significance of these two ideas for scientific naturalism can hardly be overestimated. They relieved naturalistic authors from having to deal with any formal ontology. In actual practice most of

26. Alvar Ellegard, "The Darwinian Theory and the Nineteenth-Century Philosophies of Science," *Journal of the History of Ideas* 18 (1957): 362–91; C. J. Ducasse, "Whewell's Philosophy of Scientific Discovery," *Philosophical Review* 60 (1951) : 59–69, 213–34; E. W. Strong, "William Whewell and John Stuart Mill: Their Controversy about Scientific Knowledge," *Journal of the History of Ideas* 16 (1955) : 209–31. On Mill's influence during the 1860s see David Masson, *Recent British Philosophy* (London: Macmillan & Co., 1865), pp. 11–13; Lewes, *Biographical History of Philosophy*, rev. and enl. (New York: D. Appleton & Co., 1866), p. xxi, note; Henry Sidgwick, "Philosophy at Cambridge," *Mind* 1 (1876) : 235.

27. Arthur J. Balfour, ed. *Papers Read before the Synethetic Society, 1896–1908* (London: Spottiswoode & Co., 1909), p. 276. In regard to the role of hypothesis in naturalistic writers, see Lewes, *Problems of Life and Mind, First Series,* 1 : 314–41; Tyndall, *Fragments of Science,* 2 : 101–34.

them oscillated between a near Berkelian idealism and a naïve realism. However, by formally ignoring the ontological issue or, like Spencer, by subsuming it under the Unknowable, naturalistic thinkers could apply scientific concepts to any area of intellectual endeavor merely by reducing the subject matter to phenomena. It made little difference whether these natural phenomena related to matters of physical nature, mind, art, society, or morals.

The dismissal of ontological considerations and the restricted view of knowledge were polemically (rather than personally) important as a means of permitting naturalistic authors to ignore questions, issues, and experiences inimical to their secular vision. The naturalistic theory of truth thus led directly to a self-serving agnosticism. The employment of agnosticism by Huxley and Leslie Stephen against the pretensions of religious writers is familiar. Any religious belief that could not be sustained by verifiable empirical facts became open game for the agnostic challenge.[28]

Agnosticism also served scientific naturalism in two other capacities. First, agnosticism was an instrument for clearing away certain metaphysical remnants in practical scientific research. This was especially true in psychology, where metaphysical terminology, such as "soul," plagued those men who wanted to turn the discipline into positive science. Henry Maudsley, a London physician and physiological psychologist raised the question, "Is metaphysics anything more than supernaturalism writ fine?" Maudsley had commenced in the 1860s to rid applied psychological theory of metaphysical concepts. He argued that the latter had no reality in thought, fact, or consequences.

> The very terms of metaphysical psychology have, instead of helping, oppressed and hindered him [the psychologist] to an extent which it is impossible to measure: they have been hobgoblins to frighten him from entering on his path of inquiry, phantoms to lead him astray at every turn after he has entered upon it, deceivers lurking to betray him under the guise of seeming friends tendering help.[29]

28. W. Irvine, *Apes, Angels, and Victorians* (Cleveland and New York: The World Publishing Co., 1964), pp. 247–63, 311–30; Noel Annan, *Sir Leslie Stephen: His Thought and Character in Relation to His Time* (London: MacGibbon & Kee, 1951), pp. 172–95.

29. Henry Maudsley, *Natural Causes and Supernatural Seemings* (London: Kegan Paul, Trench & Co., 1886), p. 104; idem, *Body and Mind: An Enquiry into Their Connection and Mutual Influence,* rev. and enl. (New York: D. Appleton & Co., 1875), p. vii.

Only after the imperceivable metaphysical fictions had been vanquished could meaningful and genuinely answerable questions be posed. The latter questions alone held the promise of health and healing.

Second, and for this study most important, agnosticism more nearly represented a cultural stance than a theory of knowledge per se. By asserting that men lacked sufficient knowledge to decide whether the universe was material or spiritual or whether it was ruled by a deity, the agnostics rejected a culture and cultural values that depended upon answers to such questions. They rejected a culture founded upon improbable answers to what they considered invalid or unanswerable questions. These questions and answers had no place in the New Nature, where only problems and experiences subject to the "vigilant Verification" of the objective method might be considered. The naturalistic theory of knowledge and the agnostic stance toward issues inaccessible to such knowledge constituted the primary intellectual apology for both the necessity and the adequacy of an entirely secular culture.

In their zeal for scientific enlightenment, the advocates of naturalism often tended to overstate their case in order to stir an audience or to provoke further public discussion. On the lecture platform or in the pages of the liberal journals, their tone was arrogant, their confidence unbounded, and their metaphysics reductionist. They always gave themselves room to retreat without surrendering the major issue at hand. This was their public side. In the privacy of letters and conversation, they were less fulsome, more introspective, and even self-doubting. No one who has read their letters and the anecdotes of friends can believe that they were grim reductionists unaware of or insensitive to the emotional requirements of human nature. However, these private selves were familiar only to intimate friends and a few students. The world at large had to await the turn-of-the-century biographies to discover this side of their characters. What contemporaries witnessed were impatient, hard-headed polemicists reluctant to yield or to compromise. To this public character reply had to be directed and reaction measured.

Christians could and did object to both the manner and substance of the naturalistic theory of truth for ignoring the Scriptures and the destiny of the human soul. However, non-Christian writers, such as

Henry Sidgwick, Samuel Butler, and James Ward, raised more impressive and pointed criticisms. As earlier suggested, Sidgwick considered empiricism an inadequate philosophy of scientific investigation. Butler thought the objective method was rooted in illusion. Ward argued that empirical examination of mental experience suggested that the activity of the mind determined part of the perception of phenomena. All of them believed there were certain unavoidable human questions that required nonempirical and nonobjectively verifiable concepts for rational answers.

In addition, non-Christians believed that the naturalistic view of truth illicitly excluded consideration of subjective empirical experiences that had practical consequences in the lives of human beings. The a priori exclusion of subjective experience meant that secular life must include only a part of the normal existence of normal human beings. In this regard, Sidgwick, Wallace, Myers, Butler, Romanes, and Ward firmly agreed with an argument William James once advanced to a group of his English friends.

> The personal and romantic view of life has other roots beside wanton exuberance of imagination and perversity of heart. It is perennially fed by *facts of experience,* whatever the ulterior interpretation of those facts may prove to be. . . . These experiences have three characters in common: they are capricious, discontinuous, and not easily controlled; they require peculiar persons for their production; their significance seems to be wholly for personal life. Those who preferentially attend to them, and still more those who are individually subject to them, not only easily *may* find but are logically bound to find in them valid arguments for their romantic and personal conception of the world's course.[30]

A view of truth and knowledge that systematically excluded the consideration of those experiences could never allow men to discover the whole truth or to understand the full dimensions of personality and existence. Moreover, a cosmology that did not take into account such experience could never adequately portray the conditions and circumstances of human life.

30. William James, "Presidential Address to the Society for Psychical Research, January 31, 1896," in *Presidential Addresses to the Society for Psychical Research, 1882–1911* (Glasgow: The Society for Psychical Research, 1912), p. 84.

The Cosmology of Scientific Naturalism

W. K. Clifford once remarked, "The character of the emotion with which men contemplate the world, the temper in which they stand in the presence of the immensities and the eternities, must depend first of all on what they think the world is." [31] The exponents of scientific naturalism endeavored to persuade their fellow Englishmen that nature was essentially a mass of uniformly evolving atoms and energy. Since careful examination of these atoms and energy revealed no supernatural beings, nature should be contemplated in a wholly secular temper.

The advocates of naturalism constructed their model of external nature from three seminal theories of nineteenth-century science, which in their hands converged into what Ward termed "absolute naturalism." These were Dalton's atomic theory, the law of the conservation of energy, and evolution. Of this triad Huxley observed in 1887:

> The peculiar merit of our epoch is that it has shown how these hypotheses connect a vast number of seemingly independent partial generalizations; that it has given them that precision of expression which is necessary for their exact verification; and that it has practically proved their value as guides to the discovery of new truth. All three doctrines are intimately connected, and each is applicable to the whole physical cosmos.

Huxley and his fellow naturalistic writers, such as Spencer, employed the three theories "to interpret the detailed phenomena of Life, and Mind, and Society, in terms of Matter, Motion, and Force." [32] Reduced to the common denominators of evolving matter and energy, all natural phenomena could be explained mechanically and interpreted without reference to God, supernatural agencies, or independent mind.

Undergirding the model of nature derived from these theories

31. W. K. Clifford, *Lectures and Essays*, ed. L. Stephen and F. Pollock (London: Macmillan & Co., 1901), 2 : 259. See also Herbert Dingle, "The Scientific Outlook in 1851 and 1951" in *European Intellectual History since Darwin and Marx*, ed. W. Warren Wagar (New York: Harper Torchbooks, 1966), pp. 159–83.

32. *Encyclopaedia Britannica*, 11th ed., s.v. "Naturalism"; Huxley, *Collected Essays*, 1 : 66; Herbert Spencer, *First Principles*, 4th ed. (New York: P. F. Collier & Son, 1901), p. 468.

was the concept of continuity, described by George Eliot as "the great conception of universal regular sequence, without partiality and without caprice." In 1866 W. R. Grove reminded the British Association for the Advancement of Science that continuity was "no new word, and used in no new sense, but perhaps applied more generally than it has hitherto been." This was very much an understatement. The seventeenth-century concept of uniform natural activity had by the 1860s been extended to chemistry, physics, biology, psychology, medicine, and the emerging sciences of society. Although the concept was a nonempirical assumption and not subject to "vigilant Verification," it was the essential postulate that allowed the scientists and naturalistic writers to interpret nature rationally. As Huxley once explained, the value of the extension of this principle was "to narrow the range and loosen the force of men's belief in spontaneity, or in changes other than such as arise out of that definite order [of nature] itself." [33] Explanations of natural phenomena that did not reduce the latter to such uniformity stood condemned as unscientific. By definition what was not subject to uniformity had no existence save in illusion.

The atomic theory of matter furnished the exponents of scientific naturalism with the primary example of the continuity of physical nature. However, the manner in which they popularized the theory illustrates why the movement could not be equated with the advance of science, why some opponents of naturalism could claim to be more scientifically advanced than the leading spokesmen of naturalism, and how the latter unnecessarily tied themselves to theories that became scientifically obsolete by the turn of the century.

Tyndall, Huxley, Spencer, and the psychologist Alexander Bain advocated Dalton's atomic theory. From the chemists' standpoint this theory allowed for a mechanical and mathematical concept of matter, the development of the law of definite proportions, and the completion of the periodic chart of the elements.[34] On the popular level,

33. George Eliot, "The Influence of Rationalism: Lecky's History," *Fortnightly Review*, (1865), reprinted in *Works of George Eliot* (New York: P. F. Collier & Son, n.d.), 12 : 138; W. R. Grove, "Presidential Address," *Report of the British Association for the Advancement of Science: 36th Meeting* (London: John Murray, 1867), p. 56; Huxley, *Collected Essays*, 1 : 39. All the naturalistic writers admitted that uniformity was an assumption which, they contended, was justified by, though not drawn from, experience.

34. D. S. L. Cardwell, ed., *John Dalton and the Progress of Science* (New York: Barnes & Noble, 1968); Frank Greenway, *Dalton and the Atom* (Ithaca, New York:

this variety of atomism permitted an easily visualized image of matter as composed of small, round, solid, indestructible particles.[35] All the material manifestations of the physical world stemmed from particular arrangements of such atoms and the molecules formed by them. However, in choosing to popularize the solid-ball theory of atoms, Huxley, Tyndall, and Spencer consciously chose among competing theories. For example, Spencer specifically dismissed Boscovich's theory. Huxley refused to accept Maxwell's views that the similarity of atoms bespoke a planned manufacture and that theoretically more than one atom might occupy the same space. Moreover, all of these writers paid scant attention to William Thomson's vortex theory, which interpreted the internal composition of atoms in terms of a flowing fluid.[36] A desire for conceptual convenience in popular explication rather than experimental or theoretical considerations primarily determined the publicists' choice of theory. They thus tied themselves and the philosophic view that they expounded to a concept of matter that became increasingly untenable in the latter part of the century when subatomic particles were discovered. By that time the "scientific" idea of matter associated with scientific naturalism was no longer associated with the scientific community.[37]

The atomic theory served to portray nature as one vast mechanical structure. The law of the conservation of energy explained the operation of the machine and established the limits to what was

---

Cornell University Press, 1966); H. L. Sharlin, *The Convergent Century: The Unification of Science in the Nineteenth Century* (New York: Abelard–Schuman, 1966), pp. 52–58.

35. A. Bain, "The Atomic Theory," *Westminster Review* 59 (1853): 125–96; Herbert Spencer, *First Principles*, pp. 43–45, 243–45, and Preface to *Epitome of the Synthetic Philosophy*, by F. H. Collins (New York: D. Appleton & Co., 1889), pp. viii–xi; Tyndall, *Fragments of Science*, 1 : 39, 2 : 51–74.

36. For competing theories and Huxley's, Tyndall's, and Spencer's rejection of them, see George M. Fleck, "Atomism in Late Nineteenth-Century Physical Chemistry," *Journal of the History of Ideas* 24 (1963) 106–14; W. H. Brock and D. M. Knight, "The Atomic Debates: 'Memorable and Interesting Evenings in the Life of the Chemical Society,'" *Isis* 56 (1965) : 5–25; and D. M. Knight, *Atoms and Elements* (London: Hutchinson and Co., 1967); Spencer, *First Principles*, pp. 43–45; Huxley, *Collected Essays*, 1 : 60–61; W. D. Niven, ed., *The Scientific Papers of James Clerk Maxwell* (New York: Dover Publications, 1965), 2 : 376–77, 445–84; Robert H. Silliman, "William Thomson: Smoke Rings and Nineteenth Century Atomism," *Isis* 54 (1963) : 461–74.

37. T. T. Flint, "Particle Physics," and W. Wilson, "The Structure of the Atom," in *A Century of Science*, ed. Dingle, pp. 39–69.

scientifically and naturally possible within the realm of nature. It held that the quantity of energy in the universe remained fixed throughout all the varied transformations of energy and atoms. The mechanism of nature remained closed to all external interference.[38] As Tyndall described energy in 1861:

> The proteus changes, but he is ever the same; and his changes in nature, supposing no miracle to supervene, are the expression, not of spontaneity, but of physical necessity. A perpetual motion, then, is deemed impossible, because it demands the creation of energy, whereas the principle of Conservation is—no creation but infinite conversion.

The contemporary significance of this law was immense and probably more destructive to a supernatural interpretation of nature than was evolution by natural selection. In 1868 the Archbishop of York declared, "The doctrine most in favour with physical philosophers at this moment is that of conservation of force." [39] The theory struck down any religious explanation entailing miracles, spirits, or God by suggesting such modes of interference would require new infusions of external energy into the closed mechanism of nature.[40]

Evolution completed the naturalistic cosmology. Despite the numerous discussions of this topic, considerable confusion still surrounds the contemporary meaning of the term. There were two primary definitions interpreted and associated respectively with physics and biology. In physics, evolution was linked with the nebu-

38. C. C. Gillispie, *The Edge of Objectivity* (Princeton: Princeton University Press, 1960), pp. 370–405; Sharlin, *The Convergent Century*, pp. 30–37; C. Singer, *A Short History of Scientific Ideas* (Oxford: Oxford University Press, 1959), pp. 375–78.

39. Tyndall, *Fragments of Science*, 2 : 4; William Thomson, *The Limits of Philosophical Inquiry: An Address* (Edinburgh: Edmonston & Douglas, 1868), p. 10.

40. Naturalistic writers were often as selective in their dealings with thermodynamics as they were with atomism. During the 1860s Huxley and other supporters of Darwin tried to ignore the second law of thermodynamics, which suggested a universal dissipation of energy whereby all motion and thus all life would come to a frozen halt. This law was believed to mean there had not been sufficient time for geological and organic evolution. Huxley, Spencer, and other naturalistic writers later seem to have accepted the second law although with little enthusiasm, for the morbid future implied by the law was incompatible with the optimism associated with the New Nature. See Loren Eiseley, *Darwin's Century: Evolution and the Men Who Discovered It* (Garden City, N.Y.: Doubleday & Co., 1961), pp. 238–41; E. N. Hiebert, "The Use and Abuse of Thermodynamics in Religion," *Daedalus* 95 (1966): 1046–1080; Stephen G. Brush, "Science and Culture in the Nineteenth Century," *The Graduate Journal* 7 (1967): 477–565.

lar hypothesis. Spencer and Tyndall were its major advocates. In its simplest form, it explained the state of the physical universe at any particular moment as the result of the continuously developing arrangement of matter and energy from all previous time. In *First Principles* Spencer set forth the following definition:

> Evolution is an integration of matter and concomitant dissipation of motion: during which the matter passes from an indefinite, incoherent homogeneity to a definite, coherent heterogeneity; and during which the retained motion undergoes a parallel transformation.[41]

This variety of physical evolution in conjunction with continuity, atomism, and the conservation of energy allowed naturalistic writers to suggest that the human mind itself might be little more than an as-yet-unexplained manifestation of atoms and energy.

Among biologists, evolution applied to the species question. Prior to Darwin and Wallace, numerous biologists had been convinced that evolution or transformation of species occurred. However, until the formulation of the theory of natural selection, biologists possessed no thoroughly mechanistic concept to account for those modifications. Natural selection, in the words of Huxley, "was a hypothesis respecting the origin of known organic forms which assumed the operation of no causes but such as could be proved to be actually at work." [42] Natural selection brought organic forms under a theory of change analogous to that under which the nebular hypothesis brought physical forms. It reduced modifications in organic structures to rearrangements of matter and energy requiring no supernatural agencies. In this regard, it is important to recognize that evolution by natural selection represented only the final element of the broader naturalistic synthesis of man and nature that had arisen over the course of the century.[43]

41. Spencer, *First Principles*, p. 334. See also Spencer, *Essays* (New York: D. Appleton & Co., 1868), 1 : 1–60; R. M. Young, "The Development of Herbert Spencer's Concept of Evolution," in *Actes du XIe congrès international d'histoire des sciences* (Warsaw, 1967), 2 : 273–78; Tyndall, *Fragments of Science*, 2 : 170–99.

42. Leonard Huxley, *Life and Letters of Thomas Henry Huxley* (New York: D. Appleton & Co., 1902), 1 : 182.

43. R. Young, "The Impact of Darwin on Conventional Thought," in *The Victorian Crisis of Faith*, ed. A. Symondson, pp. 13–35; Noel Annan, "Science, Religion, and the Critical Mind: Introduction," in *1859: Entering an Age of Crisis*, ed. Appleman, Madden, and Wolff, pp. 31–51.

The exponents of naturalism derived their idea of man directly from their view of physical nature. As Henry Maudsley explained, "There are not two worlds—a world of nature and a world of human nature—standing over against one another in a sort of antagonism, but one world of nature, in the orderly evolution of which human nature has its subordinate part." [44] The cosmology of scientific naturalism, like its epistemology, simply excluded all those facets of human nature that did not fit into the preconceived pattern of physical nature.[45] Naturalistic authors could and did answer the questions about man that Huxley propounded in *Man's Place in Nature.*

> The question of questions for mankind—the problem which underlies all others, and is more deeply interesting than any other—is the ascertainment of the place which Man occupies in nature and of his relations to the universe of things. Whence our race has come; what are the limits of our power over nature, and of nature's power over us; to what goal are we tending; are the problems which present themselves anew and with un-diminished interest to every man born into the world.[46]

So long as the discussion was limited to the "universe of things," naturalistic writers could discuss man. He was an animal descended from more brutish animals. Science gave him power over physical nature so that he might progress toward his end, which was the civilization of the New Nature. But of man considered as a problem to himself and within himself or of man confronting existential dilemmas, such as death, naturalistic writers could not and would not speak in public. Those issues were not relevant to the New Nature.

The Christian censure of the evolutionary and naturalistic view of man and nature is well known. However, naturalistic evolution

44. Henry Maudsley, "Hallucinations of the Senses," *Fortnightly Review* 30 (1878): 386.

45. See John C. Greene, "Darwin and Religion," in *European Intellectual History since Darwin and Marx,* ed. W. W. Wagar, pp. 31–34. Herbert Dingle once observed, "The reason why the Victorian world [of science] contained nothing corresponding to religious experience is . . . because religious experience had not been taken into account in building it up." Herbert Dingle, *The Sources of Eddington's Philosophy* (Cambridge: Cambridge University Press, 1954), p. 26.

46. T. H. Huxley, *Man's Place in Nature and Other Essays* (London: J. M. Dent & Co., 1910), p. 52.

could be considered incompatible not only with Christian doctrines and the scriptures but also with the secular doctrine and ideal of moral progress associated with rationalist and enlightenment thought. Writers such as Wallace, Myers, Butler, and Ward desired a concept of evolution that would, at least in the case of man, provide for genuinely qualitative change in the universe rather than for rearrangement of qualitatively unchanging atoms and energy. The realization of the non-Christian ideal of moral improvement required a universe of "becoming" rather than one of "being-in-process." Long before Bergson, they recognized that Spencer "had promised to trace out a genesis, but he had done something quite different; his doctrine is an evolutionism only in name." [47] They sensed a radical incommensurability between mankind's collective and individual moral awareness and the nature described in the cosmology of scientific naturalism. Like the scientific publicists, they considered man an integral part of nature. However, they contended that if man were such a part of nature, his own moral character and inner experiences must be acknowledged when describing nature as a whole. To at least some degree the macrocosm must be interpreted through the microcosm. This was exactly what the advocates of naturalism refused to do.

Moreover, the figures in this study thought man had evolved a mental nature and displayed intellectual sensibilities for which the scientific cosmology could neither account nor provide future development. If bound by that reductionist cosmology, they could only conclude with Thomas Hardy, "We have reached a degree of intelligence which Nature never contemplated when framing her laws, and for which she consequently has provided no adequate satisfactions." [48] Sidgwick, Wallace, Myers, Romanes, Butler, and Ward were not prepared to accept that predicament. They believed that nature must be commensurate with man's intelligence and ideals. In various ways, they set out to prove that nature included realities and experiences that would satisfactorily account for such intellect and permit the realization of human ideals.

47. Henri Bergson quoted by A. O. Lovejoy in "Schopenhauer as Evolutionist," in *Forerunners of Darwin, 1745–1859*, ed. B. Glass, O. Temkin, and W. L. Strauss, Jr., (Baltimore: Johns Hopkins Press, 1959), p. 433.

48. Quoted in F. E. Hardy, *The Early Life of Thomas Hardy, 1840–1891* (New York: Macmillan Co., 1928), p. 213.

THE CHALLENGE TO RELIGIOUS CULTURE

Already reeling under the attacks on the scriptures from rationalism and the higher criticism, Christianity now faced from scientific naturalism a challenge to the actual validity of religion itself.[49] Frederic Myers succinctly described the new turn of mind.

> The essential spirituality of the universe, in short, is the basis of religion, and it is precisely this basis which is now assailed. . . . The most effective assailants of Christianity no longer take the trouble to attack, as Voltaire did, the Bible miracles in detail. They strike at the root, and begin by denying—outright or virtually—that a spiritual world, a world beyond the conceivable reach of mathematical formulae, exists for us at all. They say with Clifford that "no intelligences except those of men and animals have been at work in the solar system"; or, implying that the physical Cosmos is all, and massing together all possible spiritual entities under the name which most suggests superstition, they affirm that the world "is made of ether and atoms, and there is no room for ghosts." [50]

Most naturalistic thinkers drew two conclusions from those assertions. First, as Myers suggested, they considered all existing religion a form of superstition, primitive survival, or illusion. Second, and in general departure from previous critics of religion who called for a purified faith, they argued that traditional religion, especially Christianity, and men in religious occupations were culturally dysfunctional. They called for the replacement of a religiously directed culture with a scientifically directed culture dominated by scientifically oriented men.

Among the naturalistic coterie the rising sociologists proved to be the most insidious enemies of religious culture. Tylor, Spencer,

49. F. L. Baumer, *Religion and the Rise of Scepticism* (New York: Harcourt, Brace, & Co., 1960), pp. 128–86; Howard R. Murphy, "The Ethical Revolt against Christian Orthodoxy in Early Victorian England," *American Historical Review* 60 (1955) : 800–17; Herbert G. Wood, *Belief and Unbelief since 1850* (Cambridge University Press, 1955).

50. F. W. H. Myers, *Science and a Future Life with Other Essays* (London: Macmillan & Co., 1893), pp. 131–32. Even the opponents of Christianity argued among themselves on the nature of religion and what, if any, religion men should adopt. See Sidney Eisen, "Frederic Harrison and Herbert Spencer: Embattled Unbelievers," *Victorian Studies* 12 (1968–69) : 33–56.

McLennon, and Lubbock, though disagreeing on particulars, were of one mind in arguing that religion had originated naturally with no divine aid or revelation.[51] They interpreted its origins in such a manner that religion should naturally and necessarily give way to advancing science.

Tylor considered "a minimum definition of Religion" to be "the belief in Spiritual Beings." This belief and the religion it nurtured had originated in the attempts of primitive men to understand the operation of nature by ascribing natural processes to the activity of spirits. All religion might in one manner or another be reduced to a survival of this primitive animism.

> Animism characterizes tribes very low in the scale of humanity, and thence ascends, deeply modified in its transmission, but from first to last preserving an unbroken continuity, into the midst of high modern culture. . . . Animism is, in fact, the groundwork of the Philosophy of Religion, from that of savages up to that of civilized men.

Tylor admitted that some later religions had added ethical systems to animism, but this addition did not change the nature of religion itself. Ethics was not intrinsically related to religion. Moreover, according to John Lubbock, the higher religions were essentially no better or no purer than the lower. He remarked, "The higher faiths . . . merely superimposed themselves on, and did not eradicate, the lower superstitions." [52] Contemporary religion consequently remained stigmatized by the original sin of its primitive founders.

This sociological analysis of religion permitted the spokesmen of scientific naturalism to contend that redemption of the primitive sin lay near at hand. The doctrines and theories of science could now correct that original misunderstanding of nature. Scientific ideas, therefore, did not rob men of their religion but rather fulfilled those very yearnings of human curiosity that had for centuries been mis-

51. E. Tylor, *Primitive Culture* (London: J. Murray, 1871); J. F. McLennon, "The Worship of Animals and Plants," *Fortnightly Review* 12 (1869) : 407–27 and 13 (1870) : 194–216; J. Lubbock, *The Origin of Civilization and the Primitive Condition of Man* (London: Longmans, Green, & Co., 1870); H. Spencer, "The Origin of Animal Worship," *Fortnightly Review* 13 (1870) : 535–50.

52. Tylor, *Primitive Culture*, 1 : 383 (See J. W. Burrow, *Evolution and Society: A Study in Victorian Social Theory* [Cambridge: Cambridge University Press, 1966], pp. 234–59); ibid., p. 385; Lubbock, *The Origin of Civilization*, p. 255.

directed into superstitious behavior. Tyndall explained, "The same impulse, inherited and intensified, is the spur of scientific action today." [53] This assertion constituted the foundation for the claim of naturalistic writers to replace the clergy as new leaders of English culture.

Certain naturalistic authors did not rest content with this sociological examination of religion. It sufficed only to exorcise religious doctrine and social justification for religious institutions. The chief stronghold of nineteenth-century religion had been and continued to be the subjective religious experience in the form of conversion, ecstasy, or some other antinomian manifestation. Henry Maudsley argued that such experiences were invalid for two reasons. First, being subjective they could not be investigated by the objective scientific method. No idea, knowledge, or intuition so received could be considered genuinely true because it could not be communicated as part of the universal experience of sensible men. Such experiences could not reveal truth.

> The authority of direct personal intuition is the authority of the lunatic's direct intuition that he is the Messiah; the vagaries of whose mad thoughts notoriously cannot be rectified until he can be got to abandon his isolating self-sufficiency and to place confidence in the assurances and acts of others.

Second, the religious experience could be naturally explained and dismissed as hallucination or illusion. Maudsley perceived no difference in kind between the vision of a saint and the delusion of a madman. "Whatever its inner essence, the spiritual ecstasy in which a person is carried *out of himself* by divine action, has all the outward and visible character of the ecstasy in which he is *beside himself* through morbid action." [54] With such analysis Maudsley summarily dismissed the religious experiences of mankind from Saul on the road to Damascus to the converts of nineteenth-century revivals.

Through the epistemological limits ascribed to human knowledge, the portrayal of nature without supernatural entities, and the reduction of religious practices to a primitive survival and of religious

53. Tyndall, *Fragments of Science*, 2 : 135. See also Herbert Spencer, *The Principles of Sociology* (New York: D. Appleton & Co., 1897), 2 : 247–60.

54. Henry Maudsley, *Body and Will* (London: K. Paul, Trench & Co., 1883), p. 44; idem, *Natural Causes and Supernatural Seemings*, p. 271.

experience to mental disorder, the advocates of scientific naturalism sought to displace the existing clerical and literary intellectual elite. A culture based on science must replace one founded on religion. This was what Huxley intended to indicate near the close of his life when he wrote that "the future of our civilization . . . depends on the result of the contest between Science and Ecclesiasticism which is now afoot." [55] The real issue at stake in the contest was whether men could lead secular lives in which their occupations, institutions, values, and aspirations would be determined through scientific method with little or no reference to matters beyond the range of naturalistic epistemology and outside the framework of the naturalistic cosmology or whether their lives should be guided by knowledge drawn from science as supplemented by revelation, intuition, or creative reason.

The emergence of the New Nature had opened a vast new realm for human life and achievement, the cultural values and leadership of which had yet to be determined. R. H. Hutton, the liberal Christian editor of the *Spectator,* described the novel situation.

> A very great part of the best thought of the best men is occupied in very large degree with interests which have all the largeness and catholicity, as one may say, of something quasi-spiritual, and yet no vestige of the true spiritual world in them, no vestige in them of the great conflict between darkness and light, between evil and good, between temptation and grace. The area of perfectly disinterested and perfectly innocent and wholesome interests which are not in the least moral or spiritual interests has grown vastly in the modern world, and the effect of this is that a much larger portion of the permanent mind of good men is usually eagerly at work in tracking out clues which have neither the taint of moral danger about them on the one side, nor the inspiration of spiritual help on the other. A great part of the minds of good men is thus invested in secular interests which are not in the bad sense worldly, and which are indeed in a very real sense unworldly, though they cannot be called moral or spiritual, nay, which, far from calling upon the vision of an

55. T. H. Huxley, "Mr. Balfour's Attack on Agnosticism," *The Nineteenth Century* 37 (1895) : 530.

unseen world, only tend to give a deeper intellectual fascination to the spectacle of the seen world.[56]

Over the cultural domination of this emergent secular society and secular achievement the combatants of science and religion fought. Here Francis Galton hoped there might arise "a scientific priesthood" that would tend to the health and welfare of the entire nation. New men as well as new ideas must direct the life of the New Nature.[57]

Once the intellectual and cultural ambitions of the naturalistic coterie stand recognized, it is readily perceivable why men who were themselves no longer Christians and who supported the onward movement of scientific investigation, could still vigorously oppose the pretensions of naturalistic writers. Men such as Henry Sidgwick, Samuel Butler, and James Ward, who had painfully liberated themselves from bondage to Christian doctrine, could not long tolerate or submit to a new enslavement to narrow, often intellectually shallow, scientific dogma, propagated by another intolerant and sometimes uncritical secular priesthood. They and the other figures in this study knew enough about science to realize that in and of itself science would fail to provide adequate guidance even for a secular culture. They knew that religion amounted to more than a prescientific interpretation of nature and that it encompassed dimensions of life and experience unrecognized within the context of scientific naturalism. Moreover, all of these writers believed human beings inevitably confronted situations and questions leading to ideas—such as God and immortality—that religions had contemplated but that naturalism tried to ignore. The conviction that issues such as ethics, death, and the purpose of human life must be addressed by thinking men inevitably led the figures in this study away from scientific naturalism.

Perhaps no man in late nineteenth-century England so articulately and persistently defended the necessity of considering those unanswered questions that lay at the heart of human life than did Henry Sidgwick. Like the late Paul Tillich, he understood that "the positivistic, empirical attitude can be both a humble acknowledg-

56. Hutton, *Aspects of Religious and Scientific Thought*, pp. 27–28.
57. Galton, *English Men of Science*, p. 195.

ment of man's finitude and an arrogant dismissal of the question of
the truth which concerns us ultimately." [58] Sidgwick strove to live
within the finitude of empiricism without dismissing those persistent
questions of the human condition. Sidgwick's defense of the legitimacy of those issues, his criticism of the fallacies of naturalistic solutions, and his own tenacity revealed the existential, intellectual, and
moral bankruptcy of scientific naturalism.

Henry Sidgwick refused to accept the proposition implicit in all
naturalistic thought that human beings had approached the limits of
their apprehension of truth. He considered the negativism of that
position intellectually and emotionally reprehensible. As he once
explained to a class:

> If a man says to me that he and his friends have really no in-
> terest in solving the universe, I have nothing to answer but
> "Then in heaven's name leave the universe alone." But if he
> tries to prove that anyone else ought to leave it alone, I ask by
> what empirical arguments he proves that this crisis in the
> history of human thought has been reached: that the endeavor
> to grasp the golden robe of complex wisdom will no longer as
> of old leave a fragment thereof in our hands.[59]

To surrender the hope of achieving complex wisdom was intellectually premature and morally defeatist. It led directly to a universal
skepticism that foreclosed the possibility of pursuing a rational life.

Sidgwick feared that should the advocates of scientific naturalism
achieve domination of English culture, the path to the discovery of
new truth would stand forever blocked. Proposing that men live in a
universe of open inquiry, he became a philosopher of infinite
patience who preferred to leave questions unsolved or provisionally
answered rather than to close the door to new truth by declaring
those queries unanswerable or irrelevant. He believed that the limits
of human intellectual endeavor should be set by neither contemporary scientific methods nor presently recognized human faculties.
Rather, those limits should be established only by the questions
and aspirations of which human beings were capable. Consequently,

58. Paul Tillich, *Theology of Culture* (New York: Oxford University Press, 1968),
p. 171.
59. H. Sidgwick, "Is Philosophy the Germ or the Crown of Science?", Henry Sidgwick
Papers, Trinity College, Cambridge, add. MSS. c96.2, p. 8.

when he died in 1900, Sidgwick left more issues unresolved than answered, but other men continued to pursue them. In a sense this persistent posing of questions was perhaps the chief monument to Henry Sidgwick's intellectual integrity. For this reason Lord Morley could declare, "If any Englishman ever belonged to the household of Socrates, Sidgwick was he." [60]

60. Morley, *Works of Lord Morley,* 1 : 114.

3

Henry Sidgwick: The Pursuit of Complex Wisdom

THE UNBELIEVER AND HIS APPRECIATION OF RELIGION

Henry Sidgwick entered Trinity College, Cambridge, in October 1855. He was a product of Rugby, where he had been taught by Edward Benson, his future brother-in-law and later Archbishop of Canterbury. Sidgwick had enjoyed a successful career at Rugby, and at Cambridge he continued to win academic honors, including the Chancellor's Medal. The university remained his home until he died in 1900 at the age of sixty-two.[1] Yet Sidgwick was never an academic recluse. He scorned scholars who remained within the safe confines of their own colleges and the settled theories of their own disciplines. An exponent of curricular reform, he became one of the leaders of the "revolution of the dons" that transformed and modernized British higher education during the second half of the century.[2] He also devoted his energy, time, and money to the advancement of women's education. In this endeavor he was aided by his brilliantly gifted wife, the former Eleanor Balfour. After their marriage in 1876, Sidgwick gained informal entrée into the political circle of Arthur Balfour, Eleanor's brother and his own former student.

While still an undergraduate at Trinity, Henry Sidgwick accepted an invitation to join the Apostles, the most distinguished of all undergraduate discussion societies. That commenced his long participation in the most eminent debating groups of the day, including the Metaphysical, the Aristotelian, and the Synthetic societies.[3] His never-palling conversations at these gatherings bore witness to his receptive mind, his unflagging faith in the possibility of finding

1. For details of Sidgwick's life, see books listed under his name in Bibliographical Essay.

2. S. Rothblatt, *The Revolution of the Dons: Cambridge and Society in Victorian England* (New York: Basic Books, 1968), pp. 133–55.

3. A. W. Brown, *The Metaphysical Society: Victorian Minds in Conflict 1869–1880* (New York: Columbia University Press, 1947), pp. 20–34, 238–60.

rational answers to the deepest human problems, and his general dissatisfaction with the resolutions of those issues proposed by his contemporaries.

This mental temper first displayed itself during his period of religious "storm and stress" in the sixties.[4] Like so many young men who achieved intellectual adulthood during those years, Sidgwick encountered and eventually succumbed to religious doubt. Acquaintance with the higher criticism, reading of Renan, and a long study of comparative religion shook his belief in the unique character of Christianity. The hostile reception accorded *Essays and Reviews* disenchanted him with the intellectual leadership of the Anglican Church and helped to convince him that the establishment would not adjust itself to new ideas. As Mill, Comte, and Spencer in turn influenced his developing mind, Sidgwick became uneasy about the Christian miracles. Finally, his absolute inability to accept or in some manner to rationalize the doctrine of the Virgin Birth caused his formal departure from the Christian faith.[5]

For some men this separation simply posed a speculative or religious dilemma. For Sidgwick it occasioned an ethical crisis. He held a Trinity College Fellowship that presupposed the unofficial affirmation of the Apostles' Creed. Sidgwick decided he could not honestly retain the fellowship. In June 1869, after much thought and discussion, he chose to resign the fellowship rather than to persist in what he considered the implicit hypocrisy of retaining it. Trinity immediately appointed him lecturer in Moral Sciences, a position that paid a considerably smaller salary but implied no creedal affirmation. His resignation represented not only a formal rejection of orthodoxy but also a renunciation of the Broad Church movement, which sought to include within the Anglican church men espousing almost any interpretation of the creed. Sidgwick believed that even the broadest church must possess some standard or else be a sham of intellectual honesty.[6]

4. A. Sidgwick and E. Sidgwick, *Henry Sidgwick: A Memoir* (London: Macmillan & Co., 1906), p. 33. Hereafter cited as Sidgwick, *A Memoir*.

5. Henry Sidgwick Papers, Trinity College, Cambridge, add. MSS. c96.20.

6. Sidgwick, *A Memoir*, pp. 33–38, 196–202; Owen Chadwick, *The Victorian Church* (London: Adam & Charles Black, 1970), 2 : 139–40, 147–48. See also, H. Sidgwick, *The Ethics of Conformity and Subscription* (London: Woodfall & Kinder, 1870). The resignation lowered Sidgwick's salary but did not prevent his eventual promotion after the abolition of university tests in 1871. In 1869 he was appointed to a lectureship in

The resignation of his fellowship displayed perhaps the most important strain in Sidgwick's mental character. He regarded the issues of religion, philosophy, and science not as mere speculative topics, but rather as "problems on which grave practical issues depended." Consequently when these questions arose, in the words he once employed to describe Arthur Hugh Clough, "He would not accept either false solutions, or no solutions, nor, unless very reluctantly, provisional solutions." This attitude produced an ambiguous stance toward religion itself. For although he wrote to H. G. Dakyns in 1874, "I cannot take the Creed into my mouth," neither could Sidgwick dismiss the problems that Christianity had addressed.[7]

Certain dissatisfaction had tempered even Sidgwick's initial admiration for naturalistic writers. Although he fully acknowledged the doctrines of Christianity to be incompatible with reason and science, he also felt that Mill, Comte, and Spencer failed to provide an adequate substitute for the discarded faith. Toward the end of his life, while discussing his early study of Mill, Sidgwick recalled,

> [T]he nature of his philosophy—the attitude it took up towards the fundamental questions as to the nature of man and his relation to God and the universe—was not such as to encourage me to expect from philosophy decisive positive answers to these questions, and I was by no means then disposed to acquiesce in negative or agnostic answers.

The refusal to abide by negative answers did not prevent Sidgwick's ultimate departure from Christianity, but it did halt his drift toward scientific naturalism. In 1866 he confided to a friend,

> I have sold myself to metaphysics for "a time and half a time"; I do not as yet regret the bargain. Take notice that I have finally parted from Mill and Comte—not without tears and wailings and cuttings of the hair. I am at present an eclectic. I believe in

---

Moral Sciences; in 1875 he was named Praelector in Moral and Political Philosophy at Trinity College. Finally in 1883 he was elected Knightbridge Professor of Moral Philosophy. Henry Sidgwick hereafter cited in footnotes as HS.

7. HS, "Arthur Hugh Clough" (1869), in *Miscellaneous Essays and Addresses*, ed. A. and E. Sidgwick (London: Macmillan & Co., 1904), p. 65; ibid., p. 65; HS to H. G. Dakyns, February 1874, in Sidgwick, *A Memoir*, p. 286.

the possibility of pursuing conflicting methods of mental philosophy side by side.[8]

The practical consequences of questions about meaningful human existence traditionally posed in a religious context were too vital to be abandoned or to be restricted to one path of investigation. Knowledge necessary for the pursuit of rational life should be sought in various directions.

Moreover, Sidgwick could conceive of no human culture devoid of religion. During his decade of spiritual searching, he had pursued the study of comparative religion in Hebrew and Arabic sources too extensively to dismiss religion as false science, fraud, superstition, or mental illusion.[9] Religion was a cultural activity which interwove morality, the interpretation of nature, perennial human questions, and psychological experiences. In 1867 Sidgwick criticized Matthew Arnold for failing to perceive this multifaceted function of religion.

> [Arnold] has but one distinct thing to say of them [forms of religion]—that they subdue the obvious faults of our animality. They form a sort of spiritual police: that is all. He says nothing of the emotional side of religion; of the infinite and infinitely varied vent which it gives, in its various forms, for the deepest fountains of feeling. He says nothing of its intellectual side: of the indefinite but inevitable questions about the world and human destiny into which the eternal metaphysical problems form themselves in minds of rudimentary development; questions needing confident answers—nay, imperatively demanding, it seems, from age to age, different answers: of the actual facts of psychological experience, so strangely mixed up with, and

8. HS, "Autobiographical Fragment," in ibid., p. 36; HS to H. G. Dakyns, 8 December 1866, in ibid., p. 158.

9. Between 1862 and about 1867, HS, under the impetus of having read Renan, derived "the conviction that it was impossible really to understand at first hand Christianity as a historical religion without penetrating more deeply the mind of the Hebrews and of the Semitic stock from which they sprang. This led to a very important and engrossing employment of a great part of my spare time in the study of Arabic and Hebrew. . . . My studies, aimed directly at a solution of the great issues between Christianity and Scepticism or Agnosticism, had not, as I knew, led to a really decisive result, and I think it was partly from weariness of a continual internal debate which seemed likely to be interminable that I found relief, which I certainly did find, in my renewal of linguistic studies" (HS, "Autobiographical Fragment," in ibid., pp. 36–37).

> expressed in, the mere conventional "jargon" of religion . . .
> how the moral growth of men and nations, while profoundly in-
> fluenced and controlled by the formulae of traditional religions,
> is yet obedient to laws of its own, and in its turn reacts upon
> and modifies these formulae: of all this Mr. Arnold does not
> give a hint.

Such sensitivity to the complexity of religion was foreign to the
adherents of scientific naturalism as well as to Arnold. They might
abstract certain functions of religion, redirect them, and reinterpret
them; but they could not abolish or replace religion in its full
cultural role or its various manifestations. For Sidgwick religion
persisted among cultivated persons not, as Mill suggested, because of
"the small limits of man's certain knowledge, and the boundless-
ness of his desire to know," but rather because of recurring questions
and situations of practical significance.[10]

Even in the secular realm of the New Nature, human beings
could not escape situations that required a religious resolution. In
1864 Sidgwick articulated this position in an Apostles' paper entitled "Is Prayer a Permanent Function of Humanity?" Already
well into the throes of religious doubt, he raised the question of
whether religion provided moral aid to the average human being.
Like almost every other man of the age, he responded in the affirmative. He then posed a more interesting and, considering his audience,
a more pertinent query. He asked whether religion was of any value
to "symmetrical people" who "seem so really fitted for this world as
it is" and who "live to the full, the natural life, and never seem to
wish for more." [11] In other words, was religion of any ultility to the
intellectually and emotionally emancipated men and women who
would be the ideal citizens of Huxley's New Nature?

Once again Sidgwick responded in the affirmative. He contended
there was "one trial that may befall the most symmetrical—old age
which is rarely bourne as well as youth by the nonreligious." Even

10. HS, "The Prophet of Culture" (1867), in *Miscellaneous Essays and Addresses*,
p. 47; J. S. Mill, *Nature and Utility in Religion* (Indianapolis: Bobbs–Merrill Co.,
1958), p. 67.

11. HS, "Is Prayer a Permanent Function of Humanity?", a typed MS in the Henry
Sidgwick Papers, Trinity College, Cambridge, add. MSS. c96.5, p. 11. Annotations suggest that the transcript was made from an original handwritten MS. It would appear
that Mrs. Sidgwick prepared the typescript for possible inclusion in *A Memoir* but
decided against printing it.

the most symmetrical, well-adjusted, happy citizen of the New Nature required some form of religious or optimistic affirmation to face the decay and diminishing vitality of old age. That affirmation was to be discovered not in physical nature or in the doctrines of scientific naturalism, but rather in a consideration of transcendental issues—issues traditionally associated with religion. As of yet no religion provided the essential cultural and psychological integration to supply "the crown of glory of a symmetrical nature." However, Sidgwick refused to despair and concluded, "I cannot believe the long elaboration of centuries to be in vain: and I look forward to a type of man combining highest pagan with highest medieval excellences." [12]

Sidgwick never wavered from this early assertion of the existential necessity for a religious affirmation of life—a necessity originating not with religious or spiritual or speculative matters, but with questions and conditions normal to any living man or woman. Nor did he ever waver from his hope for the eventual discovery of a religious or metaphysical synthesis that would complement the naturalistic view of man and nature. As late as 1894 he saw no reason to relinquish that goal.

> I think we shall agree that two centuries ago—or perhaps even a century ago—the fundamental notions and methods of natural science had not been brought to the condition of clearness and consistency that they have now reached; yet surely it would have been unphilosophical then to throw their methods and conclusions aside, and not rather to endeavour to aid in clearing them from confusion and contradiction. And that is how I would deal with Theology now, and with other subjects besides Theology—for instance, Ethics and Politics.

For Sidgwick the very naturalistic ideal of the rational pursuit of life required a policy of allowing certain questions to remain open and of giving persistent attention to certain theological queries. Science alone could not avoid moral skepticism any more than traditional religion alone could avoid mistaken theories of nature.

> Were we merely curious to learn what is, has been, and will be, we might be content with Sciences and Positive Philosophy:

12. Ibid., pp. 11–12.

were we merely desirous of obtaining a clear view of what ought
to be, we might be satisfied by an ethico-political system. It is
because we require a satisfactory synthesis of these different
fundamental conceptions that the offer of Theology, to prove
that Good somehow eternally Is, irresistibly claims our attention.[13]

That offer of theology irresistibly drew Sidgwick's attention when
he attempted to formulate a system of rational, logical ethics.

The Inadequacy of Naturalistic Ethics

In a letter of 26 June 1870 Henry Sidgwick confessed to Frederic
Myers, a former student and later his intimate friend,

I know . . . that my true self is a Theist, but I believe that
many persons are really faithful to themselves in being irreli-
gious, and I do not feel able to prophesy to them. If I have any
complaint against them, it is not that they do not believe in a
God, but that they are content with, happy in, a universe where
there is no God.[14]

That men could live happily and contentedly within a godless universe constituted an essential presupposition of the spokesmen for
scientific naturalism. Sidgwick dissented from this position. He stood
convinced that without the presence of a deity in the universe the
question "What ought I to do?" could receive no logical or rational
answer. Sidgwick could not live happily or contentedly in the
absence of such an answer to that query.

For Sidgwick the issue was both a personal and a professional concern. He had personally confronted it when making his decision
whether to retain or resign his Trinity fellowship. The ordeal had
left him with no doubt about the practical significance of the question. He was also a professional philosopher of ethics—"the most
eminent of living moralists," according to W. R. Sorley.[15] Like most
Victorian unbelievers, Sidgwick felt that if religion vanished over-

13. HS, "A Dialogue on Time and Common Sense" (1894), in *Lectures on the
Philosophy of Kant and Other Philosophical Lectures and Essays*, ed. J. Ward (London: Macmillan & Co., 1905), pp. 403–04; HS, *Philosophy, Its Scope and Relations:
An Introductory Course of Lectures*, ed. J. Ward (London: Macmillan & Co., 1902), pp.
94–95.
14. HS to F. W. H. Myers, in Sidgwick, *A Memoir*, p. 228.
15. W. R. Sorley, *On the Ethics of Naturalism* (Edinburgh and London: W. Blackwood & Sons, 1885), p. 74.

night, human morality would pass away.[16] In private, however, he
was willing to admit that should the influence of religion diminish
slowly, some form of popular morality would undoubtedly emerge.
Yet as he wrote in his diary on 16 March 1887, "My special business
is not to maintain morality *somehow,* but to establish it logically as
a reasoned system." As a professional philosopher, Sidgwick believed
neither the present empirical ethics of ultilitarianism nor the ethics
of evolutionary naturalism could provide a reasoned system of ethics.
Such a logical ethics was unattainable "if we are limited to merely
mundane sanctions, owing to the inevitable divergence, in this im-
perfect world, between the individual's Duty and his Happiness." [17]
Sidgwick elaborated this disturbing conclusion in his masterpiece
The Methods of Ethics, published in 1874.

In this volume, which C. D. Broad once termed "on the whole the
best treatise on moral theory that has ever been written," Sidgwick
sought to ascertain the most fruitful method for approaching ethical
questions.[18] He divided the methods into the "intuitive" and the
"utilitarian." The former he described as "the view of ethics which
regards as the practically ultimate end of moral actions their conformity to certain rules or dictates of Duty unconditionally prescribed." [19] Though after an extensive examination he found intuitionism wanting as a general method of ethics, he argued that any
system of ethics required at least one intuitive assumption—namely,
its definition or criteria of the good. This insight allowed Sidgwick
to reconcile intuitionism and utilitarianism since the latter intuitively posited the greatest good for the greatest number as its guiding
principle. Sidgwick thus departed from a strictly naturalistic ethics
that ideally would not have permitted the mind to make a nonempirical rational judgment.[20]

16. G. Himmelfarb, *Victorian Minds* (New York: Harper Torchbooks, 1970), pp.
300–13.

17. Sidgwick, *A Memoir,* p. 472.

18. C. D. Broad, *Five Types of Ethical Theory* (London: Routledge & Kegan Paul,
1967), p. 143. The discussion of HS's ethics in this chapter is heavily dependent on
Professor Broad's exposition. See also D. G. James, *Henry Sidgwick: Science and Faith
in Victorian England* (London: Oxford University Press, 1970), pp. 21–44, and W. C.
Havard, *Henry Sidgwick and Later Utilitarian Political Philosophy* (Gainesville, Fla.:
University of Florida Press, 1959), pp. 90–108.

19. HS, *The Methods of Ethics,* 7th ed. (Chicago: University of Chicago Press, 1962),
p. 96. Unless otherwise noted all quotations in this chapter are taken from this
edition.

20. "Professor Sidgwick agrees with Bentham, and the long line of moralists from
Epicurus downwards, in maintaining the doctrine of ethical hedonism, that pleasure is

A more significant departure from scientific naturalism occurred in Sidgwick's discussion of utilitarianism, which he defined as "the ethical theory, that the conduct which, under any given circumstances, is objectively right, is that which will produce the greatest amount of happiness on the whole; that is, taking into account all whose happiness is affected by the conduct." [21] He denoted two forms of utilitarianism. According to the first, universal hedonism, the conduct of the individual should be such as to achieve the greatest happiness for society. According to the second, egoistic hedonism, the individual should seek to maximize his own personal happiness. Sidgwick perceived more clearly than any previous utilitarian writer that an incontrovertible conflict existed between these two forms of utilitarianism. Social duty and personal happiness would not always coincide. Moreover, reasoning from strictly empirical considerations provided no rational or logical means for choosing between duty and happiness.

Sidgwick saw a solution to this dilemma only if the individual, in following the dictates of social duty, could remain certain that eventually he would achieve a greater measure of personal happiness. Otherwise he would dwell in a state of moral skepticism. Deliverance from moral skepticism, however, required two crucial nonempirical, metaphysical assumptions. First, the universe must constitute a moral order which required a God, or in Broad's words "a celestial Jeremy Bentham." [22] Second, it must be assumed that the human personality survives bodily death. Acting upon these assumptions, each man could follow his social duty and sacrifice immediate happiness

---

the only thing ultimately desirable; but, with Butler, he rejects the psychological hedonism, according to which pleasure is the only object of desire. So far from these two positions being inconsistent, it is only through the second that the first can be held in its universalistic form. The problem is, however, how to unite them. In Professor Sidgwick's theory, they are connected by the application of the ethical maxims of benevolence and equity, which an exhaustive examination of ethical intuitions has left standing as axioms of the practical reason. Though utilitarianism, therefore, is still adhered to, it is on an expressly Rational ground, not on the basis of Naturalism" (Sorley, *On the Ethics of Naturalism,* pp. 74–75). "In this conception of the independent nature of a moral judgment and the corresponding rational obligation to act on it, Sidgwick is at one with the intuitionists from the Cambridge Platonists of the seventeenth century to G. E. Moore" (Havard, *Henry Sidgwick and Later Utilitarian Political Philosophy,* p. 91).

21. HS, *The Methods of Ethics,* p. 411.
22. Broad, *Five Types of Ethical Theory,* p. 160.

with the assurance that in the long run his personal sacrifice would be compensated with future pleasure.

In the conclusion to the first edition of *The Methods of Ethics*, Sidgwick argued that, without positing the nonempirical assumptions of the existence of a deity and of human immortality, human beings possessed no means for achieving the rational ethical decisions required by daily conduct.

> Hence the whole system of our beliefs as to the intrinsic reasonableness of conduct must fall, without a hypothesis unverifiable by experience reconciling the Individual with the Universal Reason, without a belief, in some form or other, that the moral order which we see imperfectly realised in this actual world is yet actually perfect. If we reject this belief, we may perhaps still find in the non-moral universe an adequate object for the Speculative Reason, capable of being in some sense ultimately understood. But the Cosmos of Duty is thus really reduced to a Chaos: and the prolonged effort of the human intellect to frame a perfect ideal of rational conduct is seen to have been foredoomed to inevitable failure.[23]

Kant's two ethical postulates lived on. Only nonempirical and non-naturalistic assumptions separated rational moral behavior from ir-

23. HS, *The Methods of Ethics*, 1st ed. (London: Macmillan & Co., 1874), pp. 472–73. In all later editions HS removed the paragraph quoted in the text and inserted the following revised conclusion: "If then the reconciliation of duty and self-interest is to be regarded as a hypothesis logically necessary to avoid a fundamental contradiction in one chief department of our thought, it remains to ask how far this necessity constitutes a sufficient reason for accepting this hypothesis. This, however, is a profoundly difficult and controverted question, the discussion of which belongs rather to a treatise on General Philosophy than to a work on the Methods of Ethics: as it could not be satisfactorily answered, without a general examination of the criteria of true and false beliefs. Those who hold that the edifice of physical science is really constructed of conclusions logically inferred from self-evident premises, may reasonably demand that any practical judgments claiming philosophic certainty should be based on an equally firm foundation. If on the other hand we find that in our supposed knowledge of the world of nature propositions are commonly taken to be universally true, which yet seem to rest on no other grounds than that we have a strong disposition to accept them, and that they are indispensable to the systematic coherence of our beliefs,—it will be more difficult to reject a similarly supported assumption in ethics, without opening the door to universal scepticism" (*The Methods of Ethics*, pp. 508–09). However, all of HS's private letters, notes, and journal entries suggest that he never wavered from his first conclusion.

rational moral chaos.[24] Rational human conduct on utilitarian premises—even within the New Nature—demanded the existence of a being outside the New Nature and not encompassed within the cosmology of scientific naturalism, as well as the survival of human personality beyond its life in the physical world. To naturalistic thinkers a less welcome conclusion could hardly be imagined.

Sidgwick not only defended the rational necessity of his non-empirical assumptions but also vigorously rejected the popular alternative of evolutionary ethics. In setting forth these latter systems, Spencer, Clifford, Stephen, and other writers had sought to ground ethics in the evolutionary process and to reduce consideration of ethical issues to contemporary scientific categories.[25] Sidgwick, though in no manner doubting the fact of evolution or the function of natural selection, questioned the philosophical validity of evolutionary ethics on several points. He thought large parts of these systems were essentially irrelevant to ethics, that evolution itself provided no ethical guidance, and that no ethical conclusions could be derived from the empirical observation of nature.

By "ethics" Sidgwick meant the attempt to "determine what individual human beings 'ought'—or what it is 'right' for them—to do, or to seek to realise by voluntary action." He regarded the naturalistic theories concerning the origin and development of the moral faculties in man as having "little or no bearing upon ethics." The delineation of such origins usually constituted a large segment of treatises on evolutionary ethics. However, about this entire approach Sidgwick complained:

> For all the competing and conflicting moral principles that men have anywhere assumed must be equally derivative: and the mere recognition of their derivativeness, apart from any particular theory as to the *modus derivandi,* cannot supply us with any criterion for distinguishing true moral principles from false. . . . It is obviously absurd to make the validity or invalidity of any judgments depend on the particular stage in the process of development at which this class of judgments

24. For HS's own account of the reasoning by which he arrived at his ethical position, see Preface to the Sixth Edition of *The Methods of Ethics,* pp. xiv–xxi.

25. W. F. Quillian, Jr., *The Moral Theory of Evolutionary Naturalism* (New Haven: Yale University Press, 1945); J. W. Burrow, *Evolution and Society: A Study of Victorian Social Theory* (Cambridge: Cambridge University Press, 1966).

first made their appearance; especially since it is an essential point of the Evolution-theory to conceive this process as fundamentally similar in all its parts.[26]

The very continuity of the evolutionary process itself precluded denoting certain stages of it as higher or lower. The nature of the particular stage was of no relevance to the person who sought to decide what he ought to do while dwelling in that stage.

Nor could the end or purpose of evolution be deduced from the process itself. Capacity for life survival was the most explicit purpose to be reasonably inferred from evolution. But once survival stood assured, the process furnished no criteria for determining the quality of life toward which the surviving creatures should strive. Sidgwick curtly noted, "In short, when fairly contemplated, the doctrine that resolves all virtues and excellences into the comprehensive virtue 'of going on, and still to be' can hardly find acceptance." [27]

Moreover, Sidgwick never tired of pointing out that evolutionary sociologists, though supposedly reasoning from the same facts, could never agree about the nature of the future society toward which civilization purportedly headed. Even if they could agree, he saw no reason to expect real ethical wisdom from their conclusions.

> I do not see how anything that it can tell can give us *positive* principles of practice. It may, indeed, give us valuable negative guidance, for it may warn us from aiming at the impossible. What is to be must be, and it is idle to fight against it: but that is no reason why we should labor to hasten its coming unless we know that it will be an improvement on the present: and this we cannot know unless we bring to our sociological inquiry a criteria of political good and evil which we certainly cannot obtain from it.[28]

26. HS, *The Methods of Ethics*, p. 1; HS, "The Theory of Evolution in Its Application to Practice," *Mind* 1 (1876): 54 and "The Historical Method," *Mind* 11 (1886): 203–19; HS, "The Theory of Evolution," p. 54. See also HS, *The Methods of Ethics*, pp. 396–97, and Havard, *Henry Sidgwick and Later Utilitarian Political Philosophy*, pp. 59–89.

27. HS, "The Theory of Evolution," p. 59.

28. HS, "The Historical Method," pp. 217–18. HS was by no means hostile to sociology per se. He believed that it might eventually attain the precision necessary for scientific prediction. However, he considered the contemporary certainty of the disci-

Sidgwick thus exposed the incapacity of evolutionary thought to determine the nature of the good life or to guide men in achieving ethical conduct. Knowledge of the human condition in the past or in the future or of the mechanism of change could not determine in and of itself what a man ought to do in the present.

Finally, Sidgwick believed the evolutionary philosophers committed the perennial error of confusing what is or will be with what ought to be. His distinguished pupil G. E. Moore later termed this error one form of "the naturalistic fallacy." Perhaps echoing the sentiments voiced by J. S. Mill in the essay on *Nature,* Sidgwick declared,

> On the whole, it appears to me that no definition that has ever been offered of the Natural exhibits this notion as really capable of furnishing an independent ethical first principle. And no one maintains that "natural" like "beautiful" is a notion that though indefinable is yet clear, being derived from a simple unanalyzable impression. Hence I see no way of extracting from it a definite practical criterion of the rightness of actions.[29]

Discovering no ethical criteria in nature nor in the scientific categories interpreting nature, Sidgwick held fast to his nonempirical postulates of a deity and of human immortality so that the cosmos of duty might not fall into chaos.

In his published ethical writings, Sidgwick left these two concepts as necessary, rational, but nonempirical assumptions. Privately, however, he devoted over thirty years of his life to an intensive effort to discover an empirical basis for one of them. That quest led him into one of the strangest and least explored bypaths of nineteenth-century thought—psychical research.

Psychical Research

Henry Sidgwick admitted that the suppositions of the existence of a deity and of human immortality were nonempirical, but he re-

---

pline to be premature and the ethical deduction associated with sociology invalid. See HS, "Political Prophecy and Sociology" and "The Relation of Ethics to Sociology," in *Miscellaneous Essays and Addresses,* pp. 216–34, 249–69, and HS, *Lectures on the Ethics of T. H. Green, Mr. Herbert Spencer, and J. Martineau,* ed. E. E. Constance Jones (London: Macmillan & Co., 1902).

29. G. E. Moore, *Principia Ethica* (Cambridge: Cambridge University Press, 1966), pp. 37–58; HS, *The Methods of Ethics,* p. 83.

fused to consider them unscientific. He claimed that the theistic assumption was as valid in the sphere of morals as was the assumption of continuity in physical nature postulated by Huxley, Tyndall, and Spencer. In 1880 Sidgwick explained to an old Rugby friend the response he would give to a scientifically minded man who questioned the validity of the theistic postulate.

> To this I answer, "What criterion have you of the truth of any of the fundamental beliefs of science, except that they are consistent, harmonious with other beliefs that we find ourselves naturally impelled to hold." And this is precisely the relation that I find to exist between Theism and the whole system of my moral beliefs. Duty is to me as real a thing as the physical world, though it is not apprehended in the same way; but all my apparent knowledge of duty falls into chaos if my belief in the moral government of the world is conceived to be withdrawn.[30]

Sidgwick believed that the theistic hypothesis would receive no further confirmation and that so far as the relationship of ethics to science might be concerned, it required none.

However, he actually held out hope for the discovery of empirical data that would either support or refute the assumption of human immortality. Sidgwick thought certain contemporary psychical phenomena, if discovered to be valid, might provide sufficient empirical evidence for belief in the survival of the human personality after death.[31] These phenomena included hypnotism, mesmerism, mental telepathy, apparitions, and spiritualistic communications. Such psychical occurrences might be interpreted as proof for the independence of mind and body or for the existence of nondiscursive mental faculties.

The sources for the subject matter of psychical research were

30. HS to Major Carey, 8 August 1880, in Sidgwick, *A Memoir*, p. 347. This letter is one of the few documents in which HS expressed any specific religious opinions after resigning his fellowship in 1869. The only other extended discussion he offered is to be found in two Synthetic Society papers printed in Sidgwick, *A Memoir*, pp. 600–15.

31. C. D. Broad, *Religion, Philosophy, and Psychical Research* (New York: Harcourt, Brace & Co., 1953), pp. 86–116 and *Ethics and the History of Philosophy* (New York: Humanities Press, 1952), pp. 49–69. HS did not regard the question of immortality as a theological matter. He was not sure that immortality had any necessary relationship to the question of theism. Arthur J. Balfour, ed., *Papers Read before the Synthetic Society, 1896–1908* (London: Spottiswoode & Co., 1909), p. 190.

numerous.[32] Accounts of trances, hypnotism, telepathy, and clair-
voyance were as ancient as Greece and as modern as Swedenborg and
the religious revivals of the late fifties. Mesmerism, as a formal movement, originated on the continent toward the close of the eighteenth
century and quickly spread into England under various guises.
Spiritualism arose in the United States in the late 1840s and was soon
transported across the Atlantic by traveling mediums. It penetrated
all European countries including Russia, where Tolstoy alluded to
it in his novels. In England, key literary figures, such as the Brown-
ings, displayed more than a passing interest. Spiritualism often
attracted the attention of upper middle-class men and women, such
as Sidgwick and Frederic Myers, who, having lost faith in Christianity, still retained yearnings for some variety of religion. It also
sparked favorable curiosity among persons from the working-class
culture, such as Alfred Russel Wallace, who found the doctrines
of spiritualism more rational than those of Christianity. None of
these movements surrounding psychic phenomena was of minor
importance. Each commanded the allegiance of significant numbers
of supporters throughout the Western world during the nineteenth
century.

The interest aroused by these mysterious occurrences and the
importance attached to them by sensible men were not without
parallels in English history. During the seventeenth century when
the discoveries of the virtuosi threatened to undermine religion,
Henry More, Thomas Browne, and Joseph Glanvill had firmly
believed alleged cases of demonic possession and witchcraft to be
manifestations of a spiritual or supernatural realm. As Professor
Willey explained, "Witchcraft . . . furnished the only available
contemporary evidence of a tangible kind for the existence of super-

32. W. R. Cross, *The Burned-Over District* (New York: Harper Torchbooks, 1965);
R. Darnton, *Mesmerism and the End of the Enlightenment in France* (Cambridge:
Harvard University Press, 1968); E. R. Dodds, *The Greeks and the Irrational* (Berkeley:
University of California Press, 1951); A. Gauld, *The Founders of Psychical Research*
(New York: Schocken Books, 1968); R. Laurence Moore, "Spiritualism and Science:
Reflections on the First Decade of the Spirit Rappings," *American Quarterly* 24
(1972) : 474–500; G. K. Nelson, *Spiritualism and Society* (London: Routledge & K. Paul,
1969); K. H. Porter, *Through a Glass Darkly: Spiritualism in the Browning Circle*
(Lawrence: University of Kansas Press, 1958); Keith Thomas, *Religion and the
Decline of Magic* (New York: Scribner's, 1971); R. K. Webb, *Harriet Martineau: A
Victorian Radical* (London: Heinemann, 1960), pp. 234–47.

natural activity." [33] The psychical phenomena of the late nineteenth century furnished Sidgwick, Myers, and Wallace with similar evidence of existing beings not included in the cosmology of scientific naturalism. For minds whose aspirations could not be realized within that cosmos, the mesmerist trances, table-turnings, mediumistic messages, and other alleged psychical phenomena suggested the possibility of a natural world richer in existing realities and more spiritually satisfying than that described by the scientific publicists. Psychical research held forth the possible discovery of natural entities that could render the natural order commensurable to the ideals of the human beings dwelling therein.

Sidgwick first became involved with spiritualism in 1860 when he began to attend seances in London.[34] During this decade of personal religious turmoil seances supplemented his academic study of comparative religion. He considered the rappings of spirits as a possible manifestation of primitive religious phenomena from which all religions had perhaps originated. Yet he could come to no firm conclusion as to the validity of the messages and physical manifestations of the spirits. In 1873 he told Myers,

> As for Spirit-rapping, I am exactly in the same mind towards it as towards Religion. I believe there is something in it: don't know what: have tried hard to discover, and find that I always paralyze the phenomena; my taste is strongly affected by the obvious humbug mixed with it, which, at the same time, my reason does not overestimate.[35]

This note marked the end of Sidgwick's strictly religious interest in the spirits. He was then hard at work on *The Methods of Ethics* and moving toward its disconcerting conclusion. Henceforth, he would look to psychical research as a means of discovering empirical evidence for human immortality.

In 1874, with Myers, Edmund Gurney, A. J. Balfour, and his future wife Eleanor Balfour, Sidgwick commenced a systematic in-

33. Basil Willey, *The Seventeenth Century Background* (Garden City, N.Y.: Doubleday Anchor Books, 1953), p. 195, also pp. 60–62, 169–71, 195–203.

34. See Sidgwick, *A Memoir*, pp. 43–44, 52–55, 103–06, 162–71. Prior to his first seances HS had been a member of the Ghost Society at Cambridge. Gauld, *The Founders of Psychical Research*, pp. 88–136.

35. HS to F. W. H. Myers, 30 October 1873, in Sidgwick, *A Memoir*, p. 284.

vestigation of psychical phenomena with their bearing on the issue of immortality foremost in his mind. This endeavor set Sidgwick between the forces of contemporary religion and science. By and large, the clergy disregarded spiritualism on the grounds that it was either fraud or a work of the devil. With a few notable exceptions, including William Crookes, William Barrett, and Alfred Russel Wallace, men of science and naturalistic writers also dismissed hypnotism, mesmerism, telepathy, and spiritualism.[36] Like the clergy, most scientists considered the psychical occurrences fraudulent. A few actually did investigate seances. The scientific reductionism of others made them ill-disposed to consider the possibility that mind might exist separately from its physical organism. Most important, naturalistic writers, satisfied with life in the New Nature and with their own systems of evolutionary ethics, could not attach to psychical research the significance it held for a man such as Sidgwick.

The indifference of the clergy did not surprise or bother Sidgwick. He had long ago emancipated himself from the narrow religiosity of orthodox clergymen. The general indifference and hostility of men of science were another matter. As he once argued, "It is not a scientific way of dealing with a mass of testimony to explain what you can, and say that the rest is untrue. It may be common-sense; but it is not science." Consequently, in 1882, in the words of William James, "scandalized by the chaotic state of opinion regarding the phenomena now called by the rather ridiculous name of 'psychic'— phenomena, of which the supply reported seems inexhaustible, but which scientifically trained minds mostly refuse to look at," Sidgwick's original group joined with other interested parties to found the Society for Psychical Research.[37] Its purpose was to investigate

36. W. Crookes, "Spiritualism Viewed by the Light of Modern Science," *Quarterly Journal of Science* 7 (1870) : 316–21; "Experimental Investigation of a New Force" and "Some Further Experiments on Psychic Force," *Quarterly Journal of Science* 8 (1871) : 339–49, 471–93. For A. R. Wallace's relationship to spiritualism, see chapter 4. Barrett read a paper on the subject to the Anthropological Section of the British Association for the Advancement of Science in 1876 (Gauld, *The Founders of Psychical Research*, p. 137). For a hostile reception by a scientist, see J. Tyndall, *Fragments of Science*, 6th ed. (New York: D. Appleton & Co., 1892), 1 : 444–52.

37. HS, "Presidential Address, July 18, 1883," in *Presidential Addresses to the Society for Psychical Research* (Glasgow: Society for Psychical Research, 1912), p. 15; John J. McDermott, ed., *The Writings of William James* (New York: The Modern Library, 1968), pp. 787–88. "It was hardly possible to maintain, without writing oneself down as an ass, that a society over which Sidgwick presided and in whose work

what scientists would not investigate and thereby to combat the intellectual negativism of scientific naturalism. Eventually, through this organization numerous British intellectuals entered the international network of writers and investigators probing various manifestations of man's irrational nature. At one time or another William James, Henri Bergson, and Carl Jung cooperated with the society.

In 1888 Sidgwick reminded the Society for Psychical Research of its original purposes.

> Now our own position was this. We believed unreservedly in the methods of modern science, and were prepared to accept submissively her reasoned conclusions, when sustained by the agreement of experts; but we were not prepared to bow with equal docility to the mere prejudices of scientific men. And it appeared to us that there was an important body of evidence— tending *prima facie* to establish the independence of soul or spirit—which modern science had simply left on one side with ignorant contempt; and that in so leaving it she had been untrue to her professed method, and had arrived prematurely at her negative conclusions.[38]

This active prejudice on the part of men of science completed Sidgwick's alienation from scientific naturalism. His ethical studies had persuaded him that the scientific publicists could not successfully or rationally address certain inevitable human questions. Their refusal to investigate psychical phenomena in a systematic manner convinced him that they were not prepared even to consider the implications of those occurrences, but preferred to turn their backs on the pursuit of truth and on new evidence that might bring their present ideas into doubt. They were unfit to claim the leadership of English thought.

Sidgwick's involvement in psychical research also occasioned a crisis in his own mental life which brought his most cherished beliefs and ideas into question. In 1887 the Society for Psychical

---

he was actively interested consisted of knaves and fools concealing superstition under the cloak of scientific verbiage" (Broad, *Religion, Philosophy, and Psychical Research*, p. 94). See also Gauld, *The Founders of Psychical Research*, pp. 137–42.

38. HS, "Presidential Address, July 16, 1888," in *Presidential Addresses to the Society for Psychical Research*, p. 35.

Research had been in existence for five years. It had conducted several significant investigations, the most important of which was recorded in *Phantasms of the Living,* a systematic study of apparitions carried out by Myers, Edmund Gurney, and Frank Podmore.[39] Nevertheless, little or no light had been shed on the issue that most vitally concerned Sidgwick—human immortality. On 28 January 1887 Sidgwick noted in his journal that he had been "passing through a mental crisis" as he drifted steadily toward the conclusion "that we have not, and are never likely to have, empirical evidence of the existence of the individual after death." A grave personal dilemma confronted him.

> Soon, therefore, it will probably be my duty as a reasonable being—and especially as a professional philosopher—to consider on what basis the human individual ought to construct his life under these circumstances. . . . If I decide that this search is a failure, shall I finally and decisively make this postulate [i.e., immortality]? Can I consistently with my whole view of truth and the method of its attainment? And if I answer "no" to each of these questions, have I any ethical system at all? And if not, can I continue to be Professor and absorb myself in the mere erudition of the subject—write "studies" of moralists from Socrates to Bentham. . . .

He continued to muse on the difficulty, noting on March 22, "More meditations on the same subject—with no progress. . . . Still, it is premature to despair, and I am quite content to go on seeking while life lasts; that is not the perplexing problem; the question is whether to profess Ethics without a basis." [40]

Sidgwick had reasoned his way beyond the scope of rational decision. He had argued in *The Methods of Ethics* that rational decisions could only be achieved on the presupposition that the human personality was immortal. Now he faced what was by his own standards the impossible task of making a rational ethical decision without any empirical basis for that crucial assumption. He reached the depths of despair on 14 April 1887, as his cosmos of duty dissolved into a personal chaos.

39. Gauld, *The Founders of Psychical Research,* pp. 153–86.
40. Sidgwick, *A Memoir,* pp. 466–67, 472–73.

> I find myself without impulse to write anything of my inner life in this journal; the fact is that while I find it easy enough to *live* with more or less satisfaction, I cannot at present get any satisfaction from *thinking* about life, for thinking means—as I am a philosopher—endeavouring to frame an ethical theory which will hold together, and to this I do not see my way. And the consideration that the morality of the world may be trusted to get on without philosophers does not altogether console. The ancient sage took up a strong position who argued, "We must philosophize, for either we ought to philosophize or we ought not; and if we ought not to philosophize, we can only know this by studying philosophy." But tradition does not say what course the sage recommended to a philosopher who has philosophized himself into a conviction of the unprofitableness of philosophy. He must do something else; but how is he to do it on rational grounds without philosophy? and [when] whatever impulses nature may have given him—as to other men— to do things *without* rational grounds have been effectually suppressed by philosophy.

Almost a year passed before he emerged from this dilemma that he called his "tunnel." [41]

As late as 8 January 1888, still on the brink of the skeptical abyss, Sidgwick noted, "For my inner life, I have nothing new to say. I think over 'Gordian Knots,' but come to no further solution. Silence is best." Then for three months there was only silence. But on 12 April 1888 he commenced anew with genuine, if subdued, freshness.

> To-day I recommence my journal, with a determination to continue it. . . . The change is great in my own mind since I left off the journal; and though the loss is great, I am obliged to confess to myself that the change is not altogether for the worse. I take life more as it comes, and with more concern for small things. I aim at cheerfulness and I generally attain it . . . and though I still feel what Carlyle calls the "Infinity of Duty," it is only in great matters I feel it; as regards the petty worries of life, I feel that both the Universe and Duty *de minimis non*

41. Ibid., pp. 475, 485.

> *curant:* or rather the one Infinite duty is to be serene. And
> serene I am—so far! [42]

What had occurred during the interval of silence? Unfortunately, it
is not certain; but Sidgwick had tempered his rational expectations
of life and overcome his inability "to do things *without* rational
grounds."

Three hints of the nature of his inner resolution emerged in a
letter he wrote to J. A. Symonds on 8 April 1888. He told Symonds
that he had been laboring under the illusion that he "must settle
down into decidedness tomorrow or the day after: and that when
this moment comes the existence I am leading in a kind of tunnel
under the surface of ordinary human life will have come to an
end." [43] He apparently decided to purge himself of that illusion and
to make no decision.

Second, Sidgwick had learned something new about making
personal ethical decisions. He told Symonds, "What I intended to
say is that I have [now] emerged from my tunnel by an act of will,
and do not mean to let my mind turn on this hook any more for the
present." By that act of will Sidgwick had overcome his disinclina-
tion to act on nonrational grounds. He exercised what his friend in
the American Cambridge would later term "the will to believe." [44]
Like William James, Sidgwick decided that it was better to pursue
truth than to avoid error. He agreed within himself to affirm, on
neither rational nor empirical grounds, that the universe and man's
relationship to it was rational and to pursue his personal and professional life according to that affirmation. The life of reason was possible only after at least one nonrational act of his will. In this regard,
Sidgwick resembled George Romanes, Samuel Butler, and James
Ward, who considered reason as only one faculty or tool whereby
men lead their lives and interpret their situation in the universe.

Finally, Sidgwick came to perceive that the standards of contemporary religion and science provided inadequate grounds for classify-
ing his intellectual pursuits.

> Ethics seems to me in a position intermediate between Theology
> and Science, regarded as subjects of academic study and profes-

---

42. HS, MS Journal, Henry Sidgwick Papers, add. MSS. c97.25, p. 129; Sidgwick, *A
Memoir*, pp. 485–86.

43. Sidgwick, *A Memoir*, p. 484.

44. Ibid., p. 485; McDermott, *The Writings of William James*, pp. 717–34.

sion, in this way:—No one doubts that a Professor of Theology, under the conditions prevailing in England at least, is expected to be in some way constructive; if not exactly orthodox, at any rate he is expected to have or to be able to communicate a rational basis for some established creed and system. If he comes to the conclusion that no such basis is attainable, most sensible persons would agree that he is in his wrong place and had better take up some other calling. On the other hand the professor of any branch of science is under no such restriction; he is expected to communicate unreservedly the results to which he has come, whether favourable or not to the received doctrines: if (e.g.) he were the solitary Darwinian in a society of Creationists, that would be no reason for resigning his chair—rather for holding on. Now my difficulty is to make up my mind which of these analogies I ought to apply to my own case—and I have not yet done so.[45]

In the years that lay ahead he concluded that philosophy per se pertained to neither religion nor science but that in reality both, but especially science, presupposed the activity of the professional philosopher. He tied an earlier criticism of empiricism to a renewed faith in the role of philosophy as the queen of the sciences and handmaiden to none. He came to believe that the philosopher as well as the man of science must influence culture if society is to permit the full pursuit of truth and the proper consideration of essential human questions.

Sidgwick did not abandon psychical research but continued to pursue it even more intensely. He never received what he considered adequate proof of immortality. However, he did accept the validity of telepathy.[46] That conviction encouraged him to feel the course of investigation still held out hope for further discovery. Thus, though psychical research did not prove what he had hoped it might, the crisis in his own mental life that it occasioned in 1887 and 1888 resolved itself into a new assurance that philosophy and his profes-

45. HS to J. A. Symonds, 8 April 1888, in Sidgwick, *A Memoir*, p. 485.

46. In 1894 HS signed the conclusion to the Society for Psychical Research Report on the Census of Hallucinations. It stated, *"Between deaths and apparitions of the dying person a connection exists which is not due to chance alone.* This we hold as a proved fact. The discussion of its full implications cannot be attempted in this paper; —nor perhaps exhausted in this age" (*Proceedings of the Society for Psychical Research* [1894], 10 : 394).

sional pursuit of philosophy were essential for the consideration of issues not addressed by the spokesmen for naturalism. Consequently, he became increasingly critical of the philosophical adequacy of naturalistic doctrines.

THE INCOHERENCE OF EMPIRICISM

Henry Sidgwick recognized one of the most profoundly significant features of the intellectual life of the late nineteenth century when in 1899 he told the Synthetic Society, "Probably there never was a time when the amount of beliefs held by an average educated person, undemonstrated and unverified by himself, was greater than it is now." [47] Knowledge and the pursuit of knowledge had become so fragmented that any educated man must depend, as never before, on the authoritative judgment of other thinkers in other fields of investigation. The paradox of the new empirical era was that the experience according to which men acted was not their own but that of others communicated through the various channels of professional expertise.

Sidgwick realized that as he spoke one group of experts, the men of science, exerted undue, and he believed illicit, authority over the minds of men. No other single group so boasted of the empirical basis of their pronouncements, and no other group so benefited from the common resort to experts.

> [M]en are more and more disposed only to accept authority of a particular kind: the authority, namely, that is formed and maintained by the unconstrained agreement of individual experts, each of whom is believed to be seeking truth with unfettered independence, and declaring what he has found with perfect openness and the greatest attainable precision. This authority, therefore, is conceived as the authority of the living mind of humanity, and as containing within itself, by the very nature of its composition, adequate guarantees for the elimination of error by continual self-questioning and self-criticism; . . . It is for this kind of authority that the wonderful and steady progress of physical knowledge leads educated persons to entertain a continually increasing respect—accompanied, I think, by a cor-

47. HS, "Authority: Scientific and Theological," in Sidgwick, *A Memoir*, p. 609.

responding distrust of any other kind of authority in matters intellectual.[48]

Sidgwick did not dispute the astounding success of the scientific experts nor did he question the truth and meliorative influence of their discoveries. He did, however, stridently deny that theirs was the only intellectual authority to which men should demur and that they could explain their theory and activity on strictly empirical grounds. He thus denied the right of men of science to be the undisputed leaders of English culture.

During the last two decades of his life Sidgwick became an untiring critic of empiricism. In an article published in 1900, the year of his death, he outlined his general objection.

> I take the principle of Empiricism, as an epistemological doctrine, to be that the ultimately valid premises of all scientific reasonings are cognitions of particular facts; all the generalizations of science being held to be obtained from these particular cognitions by induction, and to depend upon these for their validity. I do not accept this principle; I think it impossible to establish the general truths of the accepted sciences by processes of cogent inference on the basis of merely particular premises; and I think the chief service that J. S. Mill rendered to philosophy, by his elaborate attempt to perform this task, was to make this impossibility as clear as day.

Explaining that his criticism of empiricism was not a denial of the truth of scientific theory or discovery, he had declared in 1882, "It is possible to combine a practically complete trust in the procedure and results of empirical science with a profound distrust in the procedure and conclusions—especially the negative conclusions—of Empirical philosophy." [49]

The arrogance and cultural pretensions of the scientific publicists rested largely on their empirical theory of truth, which both supported their own ideas and allowed them to dismiss those of opponents. They also credited empiricism for the general progress of

48. Ibid., pp. 609-10. HS made a very similar statement in "The Ethics of Religious Conformity" (1893), in HS, *Practical Ethics: A Collection of Addresses and Essays* (London: S. Sonnenschein & Co., 1898), pp. 124-25.

49. HS, "Criteria of Truth and Error" in *Lectures on the Philosophy of Kant*, p. 442; HS, "The Incoherence of Empirical Philosophy" in ibid., p. 391.

scientific thought and achievement. To challenge the philosophical adequacy of empiricism or to deny its relationship to concrete scientific advances was to strike at the heart of scientific naturalism. This was what Sidgwick did as he pointed to the "incoherence of the Empirical philosophy." He stated quite simply that he was unable "to work out a coherent theory of the criteria of knowledge on an Empirical basis." [50] His epistemological difficulties with empiricism were analogous to his ethical difficulties with the same doctrine. For Sidgwick a coherent epistemology, as well as a coherent system of ethics, had to go beyond the immediate data of the senses. Samuel Butler and James Ward also dissented from empiricism and even suggested that human knowledge and activity possessed a nonrational foundation. Except in the privacy of his journal during his mental crisis of 1887 and 1888, Sidgwick could not go that far. Publicly, he was satisfied to argue that men of science and their supporters did not do in fact what they claimed to be doing when they boasted of the empirical basis of their discoveries and theories.

In an 1882 article for *Mind* Sidgwick explained that he regarded empiricism as "a doctrine that is concerned with knowledge in respect of its validity, laying down the general criteria by which true or real knowledge may be distinguished from what is merely apparent." Had he stopped at this point and commenced his criticism, his essay would clearly have dealt with empiricism as an epistemological issue. Instead he made crystal clear that his interest in the incoherence of empiricism related to the employment of that theory by the adherents of scientific naturalism.

> [W]e may say that Empiricism of some kind is the philosophy which students of Natural Science, at the present day, generally have, or tend to have; *and also other persons who cannot be called students of Natural Science, but whose minds are impressed and dominated by the triumphant march of modern physical investigation.* Such persons have a general, unanalyzed conviction, independent of close reasoning of any kind, that the recent conquests of the human intellect over the world of concrete fact are mainly due to that precise, patient, and elaborate questioning of experience which has certainly been an indispensable condition of their attainment; that the extension and

50. Ibid., pp. 372, 374.

steady growth of these conquests constitute at the present time the most important fact for one who wishes to philosophize; and that any philosophy that is not thoroughly competent to deal with this fact has therefore a presumption against it that it is behind its age.[51]

Sidgwick challenged the naïve assertions of supporters of empiricism by arguing that the discoveries and concepts of scientists simply were not rooted in empiricism. By the 1890s he would claim that the scientists could do little or nothing until the philosopher had spoken.

Sidgwick stressed that despite the naturalistic theory of truth scientists and scientifically oriented men did not employ immediate empirical cognitions in formulating their theories. Rather, "in the course of their use as instruments of scientific reasoning" those cognitions underwent various transformations.[52] For example, in chemistry the immediate empirical cognition of acid ascertained either by taste or reaction to litmus paper was very different from the idea of acid or salt employed in scientific reasoning. Such reasoning transformed immediate laboratory experiences into theoretical elements that were not identical with the experiences. There was little relationship between the empirical data of the sciences and the conceptual framework into which the data were incorporated. Yet until so incorporated, the data were useless and meaningless. The conceptual framework determined the interpretation of the empirical data. Consequently, Sidgwick held, contrary to G. H. Lewes, that even with the objective scientific method, thought still determined things. Implicit in most of Sidgwick's thought on epistemology was the unstated assumption that the mind was much more active than most naturalistic psychologists admitted.[53] However, he left the task of formulating a psychology of the active mind to his student James Ward.

Not only the interpretation of empirical data, but also the criteria of what constituted such data, Sidgwick argued, had been and continued to be subject to change. The criteria were nothing more than a conventional arrangement achieved by the consensus of a particular group of experts. At the moment men of science formed that

51. Ibid., pp. 372, 373 (FMT's emphasis).
52. Ibid., p. 378.
53. HS also could not accept the Kantian view of reality. He appears to have embraced a naïve realism. See HS, *Lectures on Kant*, pp. 69–77, 406–29.

group. However, they based their particular criteria on considerations of conceptual convenience having little or no relationship to the empirical data itself. The current "empirical" explanation of scientific method and discovery represented a post facto explanation and justification for ideas achieved in a different fashion.[54] As he told the Metaphysical Society in 1879, "We cannot get along without the empirical sciences. But we might perhaps make a shift to dispense with Empirical Philosophy." [55]

Following his mental crisis of 1887–88, Sidgwick became even more critical of the empirical philosophy and its use by the exponents of scientific naturalism. He was especially eager to demonstrate that scientists and those writers deriving their ideas from science were not intellectually self-sufficient. His articles challenged Huxley's contention that "in truth, the laboratory is the fore-court of the temple of philosophy; and whoso has not offered sacrifices and undergone purification there, has little chance of admission into the sanctuary." [56] He thought Huxley had confused the chambers.

Sidgwick contended that the present scientific concept of an empirical fact did not arise out of vigilantly verifiable sense experience but instead rested upon a particular unexamined metaphysical interpretation of the past and future. This was the principle of continuity according to which naturalistic writers assumed that the past had been like the present and that the future would continue in the same manner. The proposition might or might not be true, but its validity had nothing to do with empiricism or with scientific proof.

> Now no proposition with regard to the past can be directly verified by sensible experience: so far as we ever regard it as so verified, reflection always shows that we do this on the basis of certain assumptions as to the uniformity of natural laws and causes. Suppose then that any dispute is raised as to the validity of such assumption, how are we to settle it? It does not exactly

54. HS, "The Incoherence of Empirical Philosophy" and "Criteria of Truth and Error," in ibid., pp. 386–90, 431–32.

55. HS, *Incoherence of Empirical Philosophy* (privately printed to be read on 14 January 1879 at the meeting of the Metaphysical Society), p. 10. This rare pamphlet (British Museum, Cup. 400.c2.(37.).) is an early draft of the article with the same title published in *Mind* in 1882. The differences are generally minor, but in the original paper, unlike the later article, HS included himself among those who often assumed philosophy must be guided by science.

56. T. H. Huxley, *Hume* (London: Macmillan & Co., 1881), pp. 51–52.

seem to belong to any physical science to settle it decisively, as the methods characteristic of such sciences seem to be not available for its solution.[57]

Since men of science and of scientific naturalism could not by their own professed method justify the philosophical presupposition of continuity, they could never be the sole arbiters of culture. The work of the scientists rested upon that of other men—the philosophers.

Sidgwick was not so naïve or professionally chauvinistic as to believe that philosophers possessed certain knowledge, a corner on truth, or final intellectual authority. Like the scientists, they could achieve nothing more than some form of expert consensus. However, until the philosophic consensus had been attained, the scientific consensus must be held in abeyance. Sidgwick did not claim a dominant position for the philosopher in contemporary culture, but he did demand recognition of the intellectual inadequacy of men of science as sole arbiters of English thought.

In a sense Sidgwick envisioned a form of cultural eclecticism similar to the personal philosophic eclecticism that he had adopted in 1866. The philosopher must continue to consider the question of ethics because scientific writers had not successfully addressed the issue.[58] Of equal importance, the professional philosopher must keep alive metaphysical questions that the exponents of naturalism eschewed but about which thinking men must always ponder.

> I cannot admit—because I do not find that Science can admit —that Science is not concerned with Reality, but only with appearance: on the other hand, I cannot but admit that the Universe as a whole has or may have characteristics other than those with which the Sciences, especially at any rate the Sciences recognized by Spencer, are concerned, and therefore that knowledge is possible with regard to it other than that attained by the consolidation of these Sciences. But even if I were as Agnostic as Mr. Spencer professes to be . . . I should not import my Agnosticism into a definition of the Scope of Philosophy.

57. HS, *Philosophy, Its Scope and Relations,* p. 100. See A. N. Whitehead, *Adventures of Ideas* (New York: Mentor Books, 1962), p. 130, and Stephen Toulmin, *The Philosophy of Science: An Introduction* (London: Hutchinson's University Library, 1953), pp. 152–53.

58. HS, *Philosophy, Its Scope and Relations,* p. 33.

> For my aim is to give a definition which all schools may accept:
> and my plan of attaining this is . . . to define the scope of
> Philosophy by ascertaining the questions which it asks, rather
> than the right answer to these questions.[59]

Only when such speculative issues were raised and discussed was
there hope for rationally coordinating human experience.

Keeping alive metaphysical questions not only served to satisfy
human curiosity but also paid genuine dividends to science by
providing impetus to new discovery. Sidgwick pointed to the ferment of scientific thought roused by philosophical speculation from
the Greeks to Descartes, Leibnitz, and Hegel. In one of his classes
he declared, "Philosophy is the central vital force which causes
new sciences to bud on the tree of knowledge: each philosophical
system is a pulsation of new sap and buds with branch or twig of
more [?] or less [?] value." [60] Philosophy assured the discovery of
further truth by raising and examining unresolved issues and questions that men of science chose for the time being to ignore.

Unlike the adherents of scientific naturalism, Sidgwick believed
that man had yet to approach the end of his discovery of truth
about the universe and of man's place therein. He scorned anyone

> who would say that man is now mature: his time for stimulat-
> ing dreams of youth is over; he is deeply impressed with the
> vanity of attempting ever anew the solution of the insoluble;
> and he has been impressed with this in time, because the
> individual profit of these vain attempts has ceased.

This stance, which was so prevalent among the men of scientific
naturalism, appeared to Sidgwick as "a flagrant abandonment of just
the basis of experience on which the arguer plants his feet." [61] Men
who trod the path of intellectual exclusion, premature certainty, and
implicit premature despair could never preside over a culture in
which all the truth of man and nature would stand revealed or
even be pursued. Their society would never permit the full manifestation of human nature nor provide a moral life resting on logical,
rational foundations.

59. Ibid., p. 15.
60. HS, "Is Philosophy the Germ or the Crown of Science?" Henry Sidgwick Papers,
add. MSS. c96.2, p. 7.
61. Ibid., p. 8.

Sidgwick refused to accept the inevitability of such an intellectually limited and morally impotent culture. He persisted in raising and addressing those human questions that inevitably led him beyond empiricism and the categories of science. He provided neither himself nor his generation with answers to those questions. In this regard his intellectual career resembled that of Clough, whose life Sidgwick once described in terms applicable to his own. "In one sense, no doubt, that work was incomplete and fragmentary; the effort of the man who ponders insoluble problems, and spends his passion on the vain endeavour to reconcile aspirations and actualities, must necessarily be so; the incompleteness is essential, not accidental." [62] Sidgwick stood as a figure of undisputed intellectual integrity who prevented other men from embracing unwarranted certainty and from becoming disheartened by a sense of premature futility. He convinced men of the legitimacy of yet unanswered questions and suggested that the methods and theories of scientific naturalism could provide no valid reasons for dismissing such problems or for regarding them as hopeless. Perhaps most important, he pointed out that the very goals of life lived according to rational and logical rules and of nature interpreted rationally and logically required the acceptance of nonempirical assumptions, the consideration of experiences not recognized by most scientifically oriented men, and a reconsideration of the naturalistic cosmology.

To pass from the urbane Henry Sidgwick lecturing to upper-middle-class and aristocratic students in his classroom at Trinity College to Alfred Russel Wallace exploring the Malay Archipelago or arranging his collections in Croyden is to move into a different sphere of nineteenth-century English life. Sidgwick's was the world of the public school, the university, the philosophical societies, and the corridors of Victorian political power. Wallace's was the world of the mechanics institutes, the provinces during the railway boom, the jungles of Southeast Asia, the Victorian scientific societies, and utopian socialist groups. Yet in their different worlds and from their separate backgrounds, both Sidgwick and Wallace concluded that scientific naturalism was incommensurate with the rational ideals that guided their lives.

62. HS, "Arthur Hugh Clough" (1869), in *Miscellaneous Essays and Addresses*, p. 63.

4

Alfred Russel Wallace: The Wonderful Man of the Wonderful Century

THE ENIGMA OF ALFRED RUSSEL WALLACE

Alfred Russel Wallace was the "other man" who discovered evolution by natural selection.[1] From the summer day in 1858 when his hastily penned sketch of the theory arrived in Charles Darwin's mail, Wallace never ceased to surprise and even to astonish scientific contemporaries by his independent judgment and initiative. In 1861, while exploring in the Dutch East Indies, he wrote to a friend, "I am here in one of the places unknown to the Royal Geographical Society, situated in the very center of East Sumatra, about one hundred miles from the sea in three directions."[2] The remark was both typical and indicative of a man who was rarely to be found in any area prescribed by the map of official opinion.

To describe something or someone who provided frequent surprise or astonishment, the Victorians employed the word *wonderful.* Wallace used it to describe the nineteenth century, which astonished him both in its scientific and technical achievements and in its social and moral failures.[3] *Wonderful* provided an equally appropriate description of Wallace himself, whose ideas and opinions were as astonishing as the century through which he lived. This ever wonderful man deviated from his own theory of natural selection, condemned other men of science for furthering the New Nature, supported phrenology, and fervently advocated the validity of spiritualism.

A certain otherness marked Wallace's entire life. A naïve, almost

1. H. Lewis McKinney, *Wallace and Natural Selection* (New Haven: Yale University Press, 1972); Barbara Beddall, "Wallace, Darwin, and the Theory of Natural Selection," *Journal of the History of Biology* 1 (1968) : 261–323.

2. A. R. Wallace to George Silk, 22 December 1861, in A. R. Wallace, *My Life: A Record of Events and Opinions* (New York: Dodd, Mead, & Co., 1905), 1 : 380. A. R. Wallace hereafter cited in footnotes as ARW.

3. ARW, *The Wonderful Century* (New York: Dodd, Mead & Co., 1899).

archaic, individualism touched all his thought; but neither affecta-
tion nor self-styled eccentricity accounted for the independent, sometimes idiosyncratic, streak in his character. Wallace was different
from most of his scientific contemporaries because his life had been
quite different from theirs.[4] Those typical English institutions of
the family, the church, the public school, the military, and the
university did little or nothing to mold his character. His family
was poor and never closely knit. His father had been trained as a
lawyer but never practiced; he lost what little fortune he had
inherited. Consequently, the children were apprenticed to manual
trades. For six years (1830–36) the young Wallace did attend grammar school, where he helped to defray the tuition payments by
aiding the teacher. More than sixty years later he bitterly recalled
the misery of that "anomalous" and 'hybrid" position of being both
pupil and teacher and thus different from everyone else.[5] In a
sense Wallace was always a "hybrid."

The years of adolescence, when wealthier boys such as Henry
Sidgwick and Frederic Myers attended Rugby and Cambridge,
found Alfred Wallace working for his elder brother, a surveyor.
The occupation did not permit long residence in any particular
area. For eighteen months following his twenty-first birthday in 1844,
Wallace taught English at the Collegiate School in Leicester. Then
he returned to surveying and the unsettled existence of that trade.

Throughout these rootless years Wallace studied botany, zoology,
geology, and natural history from the major texts of the day. He
attended the mechanics institutes and listened to anyone who would
talk to him about science. However, except for collecting specimens
of beetles and other insects, his scientific training was almost
entirely literary. In 1847 Wallace left England for South America
and four years of exploring and collecting.[6] He returned to England
in 1852 only to leave again in 1854 for new research in the Malay
Archipelago, where he remained for eight years.[7] Yet these two long
expeditions differed from the more famous voyages of Darwin and
Huxley. Though in 1853 Wallace had received a travel grant from

4. ARW, *My Life*, 1 : 1–263, and James Marchant, *Alfred Russel Wallace: Letters
and Reminiscences* (New York: Cassell & Co., 1916), 1 : 1–71.
5. ARW, *My Life*, 1 : 58.
6. ARW, *A Narrative of Travels on the Amazon and Rio Negro* (London: Reeve &
Co., 1853).
7. ARW, *The Malay Archipelago* (New York: Dover Publications, 1962).

the Royal Geographical Society, little or no official business was connected with his trip. Wallace was not attached to an English naval vessel, and he knew almost none of the English companionship that Darwin and Huxley both enjoyed and chafed under while aboard the *Beagle* and the *Rattlesnake*.

A shipwreck on the way home in 1852 destroyed most of the specimens from South America, but Wallace was more fortunate with his collections from the Malay Archipelago. There he gathered over 125,000 specimens of natural history, a feat Darwin termed "heroic." [8] Later, while arranging and pondering over his collection, Wallace pioneered the study of the geographical distribution of plants and animals. He discerned a division within the flora and fauna of the Australasian islands following a line of demarcation known to this day as the Wallace Line. His distinguished volumes on *The Geographical Distribution of Animals* marked him as the founder of the science of zoogeography.[9] Wallace was the first great anthropologist to live for an extended period among the primitive peoples whom he studied. Moreover, he displayed a sympathy and understanding for primitive civilization that was a half-century ahead of its time.[10] But supreme among those accomplishments stood his independent formulation of the theory of evolution by natural selection.

With that discovery, Wallace suddenly became "the other man." Yet neither this achievement nor his experience prior to it were such that Wallace should emerge as a creature of conventional scientific opinion. The months and years of wandering and solitude spent outside the institutions of middle-class social and intellectual life allowed him to develop little empathy for the professional goals, cultural values, and social prudence of most of his scientific friends. Since at no time in his long life did he hold a professional scientific appointment, he possessed little sense of belonging to a profession that sought to remold English thought and culture.[11] This independence

8. Ibid., p. xii; C. Darwin to ARW, 22 March 1869, in Marchant, *Alfred Russel Wallace*, 1 : 237.

9. Wilma George, *Biologist Philosopher: A Study of the Life and Writings of Alfred Russel Wallace* (New York: Abelard-Schuman, 1964), pp. 97–115, 122–55, 163–83; Karl P. Schmidt, "Animal Geography" in *A Century of Progress in the Natural Sciences*, ed. E. L. Kessel (San Francisco: California Academy of Sciences, 1955), pp. 769–71.

10. Loren Eiseley, "Alfred Russel Wallace," *Scientific American*, February 1959, p. 70.

11. ARW, *My Life*, 1 : 415–17; Marchant, *Alfred Russel Wallace*, 1 : 306.

granted him the liberty of questioning the goals and values of his professional friends and of daring to consider metaphysical ideas incompatible with the thought of the advocates of scientific naturalism.

Nothing could tempt Wallace to become a creature of conventional opinion. Even the multitude of honors that he received—the Royal, the Darwin, and the Copley Medals of the Royal Society; membership in that society; the Founders' Medal of the Royal Geographical Society; the Darwin–Wallace Medal of the Linnean Society; honorary degrees from Oxford and Dublin; a royal pension; and royal appointment to the Order of Merit—in no way enticed Wallace to truckle to professional authority.[12] His scientific peers could honor his accomplishments and deplore his admiration for phrenology and spiritualism, but they could neither dominate his spirit nor circumscribe his intellectual freedom and individuality.

When Alfred Wallace died in 1913, the author of the obituary in *Nature* remarked, "There was a great humanity about Alfred Wallace." [13] Though an exceptionally modest man, Wallace would have taken quiet pleasure in that compliment. The years of social isolation and intellectual solitude had nurtured in his mind a very real and almost tangible concept of humanity. For Wallace, "humanity" represented mankind's capacity to rise above the circumstances of physical nature and to formulate and to act according to moral values. All else in life stood subordinate to that end. Science, knowledge, technology, and religion were of value only insofar as they aided mankind in attaining the badge of its humanity—the exercise of moral faculties. This lively sense of the "potential moral beauty" of the human personality within the human animal accounted for Wallace's dissent from both Christianity and scientific naturalism.[14] The doctrines of the former discouraged human morality, and the doctrines of the latter failed to recognize the autonomous integrity of the human personality.

Not until 1864 did Wallace's naturalistic friends become acquainted with the metaphysical and moral opinions of the other man who had discovered natural selection. As Wallace continued

12. George, *Biologist Philosopher*, pp. 279–86; Marchant, *Alfred Russel Wallace*, 2 : 113.

13. "Alfred Russel Wallace," *Nature* 92 (1913) : 322.

14. Loren Eiseley, *Darwin's Century: Evolution and the Men Who Discovered It* (Garden City, N.Y.: Doubleday & Co., 1961), p. 324.

to enunciate views increasingly incompatible with naturalistic thought, most of his scientific contemporaries simply shook their heads in bewilderment. For example, Joseph Hooker, while reading *Island Life* in 1881, wrote to Darwin: "I am only two-thirds through Wallace and it is splendid. What a number of cobwebs he has swept away. That such a man should be a Spiritualist is more wonderful than all the movements of all the plants." [15] Later writers such as Loren Eiseley and Wilma George have been little more successful in penetrating the enigma of Wallace's character. Eiseley, though treating Wallace with considerable sensitivity and sympathy, separated his spiritualistic thought from his legitimate scientific work and mistakenly assigned Wallace's occult interests to the latter part of his life.[16] Ms. George attempted to consider three of Wallace's late books as serious science when, by his own admission, spiritualistic ideas and the hope of establishing a natural religion had guided his thinking.[17]

Alfred Wallace became and remained an enigma because both his contemporaries and the historians confused the man with his discovery. Natural selection represented a key feature of the naturalistic cosmology and one of the prize theories of the emerging professional men of science. However, Wallace's mind operated within a framework possessing points of reference quite different from those of the advocates of scientific naturalism. Other scientists, such as Darwin, Hooker, and Huxley, came to know Wallace only after he had become the "other man." They quite naturally, but mistakenly, assumed that he viewed nature and the purpose of scientific endeavor as they did; hence, their never-ending astonishment with the man.

A letter that Wallace wrote in 1860 to his lifelong friend George Silk may serve to illustrate the cast of mind with which Wallace approached scientific investigation. He told Silk,

---

15. J. D. Hooker to C. Darwin, 24 November 1881, in Leonard Huxley, *The Life and Letters of Sir Joseph Dalton Hooker* (London: J. Murray, 1918), 2 : 244.

16. Eiseley, *Darwin's Century*, pp. 290–324.

17. George, *Biologist Philosopher*, pp. 274–78, 281–84. Ms. George admits the spiritualistic concern of his later works but sees it very much as a side issue to the scientific problems discussed. ARW's prefaces and published correspondence leave no doubt that the spiritualistic questions were primary in his thinking and writing in regard to these books. See ARW, *The World of Life: A Manifestation of Creative Power, Directive Mind and Ultimate Purpose* (London: Chapman & Hall, 1910), pp. vi–vii; ARW, *My Life*, 2 : 122.

> I have been reading of late two books of the highest interest, but of most diverse characters, and I wish to recommend their perusal to you if you have time for anything but work or politics. They are Dr. Leon Durfour's 'Histoire de la Prostitution' and Darwin's 'Origin of Species.' If there is an English translation of the first, pray get it. Every *student of men and morals* should read it.[18]

This recommendation of two books 'of most diverse characters"— one concerned with social morality and the other with natural science —was highly characteristic of Wallace. He was first and foremost "a student of men and morals" for whom the ideas and research of science constituted aids for the moral development of human beings. Science was the handmaiden in the moral quest. As will be seen, this was the standpoint from which Wallace had always approached science, and it was the standpoint from which he made his first deviation from orthodox natural selection in the spring of 1864.

DEVIATION FROM NATURAL SELECTION: THE PHRENOLOGICAL BASIS

Both Alfred Wallace and Charles Darwin modified or supplemented the theory of natural selection. Darwin argued that sexual selection operated along with natural selection to modify species. Also, in later editions of the *Origin of Species* Darwin moved somewhat toward a Lamarckian position by suggesting the possibility of the inheritance of acquired characteristics.[19] Both modifications remained well within the naturalistic framework. Wallace likewise changed his position in two major respects. First, in 1864 he contended that for all practical purposes natural selection no longer affected the human body. Second, in 1869 and in 1870 he declared that natural selection could not account for the mental and moral nature of human beings. Though Darwin praised the 1864 departure, he condemned Wallace's later ideas, fearing that Wallace had "murdered too completely your own and my child." [20]

18. ARW to George Silk, 1 September 1860, in Wallace, *My Life*, 1: 372 (FMT's emphasis).
19. Charles Darwin, *The Origin of Species and the Descent of Man* (New York: The Modern Library, n.d.), pp. 567–96; Eiseley, *Darwin's Century*, pp. 203–04, 210–21; Peter Vorzimmer, *Charles Darwin: The Years of Controversy, the Origin of Species and Its Critics, 1859–1882* (Philadelphia: Temple University Press, 1970).
20. Darwin to ARW, 27 March 1869, in Marchant, *Alfred Russel Wallace*, 1 : 240.

On a March evening in 1864, two years after his return to England, Alfred Wallace addressed a meeting of the London Anthropological Society. He spoke on "The Development of Human Races under the Law of Natural Selection." [21] Wallace opened his discourse by posing the question, long debated among ethnologists, of mono-genesis and polygenesis. Did man have a single origin or several origins? Wallace suggested that the law of natural selection might cast some light on the issue.

Wallace argued that man, unlike any other living creature, had experienced two distinct stages of evolution. During the first stage the human body had developed according to the law of natural selection. Those to whom physical variations had granted a mar-ginal advantage in the struggle for existence had survived. However, once the human brain had attained a certain stage of development, natural selection no longer produced changes in man's physical nature.

> From the time, therefore, when the social and sympathetic feel-ings came into active operation, and the intellectual and moral faculties became fairly developed, man would cease to be in-fluenced by 'natural selection' in his physical form and struc-ture. As an animal he would remain almost stationary, the changes of the surrounding universe ceasing to produce in him that powerful modifying effect which they exercise over other parts of the organic world. But from the moment that the form of his body became stationary, his mind would become subject to those very influences from which his body had escaped; every slight variation in his mental and moral nature which should enable him better to guard against adverse circumstances, and combine for mutual comfort and protection, would be preserved and accumulated.[22]

The more brutal races would die out because the mind had not yet so fully matured in them. Climate would influence the mental evolution of those who did survive. Those peoples living in colder regions would more fully develop their faculties than those living in the warmer and more luxuriant climates.

21. The address originally appeared in the *Journal of the Anthropological Society* 2 (1854): clviii–clxx. ARW reprinted it in a somewhat revised form in *Contributions to the Theory of Natural Selection* (London: Macmillan & Co., 1870), pp. 302–31. (Hereafter cited in footnotes as ARW, *Natural Selection*.)

22. ARW, *Natural Selection*, pp. 316–17.

Wallace then returned to the question of the origin of human races. Was that origin one or many? His answer amounted to a compromise embracing both monogenesis and polygenesis. However, Wallace directed his compromise not to the avowed question of human origins but rather to the real question that had given rise to the dispute in the first place. Behind the scientific façade about the nature of human origins lay a moral issue. Monogenesists, arguing for the single origin of man, had provided the antislavery and humanitarian reform movements with scientific proof that primitive races were not qualitatively different or inferior to their masters or colonial administrators. Polygenesists, arguing for the separate origin of each race, had furnished the scientific defense for slaveholders, imperialists, and racial theorists. If the several races had separate origins, they were different species, some of which were qualitatively inferior or superior to others.[23] Wallace did not have to become explicit about this matter. Every member of the Anthropological Society knew the moral question at issue. His address was part of a continuing debate.[24]

Wallace set forth an imaginative and subtle solution to the controversy:

> Man may have been, indeed I believe must have been, once a homogeneous race; but it was at a period of which we have as yet discovered no remains, at a period so remote in his history, that he had not yet acquired that wonderfully developed brain, the organ of the mind, which now, even in his lowest examples, raises him far above the highest brutes;—at a period when he had the form but hardly the nature of man, when he neither possessed human speech, nor those sympathetic and moral feelings which in a greater or less degree everywhere now distinguish the race. . . . If, therefore, we are of [the] opinion that he was not really man till these higher faculties were fully developed, we may fairly assert that there were many originally distinct races of men; while, if we think that a being closely resembling us in form and structure, but with mental faculties

23. Philip Curtin, *The Image of Africa* (Madison: University of Wisconsin Press, 1964), pp. 40–41, 220–36, 365–72; John C. Greene, *The Death of Adam* (New York: Mentor Books, 1961), pp. 221–35, 362, nn. 1 and 2; Edward Lurie, "Louis Agassiz and the Races of Man," *Isis* 45 (1954): 227–42.

24. J. W. Burrow, *Evolution and Society: A Study in Victorian Social Theory* (Cambridge: Cambridge University Press, 1966), pp. 118–36; James Hunt, "On the Negro's Place in Nature," *Journal of the Anthropological Society* 2 (1864): xv–lvi.

scarcely raised above the brute, must still be considered to have
been human, we are fully entitled to maintain the common origin of all mankind.[25]

This compromise amounted to physical polygenesis and moral mono-
genesis. Physical and racial differences did indeed exist and might
be due to separate origins. However, the fact of separate origins did
not affect the common humanity of all creatures displaying moral
faculties manifested by the mind's operating through the physical
organ of the brain.[26] The mind and the moral faculties exercised
by it transformed the human animal into a human being. In other
words, something other than man's physical form and physical
nature constituted his humanity.

Wallace's concluding paragraph left no doubt that he had conceived the address as a comment on both the moral evolution of
man and the moral issue in dispute between the monogenesists and
polygenesists. Wallace predicted that the spread of advanced technology would destroy the remaining primitive peoples before they
could adjust to the new mode of life. Then as a uniform technological culture became established throughout the world, the mental and
moral constitution of mankind would continue to develop

> till the world is again inhabited by a single homogeneous race,
> no individual of which will be inferior to the noblest speci-
> mens of existing humanity. Each will then work out his own
> happiness in relation to that of his fellows; perfect freedom

25. ARW, *Natural Selection*, pp. 321–22.

26. Darwin welcomed this address and later declared it "the best paper that ever
appeared in the Anthropological Journal" (Darwin to ARW, 28 May 1864, and 26
January 1870, in Marchant, *Alfred Russel Wallace*, 1 : 154, 251). Some of the Darwin
circle must have been less than enthusiastic about the paper. Hooker apparently
thought ARW agreed with Richard Owen, a leading opponent of natural selection.
Clarifying his position, ARW replied to Hooker: "I do not at all agree with Owen's
system, and only meant to intimate that looking on man as an *intellectual being only,*
& considering the effect that intellect had produced in fixing his own external characters as well as in modifying other living beings,—there was some reason to class
him apart from the rest of organic nature,—as we practically do when we place the
reason & moral faculties of man, as opposed to the mental faculties of the animal
world. In pure zoological classification I would only give its due weight to the
structural peculiarities of the skull and brain, in combination with every other
character, and as man does certainly differ from the Galeopithicus, the AYE-AYE or
the Lemurs, I can only classify him as forming a *distinct family,* of the same *order*
which contains them all" (ARW to J. D. Hooker, 22 May 1864, Hooker Papers,
104 : 281, in the Library of the Royal Botanical Gardens at Kew).

of action will be maintained, since the well balanced moral faculties will never permit any one to transgress on the equal freedom of others; restrictive laws will not be wanted, for each man will be guided by the best of laws; a thorough appreciation of the rights, and a perfect sympathy with the feelings, of all about him; compulsory government will have died away as unnecessary (for every man will know how to govern himself), and will be replaced by voluntary associations for all beneficial public purposes; the passions and animal propensities will be restrained within those limits which most conduce to happiness; and mankind will have at length discovered that it was only required of them to develop the capacities of their higher nature, in order to convert this earth, which had so long been the theater of their unbridled passions, and the scene of unimaginable misery, into as bright a paradise as ever haunted the dreams of seer or poet.[27]

In such a future civilization, the moral and humanitarian ideal of the monogenesists would be realized. There could be no further justification for slavery or repression. Men in all climates would possess sufficient control over their physical environment to permit the complete flourishing of their latent moral faculties.

Wallace's audience was too interested in natural selection to notice that he had attempted to comment on a moral issue through a scientific address. He was apparently somewhat surprised and disappointed that his listeners failed to recognize the underlying intention of his presentation. When he replied to the critics during the discussion afterwards, Wallace observed,

27. ARW, "The Origins of Human Races and the Antiquity of Man Deduced from the Theory of Natural Selection," *Journal of the Anthropological Society* 2 (1864): clxix–clxx. See also *The Anthropological Review* 5 (1867): 103–04, where ARW clarifies the intentions of his original conclusion. He thought the present superior mind of the European races would allow them to take over the globe and thus the primitive native races were doomed to extinction. "I cannot believe that the progress of civilization and science will stop, and I can see no end to such progress, but the absorption and displacement of lower races by higher, till the world again become inhabited by a 'homogeneous race', whose command over nature and whose powers of intercommunication will be such as to prevent local conditions affecting, to more than a very slight degree, its external characteristics" (p. 104). See also a remark of similar content made 19 January 1864, in *Journal of the Anthropological Society* 2 (1864): cx–cxi. For general discussions of this 1864 address, see Eiseley, *Darwin's Century*, pp. 302–09, and Greene, *The Death of Adam*, pp. 311–16. The discussion in the present essay dissents somewhat from both of these treatments.

With regard to the poetical conclusion, I would merely say that
I began it by stating that I would point out what I considered
to be the bearings of this theory, if it is true. If it is not true,
of course, my remarks go for nothing; but I do not think myself that the concluding part of the paper is more poetical than
true.[28]

No one had mentioned the "poetical conclusion" during the discussion. Wallace made this remark in a special effort to call attention
to his closing statement.

The controversy over human origins had provided Wallace with
the occasion for his address. Herbert Spencer's *Social Statics* had, as
Wallace acknowledged, furnished the particular vision of the perfect
future society.[29] However, Wallace drew his conception of man,
which permitted the dismissal of natural selection as a present influence on the human body, from phrenological psychology.[30] In the
address he employed the terms *faculties, propensities,* and *feelings*
in a strictly phrenological manner. He never equated the mind with
the brain but was careful to refer to the brain as "the organ of the
mind." Moreover, those faculties that Wallace suggested had flourished when the evolution of the brain released man's body from the
influence of natural selection were the very faculties that phrenologists assigned to man but not to animals.[31]

28. ARW, "The Origins of Human Races," *Journal of the Anthropological Society*
2 (1864) : clxxxvii.

29. "The general idea and argument of this paper I believe to be new. It was,
however, the perusal of Mr. Herbert Spencer's works, especially *Social Statics,* that
suggested it to me, and at the same time furnished me with some of its applications"
(ibid., clxx, n.). See also Greene, *The Death of Adam,* p. 315.

30. George Combe, *Elements of Phrenology,* 3rd American ed. (Boston: Marsh,
Capen, & Lyon, 1835); *Outlines of Phrenology,* 1st American ed. from 7th Edinburgh
ed. (Boston: Marsh, Capen, & Lyon, 1838); *A System of Phrenology,* 6th American ed.
from 3rd Edinburgh ed. (Boston: Marsh, Capen, & Lyon, 1839); *The Constitution of
Man,* 3rd American ed. (Boston: Allen & Ticknor, 1834); John D. Davies, *Phrenology:
Fad and Science, A Nineteenth-Century American Crusade* (New Haven: Yale University
Press, 1955); Robert Young, *Mind, Brain, and Adaptation in the Nineteenth Century:
Cerebral Localization and Its Biological Context from Gall to Ferrier* (Oxford: The
Clarendon Press, 1970). Roger Smith has also noted ARW's debt to phrenology in
"Physiological Psychology and the Philosophy of Nature in Mid-Nineteenth Century
Britain" (Ph.D. diss., Cambridge University, 1970), pp. 263–69. I discovered Mr. Smith's
discussion too late to incorporate his work into this essay.

31. ARW, *Natural Selection,* p. 321. According to phrenology animals and man
shared the following *propensities,* i.e., faculties which do not form ideas but produce
an inclination of a particular variety: Amativeness, Philoprogenitiveness, Concentrative-

The affinity with phrenology extended beyond Wallace's terminology. He drew his conception of man as a creature possesing separate but interrelated physical, mental, and moral natures directly from the phrenological writings of George Combe, the chief British exponent of phrenological psychology. Wallace agreed with Combe that man possessed certain mental and moral capabilities that, when awakened, transformed the human animal into a human being.[32] Wallace also agreed with Combe's conclusion as to the scientific and moral implications of man's possessing those phrenological sentiments of Veneration, Firmness, Conscientiousness, Hope, Wonder, Ideality, Wit, and Imitation. Combe had argued that by virtue of man's possessing these qualities, it might be concluded that he "is designed for another and a higher destiny than is to be allotted to [the animals]." In 1864 Wallace similarly suggested that if true, his own theory provided "a new argument for placing man apart, as not only the head and culminating point of the grand series of organic nature, but as in some degree a new and distinct order of being." [33]

Wallace had become acquainted with phrenology prior to 1843 by reading George Combe's *Constitution of Man* (1828) and another of Combe's books, the title of which Wallace did not remember. While teaching in Leicester he had heard phrenological lectures by Spencer Hall. He had also purchased a phrenological model head and on two separate occasions allowed his own head to be examined.[34] Wallace never wavered in his loyalty and support for phrenology. In *The Wonderful Century* he suggested that phrenology would become the psychology of the twentieth century.

This phrenological bias accounted in large measure for Wallace's dissent from scientific naturalism. Phrenology represented one facet

---

ness, Adhesiveness, Combativeness, Destructiveness, Alimentiveness, Secretiveness, Acquisitiveness, and Constructiveness. The *Sentiments*, i.e., faculties that do not form ideas but merely produce a feeling or emotion which is joined with one of the propensities, are divided between those common to man and animals and those peculiar to man. The shared sentiments are Self-esteem, Love of Approbation, Cautiousness, and Benevolence. Those sentiments unique to man are Veneration, Firmness, Conscientiousness, Hope, Wonder, Ideality, Wit, and Imitation. Man and animals share the Perceptive Faculties of Individuality, Form, Size, Weight, Coloring, Locality, Number, Order, Eventuality, Time, Tune, and Language. They also share the reflective faculties of Comparison and Causality (Combe, *Elements of Phrenology*, passim).

32. Combe, *Elements of Phrenology*, p. 183. See ARW, *Natural Selection*, p. 325.
33. Combe, *Elements of Phrenology*, p. 183; ARW, *Natural Selection*, p. 324.
34. ARW, *The Wonderful Century*, pp. 174–77, 193; *My Life*, 1 : 234–36, 257–63.

of a much broader cultural phenomenon that swept across the English
provinces during the years when Wallace was a surveyor and school-
teacher. A contemporary described the movement as a "physical
puritanism" that "comes before the world under many names; but
the common purpose of all its manifestations is the healing, cleans-
ing, and restoration of the animal man." This new puritanism
included exponents of vegetarianism, the water cure, mesmerism,
and phrenology. These were movements of amateurs who often
tended toward political radicalism. Each movement, in the phrase
R. K. Webb applied to mesmerism, was "an engine to create a
perfect society" through the personal moral regeneration of individuals who would submit their bodies to the known principles
of physiology. Among the noted Victorians attracted at one time
or another to certain aspects of "physical puritanism" were Harriet
Martineau, George Eliot, Herbert Spencer, and Alexander Bain.[35]

"Physical puritanism" left a most enduring impact on Alfred
Wallace. Its ideas were characteristic of what G. M. Young once
termed the "belated rationalism" of intelligent members of the
working class. Wallace lived primarily among such people between
1837 and his departure for South America in 1847. Theirs were the
ideas that he had imbibed and that had molded his mind when he
left for his explorations. During the fifteen years of his absence from
England, he encountered few new ideas or influences that would
have caused him to modify his general framework of thought. The
importance of this isolation may be appreciated when it is recalled
that in the late forties and early fifties Herbert Spencer was also
an advocate of phrenology. However, when Spencer moved to London, he came under the influence of associationist and physiological
psychologists.[36] Wallace's long absence allowed him few contacts that

35. "Physical Puritanism," *Westminster Review* 57 (1852) : 409; R. K. Webb, *Harriet
Martineau: A Radical Victorian* (London: Heinemann, 1960), p. 245; and ibid., pp.
240–50; Gordon S. Haight, *George Eliot: A Biography* (New York and Oxford: Oxford
University Press, 1968), pp. 51–52, 100–01; G. B. Denton, "Early Psychological Theories
of Herbert Spencer," *The American Journal of Psychology* 32 (1921) : 5–15; R. Young,
"The Function of the Brain: Gall to Ferrier, 1808–1886," *Isis* 59 (1968) : 251.

36. G. M. Young, *Victorian England: Portrait of an Age*, 2nd ed. (New York: Oxford
University Press, 1964), p. 36. See also E. P. Thompson, *The Making of the English
Working Class* (New York: Vintage Books, 1963), pp. 711–832; J. F. C. Harrison, *Learn-
ing and Living 1790–1960: A Study in the History of the English Adult Education
Movement* (Toronto: University of Toronto Press, 1961), pp. 114–17. R. Young, "The
Development of Herbert Spencer's Concept of Evolution," *Actes du XIe congrès inter-
national d'histoire des sciences* (Warsaw, 1967), 2 : 273–79.

might have so reshaped his thought. The most important new influence he encountered in his brief London sojourn between expeditions was Spencer's *Social Statics,* which was itself based on phrenological psychology.[37]

It was the phrenology and mesmerism of "physical puritanism" to which Wallace referred when in his old age he spoke of the materialism of his youth. In 1913 he told his biographer, James Marchant, "The completely materialistic mind of my youth and early manhood has been slowly moulded into the socialistic, spiritualistic, and theistic mind I now exhibit." However, the materialism of "physical puritanism" could and often did lead directly to such a mind. The trance of the spiritualistic medium closely resembled the trance of the mesmerized subject. The concept of social cooperation was explicit in Combe's version of phrenology as was the concept of a deistic God.[38]

Perhaps most important, both phrenologists and mesmerists, though never in full agreement on the subject, defined mind in such a way as to be compatible with the later theories of spiritualism. Though associated with and influenced by the body, mind remained a separate entity.[39] As Combe explained,

> A mental organ is a material instrument, by means of which the mind, in this life, enters into particular states, active and passive. The mind is regarded as simple, and its substance or essence is unknown. It is furnished, by nature, with highly interesting susceptibilities, and a vast apparatus of mental organs, for enabling it to manifest its energies, and enter into different states.

Simultaneously, the phrenological emphasis on the shape of the cranium and the mesmerist view of physical fluids and energies gave

37. ARW, *My Life,* 2 : 235.

38. ARW to James Marchant, 1913, in Marchant, *Alfred Russel Wallace,* 2 : 181; A. Gauld, *The Founders of Psychical Research* (New York: Schocken Books, 1968), p. 18; A. Cameron Grant, "New Light on an Old View," *Journal of the History of Ideas* 29 (1968) : 293–301.

39. Davies, *Phrenology,* p. 156. One of the chief exponents of spiritualism in both America and Britain commented," Mesmerism has been—humanly speaking—the cornerstone upon which the Temple of Spiritualism was upreared" (Emma Hardinge-Britten, *Nineteenth-Century Miracles* [New York: W. Britten, 1884], p. 125). ARW quotes Mrs. Hardinge-Britten in *Miracles and Modern Spiritualism,* rev. ed. with chapters on Apparitions and Phantasms (London: Nichols, 1901), pp. 117, 121.

both phrenology and mesmerism an empirical and materialistic cast.[40] However, unlike the associationist and physiological psychologies linked to scientific naturalism, phrenology and mesmerism refrained from reducing the mind to an epiphenomenon of matter but instead viewed it as an autonomous entity. Consequently, Wallace could conceive of the continued evolution of the mind after the body had ceased to modify.

This concept of the separation of the human personality from the human body meant that Wallace considered man and the relation of science to man in a context wholly different from that of the advocates of scientific naturalism. As William Irvine once described the evolution of Huxley's mind, "He became interested in man as a physical mechanism, as an anthropoid ape, as a social unit and a citizen, as a delicate machine for the discovery of scientific truth, but never to any appreciable extent in man as a personality and a human being." Wallace's development was exactly the reverse. He was originally interested in the physical mechanism of man for the sake of the moral personality encased therein. He studied the anthropoid ape because it resembled man. He wrote on social questions in the hope that society might be so organized as to allow the moral faculties to flourish. Throughout his long and varied scientific career, Wallace was primarily concerned with what Koestler has dubbed "the ghost in the machine" rather than with the machine itself.[41]

Wallace, where possible, viewed most scientific issues in relation to man. Such was his approach to the species question. Anyone familiarizing himself with biology in the 1840s would have considered that topic, but in Wallace's mind it was always associated with man. H. Lewis McKinney has demonstrated that Wallace stood convinced of the fact of evolution in 1845 through his reading of Chambers's *Vestiges of Natural Creation*. It was of no small importance that the *Vestiges* was the work of an amateur, that it argued from

40. Combe, *Elements of Phrenology*, p. 30. In the 1864 address ARW spoke of "that subtle force we term mind" (*Natural Selection*, p. 325). H. Ellenberger, *The Discovery of the Unconscious* (New York: Basic Books, 1970), pp. 77–79, 110.

41. William Irvine, *Apes, Angels, and Victorians: Darwin, Huxley, and Evolution* (Cleveland and New York: The World Publishing Co., 1964), pp. 12–13; Arthur Koestler, *The Ghost in the Machine*, 1st American ed. (New York: Macmillan Co., 1967, 1968). Koestler borrowed the phrase from Gilbert Ryle, *The Concept of Mind* (London: Hutchinson, 1949), pp. 15–16.

phrenological psychology, and that it owed much to Combe's *Constitution of Man*.[42] Throughout the 1850s when Wallace pondered the species question, man remained in the center of his thought. One reason he chose to explore the Malay Archipelago was his conviction that the orangutan was closely related to man. Wallace had asked Darwin, prior to their mutual discovery, if he intended to discuss man in his projected book on the species question. Finally, during the fit of fever in 1858 when Wallace hit upon the insight of natural selection, he did so while reflecting on the effects of the Malthusian checks on savage population.[43] From the application to man, his thought moved to the effect of those checks on the plant and animal world.

Finally, phrenology and mesmerism accounted for Wallace's unshakable conviction that science could and should address itself to moral issues. Both movements were directed toward answering immediate, practical, moral questions. Earlier religious writers had believed that science could affirm moral truth already revealed in a religious context. Wallace, under the influence of phrenology, believed that science itself, outside any religious context, could discover new and enduring moral truths that would allow man to rise above his animal nature and to enjoy a distinctly human existence.

In the London Anthropological Society address of March 1864, Wallace continued to discuss, though in a very different kind of forum, matters that had weighed upon his mind for over twenty years. He brought into the professional scientific sphere the scientific concepts and goals that he had learned in the provincial mechanics institutes. The address was his single most important comment on man and contained the latent seeds for all his later departures from scientific naturalism. The American evolutionist John Fiske recalled that the address "seemed to open up an entirely new world of specu-

42. H. Lewis McKinney, "Wallace's Earliest Observations on Evolution: 28 December 1845," *Isis* 60 (1969): 370–73; C. C. Gillispie, *Genesis and Geology: A Study in the Relations of Scientific Thought, Natural Theology, and Social Opinion in Great Britain 1790–1850* (New York: Harper Torchbooks, 1959), pp. 149–83; Milton Millhauser, *Just Before Darwin: Robert Chambers and "Vestiges"* (Middletown, Conn.: Wesleyan University Press, 1959).

43. McKinney, *Wallace and Natural Selection*, pp. 80–96; Darwin to ARW, 22 December 1857, in Marchant, *Alfred Russel Wallace*, 1 : 133; ARW, *My Life*, 1 : 361–62; *The Wonderful Century*, pp. 139–40.

lation." [44] Such speculation was indeed new to men who had known little or nothing of "physical puritanism" or the "belated rationalism" of the working-class culture in which Wallace had come to maturity. For Wallace the paper was simply a continuation of his earlier thought. The phrenological view of mind and of man became increasingly important for him as he steadily achieved the conviction that the New Nature created by science was incapable of nurturing the moral personality of the human animal.

CRITIQUE OF THE NEW NATURE AND THE TURN TO SPIRITUALISM

Alfred Wallace had never shared in the midcentury chauvinism over the alleged superiority of European civilization. The moral decency and honesty of the primitive peoples of South America and the Malay Archipelago had profoundly impressed him. In a letter of 1855 he remarked, "The more I see of uncivilized people, the better I think of human nature on the whole, and the essential differences between so-called civilized and savage man seem to disappear." [45] After 1864 private doubts increasingly plagued Wallace in regard to the quality of life and social morality in England. By 1869 in *The Malay Archipelago* he expressed not only glowing admiration for primitive tribes, but also explicit condemnation of European civilization. He closed the volume with a scathing critique of English society, declaring that "the mass of our populations have not advanced beyond the savage code of morals, and have in many cases sunk below it." This view essentially contradicted the contention of naturalistic authors, such as John Lubbock, who in the same year suggested that, "even if for the moment we admit that science will not render us more virtuous, it must certainly make us more innocent." [46]

The phrenological division of human nature into physical, mental, and moral aspects required Wallace to distinguish between material and moral improvement. Moral progress was not a necessary con-

44. John Fiske, *A Century of Science* (Boston: Houghton Mifflin and Co., 1899), p. 104.

45. ARW to an unknown correspondent, May 1855, in Marchant, *Alfred Russel Wallace*, 1 : 55. See also ARW, *My Life*, 1 : 287–89; *Narrative of Travel on the Amazon and Rio Negro*, p. 519.

46. ARW, *The Malay Archipelago*, p. 456; John Lubbock, *Pre-historic Times* (London: Williams & Norgate, 1869), p. 587.

comitant to the progress of physical science or industrial technology. Genuine progress toward that perfect future condition of "individual freedom and self-government" was "rendered possible by the equal development and just balance of the intellectual, moral, and physical parts of our nature."[47] The material advances of the New Nature must be coordinated to aid the simultaneous evolution of all man's faculties. Improvement of the human animal did not necessarily improve the human being.

Wallace recognized that the values directing the concrete application of science lay outside the framework of scientific thought. A truly humane society must give as much attention to the ends of material progress as to the means of its achievement. He reminded his readers,

> [I]f we continue to devote our chief energies to the utilizing of our knowledge of the laws of nature with the view of still further extending our commerce and our wealth, the evils which necessarily accompany these when too eagerly pursued, may increase to such gigantic dimensions as to be beyond our power to alleviate.

Like Henry Sidgwick, Wallace realized that the evolution of society toward material civilization furnished no guarantee for the ethical correctness of either the process or the end toward which it moved. The present growth of science and technology fostered only competitive individualism and greed. These were characteristic of the phrenological propensity of acquisitiveness, which according to Combe, "produces the tendency to acquire, and the desire to possess in general, without reference to the uses to which the objects, when attained, may be applied." [48] Men shared this propensity with animals. A society based upon the development of acquisitiveness could

47. ARW, *The Malay Archipelago*, p. 456.

48. Ibid., p. 457. Compare ARW's remarks with the following statement by George Combe: "Physical has far outstripped moral science; and, it appears to me, that, unless the lights of Phrenology open the eyes of mankind to the real constitution of the world, and at length induce them to modify their conduct in harmony with the laws of the Creator, their future physical discoveries will tend only to deepen their wretchedness. . . . The science of man's whole nature, animal, moral, and intellectual, was never more required to guide him than at present, when he seems to wield a giant's power, but in the application of it to display the ignorant selfishness, wilfulness, and absurdity of an overgrown child" (*The Constitution of Man*, p. 177); Combe, *Elements of Phrenology*, p. 54. See also Combe, *The Constitution of Man*, pp. 141–77.

not produce or sustain those qualities of life that were distinctly human.

Wallace especially feared that the man of science might be drawn into the cash nexus of the acquisitive propensity. For this reason he was generally averse to the professionalization of science and government support of private research. In January 1870 Wallace began a long letter to the editor of *Nature* by declaring, "The public mind seems now to be going mad on the subject of education; the Government is obliged to give away to the clamour, and men of science seem inclined to seize the opportunity to get, if possible, some share in the public money." [49] He opposed this rush on the public treasury because it was unjust for the public to aid so small a group of men and because the private interests of the individual scientist rather than projects affecting society at large would receive support.

In the same issue, the editorial attacked Wallace's letter, and on January 20, Wallace contributed a most revealing reply, which suggested how profoundly his view of the purpose of scientific investigation differed from that of his scientific peers.

> The main result of the cultivation of science I hold to be, undoubtedly, the elevation of those who cultivate it to a higher mental and moral standpoint; while the secondary, but no less certain result, is the acquisition of countless physical, social, and intellectual benefits for the whole human race. But if these are the *secondary* and not the *primary* results of cultivating science, it seems to me to be radically unsound in principle, and sure to fail in practice, if by means of any system of State support we seek to find a short cut to these secondary results.[50]

In Wallace's mind and personal experience, the pursuit of scientific investigation was an endeavor that increasingly transformed the man of science into a more fully *human* being. Scientific research called forth the use of those particularly human faculties of wonder, ideality, wit, and imitation.

Wallace believed that the diversion of limited public funds to the support of a small coterie of researchers would risk the loss of the greater opportunity to elevate the moral qualities of the entire society through the popularization of existing scientific knowledge.

49. ARW, "Letter to the Editor," *Nature* 1 (1870): 288.
50. ARW, "Letter to the Editor," *Nature* 1 (1870): 315.

As he explained in 1869, when pleading for a museum of natural history,

> [I]f they [middle, lower classes and the young] wish to follow up any branch of natural history as an amusement or a study, it leads them into the pure air and pleasant scenes of the country, and is likely to be the best antidote to habits of dissipation or immorality. . . . The inexhaustible variety, the strange beauty, and the wondrous complexity of natural objects, are pre-eminently adapted to excite both the observing and reflective powers of the mind, and their study is well calculated to have an elevating and refining effect upon the character.[51]

Narrow professional pursuit of science and government aid to that professional pursuit would produce the doubly harmful effect of developing the acquisitive propensity of scientists while failing to develop the moral propensities of the general population.

It is against the background of his disillusionment with the New Nature, his view of the purpose of science, and his phrenological concept of human nature that Wallace's conversion to spiritualism must be considered. While still in the Malay Archipelago, Wallace had read of the strange spirit phenomena manifesting themselves in America and Europe, "and being aware, from my own knowledge of Mesmerism, that there were mysteries connected with the human mind which modern science ignored because it could not explain, I determined to seize the first opportunity on my return home to examine these matters." Almost three years passed after that return before he had an opportunity to do so. During the summer of 1865 Wallace attended his first seance and witnessed table-turning. Not long afterwards, he became convinced of the validity of the phenomena. From that time until his death in 1913, to the chagrin of his scientific friends and to the unconcealed joy and advantage of the spiritualists, Wallace advocated and defended spiritualism in letters, books, articles, and courtroom testimony.[52]

Among contemporary men of science, Wallace justified his activity as "a *new branch* of anthropology." [53] Most of them remained un-

---

51. ARW, *Studies Scientific and Social* (London: Macmillan & Co., 1900), 2 : 3.

52. ARW, *Miracles and Modern Spiritualism*, pp. 131–32. See Bibliographical Essay for a list of ARW's extensive spiritualist writings.

53. ARW to T. H. Huxley, 22 November 1866, in Marchant, *Alfred Russel Wallace*, 2 : 187.

convinced and openly disapproved. In that disapproval Wallace saw the professional blindness that had denied the validity of phrenology, that had condemned mesmerism even after its practitioners had employed it to perform painless surgical operations, and that had denied the evidence for evolution, the antiquity of man, and natural selection. Professional scientists now brought against spiritualism similar charges of fraud, charlatanism, impossibility, and lack of evidence. He regarded this opposition as one more example of intransigent professionalism blocking the progress of truth and morality.

Wallace considered spiritualism "scientific" because the spiritualistic experiences were immediate and empirical.[54] Spiritualism fulfilled his expectation that science should address itself to the moral condition of man. It provided Wallace with the final set of scientific laws required to explain human nature. As he wrote in an unpublished letter to the *Pall Mall Gazette* in 1868:

> I admire and appreciate the philosophical writings of Mr. Lewes, of Herbert Spencer and of John Stuart Mill, but I find in the philosophy of Spiritualism something that surpasses them all,— something that helps to bridge over a chasm whose border they cannot overpass,—something that throws clearer light on human history and on human nature than they can give me.[55]

Spiritualism furnished Wallace with a scientific explanation for the development of man's moral nature and brought man's total being under the rule of rational cosmic law.

In a curious manner, the theory of spiritualism provided a law for the moral world analogous to that provided by natural selection for the organic world. Natural selection removed the necessity for an arbitrary and interfering God of Special Creation. Spiritualism banished the arbitrary God of predestination and replaced Him with a uniform law of individual moral progress and of personal moral responsibility.

> The noble teaching of Herbert Spencer, that men are best educated by being left to suffer the natural consequences of their actions, is the teaching of Spiritualism as regards the transition

54. George, *Biologist Philosopher,* pp. 244–46.
55. ARW to editor of *Pall Mall Gazette,* May 1868, in Alfred Russel Wallace Papers, British Museum, add. MSS. 46439.

to another phase of life. There will be no imposed rewards or punishments; but every one will suffer the natural and inevitable consequences of a well or ill spent life. The well-spent life is that in which those faculties which regard our personal physical well-being are subordinate to those which regard our social and intellectual well-being, and the well-being of others.[56]

Spiritualism thus united those two divergent elements of Wallace's thought—individualism and social benevolence.

Spiritualism also cleared away a problem that had haunted Wallace ever since adolescence—predestination. Wallace recalled that his parents had been "old-fashioned religious people belonging to the Church of England." They employed religion to set the moral tone of their home. No profanity was ever permitted. The family attended church twice on Sunday; only religious books, such as *Pilgrim's Progress* and *Paradise Lost,* were read on that day. Of specific religious doctrines Wallace had but one memory—the teaching of arbitrary rewards and punishment after death. Preaching that he heard while living with his brother and conversations with the clergyman who ran the Collegiate School in Leicester further impressed this doctrine on his mind.[57]

Wallace learned to hate with a vengeance the injustice and irrationality of predestination. He first realized the discrepancy between this doctrine and Christian morality when he visited London with his brother and attended the Owenite Hall of Science.[58] There the young Wallace heard the teachings of Robert Owen, read the pamphlets of Tom Paine and other rationalist skeptics, and listened to discussions of Strauss's *Life of Jesus.* "Consistency," the tract by Robert Dale Owen, Robert Owen's son, particularly interested Wallace. The younger Owen, who himself also later converted to spiritualism, argued that the doctrine of predestination led to immoral living because it rendered one's eternal reward a matter of chance rather than a function of the virtue of one's life. Concurring in these arguments, Wallace moved very quietly and painlessly from faith to skepticism. His loss of faith grew directly out of a situation succinctly described by a writer later in the century: "God,

56. ARW, *Miracles and Modern Spiritualism,* pp. 222–23.
57. ARW, *My Life,* 1 : 77; ibid., pp. 53–54, 80–83, 87–88.
58. Ibid., pp. 87–91, 227–28.

and immortality, and the Bible have been so taught as to make scepticism the only refuge for morality to flee to." [59]

Wallace later identified this rational skepticism with agnosticism.
His skepticism, however, more nearly resembled deism. He did not
deny the possibility of religious knowledge or of pure religion but
rather the validity and morality of the Christian religion. Most
important, Wallace and the Owenites did not dismiss the moral significance of the questions that Christianity had addressed. The
questions of religion remained valid even if the Christian answers
were false. The Owenite criticism of Christianity made Wallace, as
well as genuine Owenites, highly susceptible to a rational religion,
such as spiritualism, that was based on empirical evidence and that
emphasized social cooperation and benevolent individualism.[60]

Although the moral theory of spiritualism attracted Wallace, he
could and certainly did reconcile himself to the physical phenomena
of the seance. Over the course of his life he eagerly witnessed practically all the stock-in-trade physical manifestations of the spirits—
rapping, table-turning, slate-writing, spirit photography, and mate-
rialization of hands, bodies, and even babies. Since phrenology and
mesmerism had already convinced him of the separation of mind and
body, it was but one more short step to the belief that the minds of
departed men and women could perform material feats. There is no
doubt that on numerous occasions Wallace was the victim of fraudulent mediums. Unlike Sidgwick or Myers, he was not a psychical
researcher. He brought little critical judgment to bear on his
spiritualistic experiences. As Frederic Myers, certainly no opponent
of spiritualism, told Oliver Lodge in regard to Wallace: "His worst
credulity as to the good faith of cheating mediums belongs to a
separate compartment of his mind—or rather forms a part of his
innocent generosity of nature, an unwillingness to believe that anyone will do anything wrong." [61]

Why did Wallace find himself so drawn to spiritualism with its
numerous charlatans? One answer, though probably not the definitive one, is that in viewing spiritualistic phenomena he underwent

59. "The Religious Heresies of the Working Class," *Westminster Review* 77 (1862):
67.

60. J. F. C. Harrison, *Robert Owen and the Owenites in Britain and America*
(London: Routledge & K. Paul, 1969), p. 251.

61. F. W. H. Myers to O. Lodge, 15 May 1892, in Oliver Lodge Papers 1331,
Archives of the Society for Psychical Research, London.

a genuine religious experience, such as Charles Y. Glock has suggested may originate in "ethical deprivation." This deprivation exists "when the individual comes to feel that the dominant values of the society no longer provide him with a meaningful way of organizing his life, and that it is necessary for him to find an alternative." Such was the state of Wallace's mind in 1865 and for many years thereafter. The physical phenomena of the seance were important because they called attention to the existence of spheres of life with values different from those of mid-Victorian England. Wallace had long needed a new ethical framework for integrating his own values and social experience. This situation may suggest why he never wavered from the assertion he voiced in 1866 in *The Scientific Aspect of the Supernatural:* "I prefer . . . to rest the claims of spiritualism on its moral uses." [62] Spiritualism was useful to Wallace because the moral guides in the surrounding society had long been failing him.

For a quarter century, Wallace had received no aid from orthodox Christianity in directing his life. He had vented his disgust with his parents' religion in 1843 while describing the life of the South Wales farmer.

> Their preachers, while they should teach their congregations moral duties, boldly decry their vices, and inculcate the commandments and the duty of doing to others as we would they should do unto us, here, as is too frequently the case throughout the kingdom, dwell almost entirely on the mystical doctrine of the atonement—a doctrine certainly not intelligible to persons in a state of complete ignorance, and which, by teaching them that they are not to rely on their own good deeds, has the effect of entirely breaking away the connection between their religion and the duties of their everyday life.[63]

Several of his letters home while exploring in the Far East included similar ethical complaints against Christianity. During these same years he expressed criticism of Protestant missionaries, who, he felt,

---

62. Charles Y. Glock, "The Role of Deprivation in the Origin and Evaluation of Religious Groups," in *Religion and Social Conflict,* ed. Robert Lee and Martin E. Marty (New York: Oxford University Press, 1964), pp. 28–29; ibid, p. 28; ARW, *Miracles and Modern Spiritualism,* p. 124.

63. ARW, *My Life,* 1 : 220–21.

worked harder to teach doctrine than virtuous living. He stated similar feelings during 1865.[64]

Second, after he returned to England, the values of English society failed to give Wallace direction or consolation in pursuit of his vocation. He not only hated the greed and competition of that society but also encountered difficulty in making his own way in it. He was turned down in his application to become secretary of the Royal Geographical Society in 1864. About the same time, he was jilted by the woman he hoped to marry. He handled the investment of his profits from the Malay expedition unwisely. Over the years he only too well fulfilled a prophecy he had made of himself in 1859 when he wrote, "It is perhaps good to *be* rich, but not to *get* rich, or to be always trying to get rich, and few men are less fitted to get rich, if they did try, than myself." [65] Spiritualism provided a set of values that suited both his character and his experience of social frustration.

Finally, as has been seen, after 1865 Wallace increasingly doubted whether moral progress could be achieved automatically through scientific advance within a commercially and competitively oriented society. In the closing lines of the 1864 address, he had spoken of almost automatic progress. It was the feasibility of such progress, if limited to physical means of accomplishment, that Wallace actively began to question. He was no longer certain that science could fulfill the moral task he envisioned for it.

The ethical and metaphysical doctrines of spiritualism addressed themselves to each facet of Wallace's ethical deprivation from the values of English society. They provided him with a practical morality according to which daily virtue determined the condition of man after death. Christianity with its predestination did not do this. Moreover, Wallace believed that the ethical systems advanced by agnostics would "be of little value in cases of great temptation." Only according to the teachings of spiritualism did the sacrifices required by the virtuous life make sense. Spiritualism furnished proof that "our condition and happiness in the future life depends, by the action of strictly natural law, on our life and conduct here." [66] Spiritualism thus met an immediate need in Wallace's life with

64. Ibid., 2 : 53–54; ARW, *Studies Social and Scientific*, 2 : 107–08.
65. ARW to T. Sims, April 1859, in *My Life*, 1 : 368. See also 1 : 415–17.
66. ARW, *Studies Social and Scientific*, 2 : 381–82.

which traditional religion and the ideas of scientific naturalism could not deal. Moreover, it allowed Wallace with his very marginal financial success to believe that there were other and higher values by which one could judge and organize one's life than those of a commercial civilization. Spiritualism proved to Wallace that man did indeed possess an eternal spiritual personality whose health was more important than that of man's physical body.

Perhaps most important, spiritualism renewed and redirected Wallace's faith in the possibility and the necessity of moral progress for the human race. The cosmos of the spiritualists that incorporated the presence and influence of benevolent spirits provided the additional required impetus for moral progress. For this reason, in 1870 when Wallace republished his 1864 Anthropological Society address, he revised the concluding paragraph to express both his new pessimism and the basis for his renewed optimism.

> Among civilized nations at the present day, it does not seem possible for natural selection to act in any way, so as to secure the permanent advancement of morality and intelligence; for it is indisputably the mediocre, if not the low, both as regards morality and intelligence, who succeed best in life and multiply fastest. Yet there is undoubtedly an advance—on the whole a steady and a permanent one—both in the influence on public opinion of a high morality, and in the general desire for intellectual elevation; and as I cannot impute this in any way to "survival of the fittest," I am forced to conclude that it is due, to the inherent progressive power of those glorious qualities which raise us so immeasurably above our fellow animals, and at the same time afford us the surest proof that there are other and higher existences than ourselves, from whom these qualities may have been derived, and toward whom we may be ever tending.[67]

The meliorist vision remained, but the means to its achievement had been modified. Only spiritualism allowed Wallace to continue to believe that man could become a creature of moral values. It is small wonder that, given the profound personal and social significance of spiritualism to Wallace, he should modify certain of his scientific views.

67. ARW, *Natural Selection*, pp. 330–31.

Spiritualism, Man, and the Cosmos

Although Wallace's conversion to spiritualism did influence his scientific views of human nature and of the teleological implications in physical nature, nevertheless broad areas of his work remained unaffected by his metaphysical ideas. His most significant scientific articles and books displayed little or no trace of spiritualism. He did not broach the subject at all in *The Malay Archipelago,* in *Island Life,* or in his two great volumes on *The Geographical Distribution of Animals.* When Wallace wrote *Darwinism,* which constitutes perhaps the clearest explication of natural selection ever written, he made no reference to preternatural influences except in the last chapter, which concerned man.

In fact, during the entire second half of the century, the original concept of natural selection as the sole agency for explaining modifications in the organic world, except for those in man, boasted no more staunch defender than Alfred Wallace. He vigorously defended the theory against all challengers and was accused of and admitted to being "more Darwinian than Darwin." [68] George Romanes even argued that in the light of Darwin's later modifications of opinion this single-minded adherence to natural selection should be termed Wallacism rather than Darwinism.[69] Nevertheless, when Alfred Wallace made his second deviation from natural selection in the case of man, he did so in no small manner.

In April 1869, toward the close of a review of Sir Charles Lyell's *Antiquity of Man,* Wallace suggested to the dumbfounded amazement of his naturalistic friends that natural selection could account neither for man's mental and moral nature nor for certain physiological features of the human body. Moreover, he declared there existed evidence "that an Overruling Intelligence has watched over the action of those laws so directing variations and so determining the accumulation, as finally to produce an organization sufficiently perfect to admit of, and even to aid in, the indefinite advancement of our mental and moral nature." Upon reading those theistic lines, Darwin wrote to Wallace, "If you had not told me I should have thought they had been added by someone else. As you expected, I

68. ARW, *My Life,* 2 : 22.

69. George Romanes, "Mr. Wallace on Darwinism," *Contemporary Review* 56 (1889) : 244–58.

differ grievously from you and I am very sorry for it." Wallace replied sympathetically, "I can quite comprehend your feelings with regard to my 'unscientific' opinions as to Man, because a few years back I should myself have looked at them as equally wild and uncalled for." There can be no question that Wallace's spiritualistic experiences had occasioned the modification of his ideas. He added in his letter to Darwin, "My opinions on the subject have been modified solely by the consideration of a series of remarkable phenomena, physical and mental, which I have now had every opportunity of fully testing, and which demonstrate the existence of forces and influences not yet recognized by science." [70]

Wallace pursued and expanded his heresy in the concluding essay of *Contributions to the Theory of Natural Selection*, published in 1870. There he recalled Darwin's contention that natural selection had "no power to produce absolute perfection but only relative perfection, no power to advance any being much beyond his fellow beings, but only just so much beyond them as to enable it to survive them in the struggle for existence." [71] The presence in man of any modification perfected appreciably beyond immediate physical needs would provide, Wallace argued, evidence that some law or power other than natural selection had been at work. He then claimed that human beings did indeed possess such overdeveloped modifications.

Wallace rested his case primarily on the issue of the human brain.[72] Reminding his readers of the general agreement among men of science as to the normally proportional relationship between brain size and mental capacity, he argued that even among the most primitive races the size of the brain far exceeded the mental require-

70. ARW, "Sir Charles Lyell on Geological Climates and the Origin of Species," *Quarterly Review* (American ed.) 126 (1869) : 205. See also ARW to Charles Lyell, 28 April 1869, in ARW, *My Life*, 1 : 427-28. C. Darwin to ARW, 14 April 1869, in Marchant, *Alfred Russel Wallace*, 1 : 243. ARW to Darwin, 18 April 1869, in ibid., pp. 243-44. On 22 February 1889, ARW wrote to E. B. Poulton of Oxford who had read the proofsheets of *Darwinism:* "I (think I) *know* that non-human intelligences exist—that there are *minds* disconnected from a physical brain—that there *is,* therefore, a spiritual world. This is not, for me, a *belief* merely, but a *knowledge* founded on the long-continued observation of facts—and such *knowledge* must modify any views as to the origin and nature of human faculty" (E. B. Poulton, "Alfred Russel Wallace," *Proceedings of the Royal Society of London,* series B, 95 (1924) : xxviii.

71. ARW, *Natural Selection,* p. 334.

72. ARW also discussed the absence of hair on the human back. He considered this a harmful trait from the standpoint of survival and one not caused by natural selection (ibid., pp. 344-49).

ments for survival in a primitive environment. The brain that man might require simply to survive would be only slightly larger than that of a gorilla. However, human beings possessed a considerably larger brain.

> We see, then, that whether we compare the savage with the higher developments of man, or with the brutes around him, we are alike driven to the conclusion that in his large and well-developed brain he possesses an organ quite disproportionate to his actual requirements—an organ that seems prepared in advance, only to be fully utilized as he progresses in civilization. . . . We must therefore admit, that the large brain he actually possesses could never have been solely developed by any of those laws of evolution, whose essence is, that they lead to a degree of organization exactly proportionate to the wants of each species, never beyond those wants—that no preparation can be made for the future development of the race—that one part of the body can never increase in size or complexity, except in strict co-ordination to the pressing wants of the whole. The brain of prehistoric and of savage man seems to me to prove the existence of some power, distinct from that which has guided the development of the lower animals through their ever-varying forms of being.[73]

The excessive size of the brain suggested not only other influences besides that of natural selection, but also the probability that man was intended for some end other than physical existence as an animal. The brain implied higher ends for human evolution.

A phrenological examination of the qualities of the human mind supported the latter suggestion. Wallace admitted certain concepts, such as justice, could have arisen naturalistically. However, another class of intellectual phenomena could not be so explained because it did not originate in a situation of marginal survival or of natural society.

> Such [faculties] are the capacity to form ideal conceptions of space and time, of eternity and infinity—the capacity for intense artistic feelings of pleasure, in form, color, and composition—and for those abstract notions of form and number which render geometry and arithmetic possible.

73. Ibid., p. 343.

These traits had no utility for physical survival. Nor was there any particular value for physical survival in the intense mystical devotion that savages directed toward objects of moral worth. Wallace believed that "a moral sense is an essential part of our nature," and that the influence of natural selection could not have generated it. Human beings possessed these innate mental faculties because they "are evidently essential to the perfect devlopment of man as a spiritual being." On the basis of these observations and reflections, Wallace concluded "that a superior intelligence has guided the development of man in a definite direction, and for a special purpose, just as man guides the development of many animal and vegetable forms." [74]

There is considerable irony in the fact that Wallace employed the brain as his primary evidence of supernatural influence. Over the course of the century, physiological psychologists increasingly tended to interpret the mind as an epiphenomenon of the material brain. So far as the clash between religious and scientific ideas was concerned, the mind/brain dispute held the greatest peril for religious thinkers.[75] Wallace did not share that misgiving because he reasoned within the framework of phrenology. As he explained in 1896, "I believe that the individual human spirit is developed *in* and *by means of* the body, and that the mental powers and faculties of the spirit are developed along with, and by means of, the brain." [76] Phrenologists took refuge in an agnostic position in regard to the exact relationship of mind and brain. However, in 1870 Wallace recognized that some attempt must be made to meet the objection that mind was simply the product of the molecular arrangement of the brain cells.

In the *Scientific Aspect of the Supernatural*, published in 1866, Wallace, using a common spiritualist image, had explained, "It is the 'spirit' of man that is man. Spirit is mind; the brain and nerves

74. Ibid., p. 351. This appears to resemble a description of the phrenological sentiment of ideality which is unique to man (Combe, *Elements of Phrenology*, pp. 79–81). ARW, *Natural Selection*, p. 355. Compare with Combe's statement: "According to Phrenology, morality and natural religion originate in, and emanate from, the primitive constitution of the mental powers themselves" (*Elements of Phrenology*, p. 177). ARW, *Natural Selection*, pp. 358–59.

75. R. Young, "The Impact of Darwin on Conventional Thought," in *The Victorian Crisis of Faith*, ed. Anthony Symondson (London: Society for Promoting Christian Knowledge, 1970), p. 21.

76. ARW, "Letter to the Editor," *Light* 16 (1896) : 298.

are but the magnetic battery and telegraph by means of which spirit communicates with the outer world." In 1870 he became somewhat more sophisticated in his argument. Ostensibly he set out to refute the statement by Huxley (taken out of context) that " 'our thoughts are the expression of molecular changes in that matter of life which is the source of our other vital phenomena.' " [77] Wallace argued, as Huxley himself had done elsewhere, that we can have no clear conception of matter. Consequently, to say that the mind arose from the matter of protoplasm was a meaningless proposition.

Wallace sought to exorcise the specter that haunted all the men in this study—the possibility that mind was actually material. He contended that if there were no consciousness in the individual molecule, consciousness could not emerge from the aggregations of molecules. He declared, "There is no escape from this dilemma,—either all matter is conscious, or consciousness is something distinct from matter, and in the latter case, its presence in material forms is a proof of the existence of conscious beings, outside of, and independent of, what we term matter." Wallace then claimed that Matter is Force and that "all force may be will-force." If such is indeed the case probably, "the whole universe, is not merely dependent on, but actually *is*, the WILL of higher intelligences or of one Supreme Intelligence." [78] Wallace carried this speculation no further. It served to provide him with sufficient rationale to support the presence of spirits who existed outside physical nature and yet as nonmaterial manifestations of force could influence matter or human minds.

This metaphysical postscript in *Contributions to the Theory of Natural Selection* was of little intrinsic interest. It was not original. Joseph Priestly had suggested a very similar interpretation of matter.[79] However, the scientific rationale according to which Wallace justified the possible existence of various levels of intelligences above that of man exerted a direct influence over Frederic Myers and James Ward. In 1870 Wallace based his view of an infinite number

77. ARW, *Miracles and Modern Spiritualism*, p. 107; ARW, *Natural Selection*, p. 362.

78. Ibid., pp. 365, 368.

79. H. W. Piper, *The Active Universe* (London: The Athlone Press, 1962), p. 27. Karl Pearson considered ARW's speculation on matter of sufficient significance to merit criticism and refutation. See Karl Pearson, *The Grammar of Science* (London: J. M. Dent & Sons, 1951), p. 342.

of levels of intellectual existence or manifestations of force on the concept of continuity.

> The grand law of continuity which we see pervading our universe, would lead us to infer infinite gradations of existence, and to people all space with intelligence and will-power; and, if so, we have no difficulty in believing that for so noble a purpose as the progressive development of higher and higher intelligences, those primal and general will-forces, which have sufficed for the production of the lower animals, should have been guided into new channels and made to converge in definite directions.[80]

Such reasoning from analogy allowed Wallace to project the possible continuity of life and mind into realms of being beyond those manifest through matter. Spirits in those ethereal realms could affect man and physical nature without abridging the law of the conservation of energy because energy was but one aspect of the will-force that underlay everything.

Wallace remained silent about spiritualism in the context of his scientific works until he published *Darwinism* in 1889. There he repeated his conviction that a cause other than natural selection must account for the mental and moral faculties of man. He extended his argument to declare that there had been three separate occasions "in the development of the organic world when some new cause or power must necessarily have come into action." [81] These were the change of matter from inorganic to organic, the appearance of consciousness that separated animals from plants, and the appearance in man of distinctly human mental faculties.

This new addition foreshadowed the line of reasoning that Wallace would assume in his last three "scientific" books—*Man's Place in the Universe* (1903), *Is Mars Inhabitable?* (1907), and *The World of Life* (1910). In these volumes Wallace attempted to provide spiritualism with a foundation in natural religion. They were the work of his very old age, but not of a feeble or deteriorated mind. Each book in a slightly different fashion vindicated the position Wallace had enunciated in *Light,* the major spiritualist publication, in 1885:

80. ARW, *Natural Selection,* p. 370.
81. ARW, *Darwinism* (London: Macmillan & Co., 1889), p. 474.

[T]he whole *raison d'être* of the material universe—with all its marvellous changes and adaptations, the infinite complexity of matter and of the ethereal forces which pervade and vivify it, the vast wealth of nature in the vegetable and animal kingdoms —is to serve the grand purpose of developing human spirits in human bodies.[82]

In *Man's Place in the Universe* Wallace employed astronomical data to prove to his own, if not to the astronomers', satisfaction that the earth was located in the middle of the universe.[83] Only a planet so located was capable of producing and sustaining human life with its moral potential. Percival Lowell's suggestion in *Mars and Its Canals* (1906) that intelligent creatures had constructed the canals on Mars drew a speedy retort from Wallace in the form of *Is Mars Inhabitable?* (1907). In this slight volume Wallace argued that the temperature on Mars could not support human life and suggested alternative geological explanations for the canals. The unique nature of the position of man on earth was thus preserved in his sight.

In *The World of Life* Wallace created nothing less than a spiritualist theodicy. Every facet of nature was intended to awaken mankind's moral faculties. Wallace again reverted to a position that he had articulated in *Light* in 1885.

The need for labour in order to live, the constant struggle against the forces of nature, the antagonism of the good and the bad, the oppression of the weak by the strong, the painstaking and devoted search required to wrest from nature her secret powers and hidden treasures—all directly assist in developing the varied powers of mind and body and the nobler impulses of our nature . . . the oppression and wrong, the ignorance and crime, the misery and pain, that always and everywhere pervade the world, have been the means of exercising and strengthening the higher sentiments of justice, mercy, charity, and love, which we all feel to be our best and noblest characteristics, and which

82. ARW, "Are the Phenomena of Spiritualism in Harmony with Science?", *Light* 5 (1885) : 256.
83. ARW, *Man's Place in the Universe* (New York: McClure, Phillips, & Co., 1903). See also ARW, *My Life*, 2 : 122.

it is hardly possible to conceive could have been developed by any other means.[84]

For Wallace the temporal suffering of humanity, to which he was highly sensitive, was not useless. It served to arouse man's moral faculties. The alleviation of suffering by actively exercising those faculties raised men to higher levels of humanity. The tribulation of the present life aided the development of the human personality toward achieving a degree of higher spirituality after death.[85]

In *The World of Life* Wallace described the earth as "a vast schoolhouse for the higher education of the human race in preparation for the enduring spiritual life to which it is destined." [86] Through the medium of lesser spiritual intelligences the guiding mind of the universe employed the cruelty and pain of earthly existence in the higher moral purpose of aiding man's evolution into a fully spiritual creature. Implicit in this argument was a concept of a limited God that Wallace shared with many of his contemporaries such as J. S. Mill, William James, and James Ward. Only such a concept of God allowed him to ascribe a moral personality to the deity and a rational and just destiny to man.

The method, reasoning, and purpose of these last books were far removed from scientific naturalism. They echoed in spirit, if not in theology, the late seventeenth-century exponents of natural religion and an almost Leibnizian optimism. For Wallace himself, they represented a direct continuation of the purpose of scientific venture that in 1843 he had advocated in his first discussion of science. That year he composed a lecture entitled "The Advantages of Varied Knowledge" apparently for delivery at the local mechanics institute in Neath. Wallace explained that man possessed the power to explore the mysteries of nature. To fail to explore nature meant man should lack knowledge that "we should be the better for knowing" and would also let "our highest powers and capacities rust for want of use." He concluded by demanding of his audience:

Shall we not then feel the satisfaction of having done all in our power to improve by culture those higher faculties that distin-

84. ARW, "Are the Phenomena of Spiritualism in Harmony with Science?", *Light* 5 (1885) : 256. See pp. 241–42 for James Ward's similar view of evil.
85. ARW, *The World of Life*, pp. 376–80; *Darwinism*, pp. 36–40; *My Life*, 2 : 254–55.
86. ARW, *The World of Life*, p. 391.

guish us from the brutes, that none of the talents with which
we may have been gifted have been suffered to lie altogether
idle? And, lastly, can any reflecting mind have a doubt that,
by improving to the utmost the nobler faculties of our nature
in this world, we shall be the better fitted to enter upon and
enjoy whatever new state of being the future may have in store
for us? [87]

Wallace himself never wavered in his response to those questions.
He never abandoned his faith that science and scientific knowledge
must provide the means to man's moral development. This was the
faith that he voiced in his last three books on nature. These were
his final statements and perhaps the final statement by any important
nineteenth-century man of science of the ameliorative expectation
that had flourished seventy-five years earlier in the Owenite Halls of
Science and in the mechanics institutes. The messages of these books
represented the last flicker from the forge of "belated rationalism"
that had molded Wallace's mind and spirit and inspired him with
the vision of the moral capacity of the human personality.

Somewhat younger men, whose minds had not experienced the
heat of that forge and whose understanding of science was derived
from the writings of the exponents of scientific naturalism, faced a
more difficult task than had Wallace in achieving an optimistic outlook on the universe. They had to reason their way or find evidence
to support the ideas that Wallace assumed because of his particular
background. For example, Henry Sidgwick had to convince himself
that the universe was a moral order. Still other men had to satisfy
themselves that human beings did possess a moral personality autonomous of the physical mechanism of the body. Such a figure was
Frederic Myers, an acquaintance of Wallace's and a close friend of
Henry Sidgwick's. Myer's life was spurred by the single driving impulse to discover that the human personality survived physical death.
These three men—Wallace, Sidgwick, Myers—were among those to
whom Carl Jung specifically declared should belong

> the immortal merit of having thrown the whole of their author-
> ity on to the side of non-material facts, regardless of public
> disapproval. They faced academic prejudices, and did not shrink
> from the cheap derision of their contemporaries; even at a time

87. ARW, *My Life*, 1 : 202–03.

when the intellect of the educated classes was spellbound by the new dogma of materialism, they drew public attention to phenomena of an irrational nature, contrary to accepted convictions. These men typify the reaction of the human mind against the senseless and desolating materialistic view.[88]

Frederic Myers not only reacted against the prevailing view of the human mind, but also, in the absence of efforts from the professional psychologists in England, attempted to formulate a dynamic psychology that could accommodate the nonmaterial facts unearthed by psychical researchers.

88. C. G. Jung, "The Psychological Foundations of Belief in Spirits," *Proceedings of the Society for Psychical Research* (1921), 31 : 76.

5

Frederic W. H. Myers: The Quest for the Immortal Part

IN SEARCH OF A SOUL

Frederic W. H. Myers possessed the temperament and pursued the craft of a poet. He received the education of a classical scholar. Class and circumstance acquainted him with the wealthy, the great, and the near great. He was by profession a school inspector and by avocation one of the most intrepid psychical researchers in late Victorian England. Affluence and leisure permitted his avocation to prevail over his profession. His most significant contribution to psychical research, *Human Personality and Its Survival of Bodily Death,* appeared in 1903, two years after his own death. Although this two-volume study has been considered representative of the Edwardian era, its ideas and concerns were the products of the intellectual tensions of the last four decades of Victoria's reign.[1] In those curious volumes, Myers wove into a single cloth, for which his life furnished the pattern, the various threads of Christian, classical, romantic, and scientific thought that characterized the Victorian mind.

Outside circles of psychical research, Frederic Myers is perhaps best remembered, if at all, for his walk and conversation with George Eliot in the Fellows' Garden of Trinity College, Cambridge, in 1873. On that rainy May evening the grave authoress, discoursing on God, Immortality, and Duty, urged her young companion to consider "how inconceivable was the *first,* how unbelievable the *second,* and yet how peremptory and absolute the *third.*"[2] Frederic Myers was thirty years old when he listened to those words. For easily half of his young life, the issues of which George

1. S. Hynes, *The Edwardian Turn of Mind* (Princeton, N.J.: Princeton University Press, 1968), pp. 138–44.
2. Frederic W. H. Myers, *Essays: Modern,* 2nd ed. (London: Macmillan & Co., 1885), p. 269. Frederic W. H. Myers hereafter cited in footnotes as FM.

Eliot spoke had haunted Myers and prevented him from coming to peace with himself. He had pondered and considered them at length with his teacher and friend Henry Sidgwick and with others of his generation at Cambridge, including Walter Leaf, Edmund Gurney, and Arthur Balfour.[3] One may surmise that hesitantly, fearfully, and even reverently, Myers had posed to the learned sage some question, previously discussed among his friends, that evoked her famous response.

George Eliot's comment, steeped in the ideals and presupposing the conclusions of scientific naturalism, afforded Myers neither comfort nor satisfactory guidance. Years later he recalled his inner reaction to her words.

> I listened, and night fell; her grave, majestic countenance turned towards me like a Sibyl's in the gloom; it was as though she withdrew from my grasp, one by one, the two scrolls of promise, and left me the third scroll only, awful with inevitable fates. And when we stood at length and parted, amid the columnar circuit of the forest-trees, beneath the last twilight of starless skies, I seemed to be gazing, like Titus at Jerusalem, on vacant seats and empty halls,—on a sanctuary with no Presence to hallow it, and heaven left lonely of a God.[4]

Quite simply Frederic Myers was not made from the stuff of that heroic stoicism George Eliot described. He was morally too uncertain and emotionally too sensitive to confront life without the larger hope.

An evangelical shorn of his faith, Myers had liberated himself from neither the fears and frailties of the flesh nor the expectation of immortality.[5] A classicist, he had imbibed too deeply the thoughts of Plato and Plotinus to abandon the belief that somehow man's moral nature partook of an invisible underlying reality of things. A

3. David Newsome, *Godliness and Good Learning: Four Studies on a Victorian Ideal* (London: John Murray, 1961), pp. 228–29.

4. FM, *Essays: Modern,* p. 269.

5. See the Bibliographical Essay for a discussion of FM's biographical sketch, *Fragments of Inner Life* (privately printed, 1893). If this is not available, see *Dictionary of National Biography,* s.v. "Frederic William Henry Myers, 1843–1901," ed. Leslie Stephen and Sidney Lee (London: Oxford University Press, 1949–1950), 22 : 1087–90; and Alan Gauld, *The Founders of Psychical Research* (New York: Schocken Books, 1968).

romantic, as suggested by his gothic description of the scene in the Fellows' Garden, he could not inwardly release himself from a sense of personal, organic, and spiritual union with nature such as Wordsworth had explored and glorified. Yet Frederic Myers was also a child of his age. He respected science and the scientific mind. In 1864, after obtaining a first class on the moral science tripos, he attempted to extend his studies for another year in order to read for the natural science examination. Though his plan failed, he had by that date certainly begun to familiarize himself with current science, wherein he sought answers to those questions that disturbed him most.

George Eliot's declaration conflicted with each of the strains in Myers's character and with the hope he had placed in scientific knowledge. The woman, who so admired the sciences, had addressed herself to the problems of the universe and delivered an answer with which Myers could not live. So he turned his back on that "heaven left lonely of a God" and lived in the hope that Henry Sidgwick had aroused in him on another walk some years earlier.

Myers shared Sidgwick's conviction that ultimate questions yet unanswered must still be confronted. In 1869 or 1871 (the date is unsure), Myers had in trembling asked his mentor

> whether he thought that when Tradition, Intuition, Metaphysic, had failed to solve the riddle of the Universe, there was still a chance that from any actual observable phenomena,—ghosts, spirits, whatsoever there might be,—some valid knowledge might be drawn as to a World Unseen. Already, it seemed, he had thought that this was possible; steadily, though in no sanguine fashion, he indicated some last grounds of hope; and from that night onwards I resolved to pursue this quest, if it might be, at his side.[6]

During the thirty years of life that lay before him, Myers unswervingly sought empirical proof of that unseen world. Unlike Sidgwick or Wallace, Myers pursued evidence of the invisible not for ethical reasons or for the moral improvement of humanity, but for the

6. FM, *Fragments of Prose and Poetry*, ed. Eveleen Myers (London: Longmans, Green, & Co., 1904), pp. 98–99. See also, Gauld, *The Founders of Psychical Research*, p. 103.

personal assurance that he would pass through the portals of death and achieve in a new realm the spiritual existence that eluded him in this life.

Myers was determined to discover by the methods of science the existence of the human soul, which earlier religious and philosophical writers had apprehended intuitively. He hoped that on empirical, scientific grounds he might demand as had St. Paul, "O death, where is thy sting? O grave, where is thy victory?" In his quest for the immortal part Frederic Myers prefigured the "modern man in search of a soul" whom Carl Jung described in 1931 as expecting "something from psychic life which he has not received from the outer world: something which our religions, doubtless, ought to contain, but no longer do contain." [7] Myers realized that Christianity no longer satisfied man's spiritual needs in the age of science and the New Nature. Yet he also perceived that scientific naturalism failed to confront the human condition in the hour of death. Consequently, he sought to expand the realm of scientific knowledge and theory that men might neither live nor die in vain and that they might become aware of the truly cosmic dimensions of human existence.

The determination to substantiate hope with empirical evidence led Myers from classics and literature to a self-mastery of the intricacies of contemporary science and psychology. William James described his friend's self-education.

> Brought up entirely upon literature and history, and interested at first in poetry and religion chiefly; never by nature a philosopher in the technical sense of a man forced to pursue consistency among concepts for the mere love of the logical occupation; not crammed with science at college, or trained to scientific method by any passage through a laboratory, Myers had as it were to recreate his personality before he became the wary critic of evidence, the skillful handler of hypothesis, the learned neurologist and omnivorous reader of biological and cosmological matter, with whom in later years we were acquainted.[8]

7. C. G. Jung, *Modern Man in Search of a Soul*, trans. W. S. Dell and Cary F. Baynes (London: K. Paul, Trench, Trubner & Co., 1933), p. 237.

8. William James, *Memories and Studies* (New York and London: Longmans, Green & Co., 1911), p. 146.

Myers became a serious psychologist. He first introduced the studies
of Freud to an English audience.[9] He was a mainstay of the Society
for Psychical Research and a leader in the early meetings of the
International Congress of Experimental Psychology. Myers considered his own achievement puzzling and often commented that
future generations would be surprised that the empirical investigation of so profound a problem as death and survival had fallen to a
self-taught amateur.

Despite this personal achievement, Myers did not "recreate his
own personality," but rather followed his earlier predispositions by
a different means. As with the thought of Fechner, von Hartmann,
Janet, Flournoy, Freud, and Jung, the system of psychology and
cosmology that Myers set forth owed much to romantic philosophy
and classical erudition as well as to empirical scientific research.
Myers thought and wrote in the romantic–idealist tradition of
Coleridge and Wordsworth. In restrospect, *Human Personality and
Its Survival of Bodily Death* more nearly represented the last great
manifesto of English romanticism than the program for future
scientific research that Myers had intended to achieve.

IF A MAN DIE . . .

In his absorption with death Frederic Myers was at one with his
age. For most nineteenth-century men and women, death represented
one of the chief facts of life. In the highly stratified society of Victorian England, death constituted a bond linking the various classes
by virtue of their common mortality. Few families of any social class
escaped the untimely passing of members from cholera, typhoid,
childbirth, or childhood disease. The deathbed scene was a much
used convention in novels and a not unfamiliar feature at one time
or another in many people's lives. Evangelicals and secularists alike
placed considerable stock in the last moments of the passing soul,
when true convictions were supposedly voiced. The rites of mourning were set and elaborate. Poor workingmen could purchase in-
surance to provide funerals for themselves. Death even became the
source for political dispute between Dissenters and Anglicans when

9. L. S. Hearnshaw, *A Short History of British Psychology 1840–1940* (New York:
Barnes & Noble, 1964), p. 159.

the former sought the legal right to be buried in the parish church-yard.[10]

For Myers, the issue of death was inextricably related to the question of the survival of the soul. Some men have been intoxicated with God, others with nature; but Frederic Myers was intoxicated with the idea and prospect of immortality. On one occasion while visiting Francis Darwin, Myers shook his friend, declaring, "Frank, let me feel you: a man who really does not WANT immortality." Myers not only wanted it, he wanted proof of it. As the psychologist William McDougall wrote in 1903, "Hitherto the belief in a future life had been a matter of faith: Myers sought to make it a matter of knowledge." [11] Myers's desire for empirical evidence of the survival of human personality represented in a peculiar fashion a reaction against the treatment of death by both Christians and men of science.

Within the late evangelical homes in which Frederic Myers, Henry Sidgwick, and Samuel Butler were reared, there were apparently frequent discussions of the afterlife.[12] Conversations about heaven and hell no doubt constituted one part of the moral training of children. In the Myers's household his mother attended to the religious teaching. Very early in his life—far too early for the good of his emotional stability—Frederic Myers was introduced to the idea of the extinction of personality.

When he was five or six years old, Myers happened upon the body of a mole crushed by a cart. As might any child reared on the idea of an afterlife, he asked his mother if the animal's soul had gone to heaven.[13] Mrs. Myers, more concerned with sound doctrine than with

10. Geoffrey Gorer, *Death, Grief, and Mourning* (Garden City, N.Y.: Doubleday & Co., 1965), pp. 192–99; Newsome, *Godliness and Good Learning*, pp. 148–94; Walter Houghton, *The Victorian Frame of Mind* (New Haven and London: Yale University Press, 1957), pp. 276–77; Owen Chadwick, *The Victorian Church* (London: Adam & Charles Black, 1970), 2 : 202–07; Geoffrey Best, "Evangelicalism and the Victorians," in *The Victorian Crisis of Faith*, ed. Anthony Symondson, (London: Society for Promoting Christian Knowledge, 1970), pp. 54–55; Susan Budd, "The Loss of Faith: Reasons for Unbelief among Members of the Secular Movement in England, 1850–1950," *Past and Present* 36 (1967) : 106–25.

11. Quoted in Gwen Raverat, *Period Piece: A Cambridge Childhood* (London: Faber, 1953), p. 189; W. McDougall, "Critical Notice of F. W. H. Myers's *Human Personality and Its Survival of Bodily Death*," *Mind*, ns. 12 (1903) : 513.

12. Best, "Evangelicalism and the Victorians," p. 55; A. F. Silver, ed., *The Family Letters of Samuel Butler* (Stanford, Calif.: Stanford University Press, 1966), pp. 40–42.

13. FM, *Fragments of Inner Life*, p. 7. For the story of another child who had a

the sensitivity of her son's feelings, replied that the mole would not live again. Forty-five years later Myers wrote:

> To this day I remember my rush of tears at the thought of that furry innocent creature, crushed by a danger which I fancied it too blind to see, and losing all joy forever by that unmerited stroke. The pity of it! the pity of it! and the first horror of a death without resurrection rose in my bursting heart.[14]

It would perhaps be no exaggeration to suggest that Myers spent the rest of his life in an effort to prove that human beings did not face the plight of that mole. That men as well as animals might face extinction dawned on Myers a few years later and in a distinctly liberal Christian context when extinction was posed as an alternative to the doctrine of hell.

This second traumatic shock did not come with his father's passing in 1851 but occurred a year or two later. Again his mother was the vehicle of gloom.

> My mother, who shrank from dwelling on the hideous doctrine of hell, suggested to me that perhaps men who led bad lives on earth were annihilated at death. The idea that such a fate should be possible for any man seemed to me appalling. I remember where I stood at the moment, and how my brain reeled under the shock.[15]

Myers's youthful reaction and his adult recollection of this incident point up a paradoxical feature of the removal of the doctrine of literal hell from liberal theology.[16] The fear or hatred of hell, as seen in the case of Alfred Russel Wallace, could result in the rejection of Christianity. However, for people like Frederic Myers, who considered themselves unworthy of salvation or who had lost faith in Christianity but retained belief in sin, the absence of a doctrine

---

similar experience, see Erik Erikson, *Childhood and Society,* 2nd ed. rev. & enl. (New York: W. W. Norton & Co., 1963), pp. 25–34.

14. FM, *Fragments of Inner Life,* p. 8.

15. Ibid.

16. FM's father seems to have embraced an advanced view of the afterlife and no doubt was the source of his wife's idea of the annihilation of evil men as a substitute for hell. See Frederic Myers, *Catholic Thoughts on the Bible and Theology* (London: W. Ibister & Co., 1874), pp. 253–72, 430–31; Owen Chadwick, *The Victorian Church* (New York: Oxford University Press, 1966), 1 : 544–50; and Bernard M. G. Reardon, *From Coleridge to Gore: A Century of Religious Thought in Britain* (London: Longman, 1971), pp. 216–19.

of afterlife could create equally grave personal anxiety. Psychologically, the prospect of annihilation may have been worse than the prospect of damnation. If hell existed, then God at least concerned himself about men—even immoral men. But if only annihilation awaited evil men or all men, even God—quite literally—did not give a damn about them. They were indeed lost forever, and their lives were devoid of transcendental meaning or significance. As Myers matured and meditated continually on death and immortality, fear of annihilation rather than of hell haunted him. As he wrote in *Human Personality*, "The worst fear was the fear of spiritual extinction or spiritual solitude." [17] These anxieties stemmed directly from concerns about his own moral life and from his religious development.

While studying at Trinity College, Cambridge, during the 1860s, Myers became deeply introspective about his personal life. There can be little question that his efforts to control his awakened sexual nature accounted for his introspection. Just as he was becoming keenly aware of the passions of the flesh, he concluded that Christianity was incapable of guiding his life. For a time he turned to revelry in Greek studies and culture but found no satisfying moral wisdom in those authors.[18]

He soon abandoned his devotion to Hellenism, when in 1865 he came under the influence of Josephine Butler, one of the most remarkable and charismatic women of the age.[19] She was the sister-in-law of the Master of Trinity College. She used her beauty and charm to seduce young men into reaffirming their Christian faith. As Myers expressed her approach, "She introduced me to Christianity, so to say, by an inner door; not to its encumbering forms and dogmas, but to its heart of fire." [20] As an active opponent of the

17. FM, *Human Personality and Its Survival of Bodily Death*, new impression (London: Longmans, Green, & Co., 1915), 2 : 281.

18. FM, *Fragments of Inner Life*, pp. 10–11; "Account of My Friendship with Henry Sidgwick, Oct. 18, 1873," F. W. H. Myers Papers, Trinity College Library, Cambridge. At the time the author consulted this letter and certain other of FM's MSS, they were in the private possession of Mrs. E. Q. Nicholson, a granddaughter of FM's. Since that time Mrs. Nicholson has deposited these papers with Trinity College Library.

19. *Dictionary of National Biography: Supplement*, s.v. "Mrs. Josephine Elizabeth Butler, 1828–1906," ed. Sidney Lee (London: Oxford University Press, 1951), 1 : 282–83; Glen Petrie, *A Singular Iniquity: The Campaigns of Josephine Butler* (New York: Viking Press, 1971); Gauld, *The Founders of Psychical Research*, pp. 95–98.

20. FM, *Fragments of Inner Life*, p. 13.

Contagious Diseases Laws, which regulated certain forms of prostitution, Mrs. Butler no doubt combined Christianity with the idea of sexual purity—a combination to which Myers was most susceptible. For about three years Myers remained content, meditated on Seeley's *Ecce Homo,* and lived a somewhat ascetic existence.

However, by 1869 the heady ecstasy of Mrs. Butler's ideas had worn away. During an attack of pneumonia, Myers realized that he had passed from Christianity to agnosticism. "There is no need to retrace the steps of gradual disillusion. This came to me, as to many others, from increased knowledge of history and of science, from a wider outlook on the world. Sad it was, and slow; a recognition of insufficiency of evidence, fraught with growing pain." [21] It would appear that the higher criticism and to a lesser degree the ideas of scientific naturalism had undermined his faith. Myers, like Sidgwick, was never happy or satisfied with agnosticism. It left his passions uncontrolled and his anxiety over annihilation all the more pressing.

It was at this time in 1869 or 1871 when he took his walk with Sidgwick and decided to seek proof of the existence of an unseen realm through psychical research. Initially he was far from enthusiastic. He later explained, "I had at first great repugnance to studying the phenomena alleged by Spiritualists;—to re-entering by the scullery window the heavenly mansion out of which I had been kicked through the front door." [22] Myers soon overcame his early reluctance and with friends and then members of the Sidgwick group began to attend seances and to evaluate evidence. Not long thereafter he came under the influence of another woman who so touched his life that his desires for immortality, sexual purity, and a transcendental meaning to life were drawn together into a single, inseparable knot. This association transformed Myers's life and the meaning and purpose he attached to psychical research.

The woman was Annie Marshall, unhappily married to one of Myers's cousins.[23] Her husband was subject to periods of pathological dejection, and her own mental health was far from stable. She and

21. FM, "Account of My Friendship with Henry Sidgwick, Oct. 18, 1873," F. W. H. Myers Papers; FM, *Fragments of Inner Life,* p. 13.

22. FM, *Fragments of Inner Life,* p. 15.

23. For the sparse details of FM's relationship with Annie Marshall, see FM, *Fragments of Inner Life,* pp. 16–28; W. H. Salter, "F. W. H. Myers's Posthumous Message," *Proceedings of the Society for Psychical Research* (1958), 52 : 5–8; Gauld, *The Founders of Psychical Research,* pp. 116–24.

Myers had met in 1871. By 1873, in one of those impossible marital situations engendered by Victorian law and mores, she and Myers fell deeply in love. It would appear that Myers, then just over thirty and with no prospect for marriage, desired an affair to which Annie Marshall would not consent. Nevertheless, an intense platonic relationship did develop in which Myers, à la Mrs. Butler, sublimated his sexual ardour into an intense spiritual love.

Annie Marshall's refusal to indulge their mutual passions awakened in Myers a mode of human affection of which he had not previously known himself capable.

> I had guessed not, did I not know, that the spirit
>   of man was so strong
> To prefer irredeemable woe to the slightest shadow
>   of wrong . . .[24]

Annie Marshall had brought out the best in him. He found that purity and morality were possible without religious or ethical sanctions. Myers discovered that human beings did possess a spiritual nature and that he himself possessed a soul capable of spiritual love.

In a letter to George Eliot written on 7 December 1872 Myers had voiced his thoughts on the nature of the relationship of love and immortality.

> Life has come to such a pass—now that there is no longer any God or any hereafter or anything in particular to aim at—that it is only coming into contact with some other person that one can be oneself. There is no longer anything to keep a [sic] isolated fire burning within one. All one can do is to feel the sparks fly from one for a moment when one strikes a kindred soul. Such contact in real life can make one feel for the moment immortal; but the necessary circumstances are so unusual! mere love, delicate or passionate, will not do: to have its best savour love must be set among great possibilities and great self-sacrifices, and must demand the full strain of all the forces within one.[25]

The love that Myers soon shared with Annie Marshall more than fulfilled these conditions and expectations. But it was cut short, and once again the issue of immortality was pressed home to Myers.

24. FM, *Fragments of Inner Life*, p. 19.
25. FM to George Eliot, in F. W. H. Myers Papers.

Not long after their final parting in 1876, Annie Marshall drowned herself. The tragedy was crucial for Myers. Perhaps he felt guilt. Perhaps he simply felt the loss of one who had led him to achieve a new awareness of his inner nature. Or perhaps he regretted the affair had been platonic. Whatever the case (and it can only remain a matter for undocumented speculation), Myers began to rationalize their ill-fated relationship as one between two immaterial souls whose love would again be renewed in eternity. It gave him new reason and determination to discover human immortality and an enduring spiritual nature in human beings. In his autobiographical sketch he wrote, "I felt that if anything still recognizable in me had preceded earth-life, it was this one profound affinity; if anything were destined to survive, it must be into the maintenance of this one affinity that my central effort must be thrown." [26]

To reach Annie Marshall's spirit as well as to find proof of his own immortality now became Myers's goal. By the end of his life the certainty that he had actually contacted her confirmed, more than any other single factor, his belief in survival. On 3 January 1899 Myers wrote Oliver Lodge, "This year 1899—after 23 years of such endeavour—has brought me *certainty*—Far more fully even than Mrs. Piper I have gained thru Mrs. Thomson the conviction that a Spirit is near me who makes my religion and also will make my heaven." [27] Twenty-three years had passed since Annie Marshall's death. In his diary throughout 1899 and 1900 there appear frequent notations of seances where Myers believed he had been in the presence of the woman he had loved so passionately and with such profound sexual and personal frustration.[28]

In 1880 Myers married the very beautiful Eveleen Tennant. The marriage was generally happy and, if the sketches of rabbits in his diary are indicative, sexually satisfying. Yet the couple were not particularly compatible intellectually. This may account for his continued desire to contact Annie Marshall. It may also have meant that in retrospect he exaggerated the felicity of the previous relationship. Whatever the case, Myers came to realize that in addition to proving survival he must also achieve a conception of the human

26. FM, *Fragments of Inner Life*, p. 38.
27. FM to Oliver Lodge, in Oliver Lodge Papers, 1528, Archives of the Society for Psychical Research, London.
28. FM's diary, F. W. H. Myers Papers.

personality that linked human relationships to a spiritual reality unrecognized by the advocates of scientific naturalism and especially by physiological psychologists.

The naturalistic writers whose books Myers studied in detail paradoxically stimulated the same fear of extinction that had been initially roused by his Christian mother. Whenever possible the scientific publicists simply avoided the issue of death or pointed with pride to Darwin's words, "I am not the least afraid to die." [29] Death could not be synthesized into the context of the New Nature. The New Nature might prolong life, but it could not abolish death. For the exponents of scientific naturalism, death was an embarrassment; immortality, an illusion. Herbert Spencer wrote of death in unusually aseptic terms.

> Death, or that final equilibration which precedes dissolution, is the bringing to a close of all those conspicuous integrated motions that arose during evolution. The impulsations of the body from place to place first cease; presently the limbs cannot be stirred; later still the respiratory actions stop; finally the heart becomes stationary, and, with it, the circulating fluids. That is, the transformation of molecular motion into the motion of masses comes to an end; and each of these motions of masses, as it ends, disappears into molecular motions.[30]

There was no immortality for a human personality that was the product of a particular arrangement of atoms and energy. Death amounted to simple extinction and return to the primal elements— dust to dust, ashes to ashes—the "final equilibration."

As Myers began to think about the nature of a human personality that could experience or re-experience a spiritual relationship, such as he had known with Annie Marshall, he saw that he must oppose and vanquish physiological psychology which reduced human life, love, and emotions to matter and energy. He told J. A. Symonds in 1884,

> The kind of adversary present to my mind is a man like Dr. Maudsley:—a man for whose private character I can well believe

29. F. Darwin, *The Life and Letters of Charles Darwin* (New York: D. Appleton & Co., 1899), 2 : 529.

30. Herbert Spencer, *First Principles* (New York: P. F. Collier & Son, 1901), p. 440.

that I should feel much respect, but who represents a school of thought which, if it prevails, will bring the world to the Nihilism of the brutes of the field. I want to snatch our young Ray-Lankesters as brands from the burning—to save the men whose minds associate religion and the mad house, psychology and the vivisection-table, Love and the Strand.[31]

So long as Maudsley's version of psychology prevailed, not only was human immortality impossible but also any form of human relationship that rose above man's animal nature.

For Myers this problem touched on the still larger issue of the religion of the future. Myers's own sensitivities and spiritual aspirations made him particularly aware of "the deep disquiet of our time." The incommensurability of man's spiritual needs and the world of the New Nature confronted him at every turn in his life.

Never, perhaps, did man's spiritual satisfaction bear a smaller proportion to his needs. . . . [T]hrough our civilized societies two conflicting currents run. On the one hand health, intelligence, morality,—all such boons as the steady progress of planetary evolution can win for man,—are being achieved in increasing measure. On the other hand this very sanity, this very prosperity, do but bring out in stronger relief the underlying *Welt-Schmerz*, the decline of any real belief in the dignity, the meaning, the endlessness of life.[32]

Christianity no longer provided life with dignity and meaning or the promise of immortality. The New Nature could not rise above its mundane origins.

Myers did not wallow in the implicit pessimism of his position. He firmly believed that mankind, at least mankind in the West, stood on the verge not of spiritual death but of a new spiritual vitality. His own era seemed to resemble the last days of the dying ancient world when Christianity had replaced paganism.

The unique effect of that great Christian impulse begins, perhaps, to wear away. But more grace may yet be attainable from the region whence that grace came. Our age's restlessness, as I

31. FM to J. A. Symonds, 28 August 1883, in J. A. Symonds Papers, University of Bristol Library, Bristol, England.
32. FM, *Human Personality*, 2 : 279.

believe, is the restlessness not of senility but of adolescence; it resembles the approach of puberty rather than the approach of death.[33]

Myers neither looked toward nor sought a revival of Christianity. Rather, he expected the emergence of a new religion that would combine the universally appealing elements of Christianity, such as immortality, with a scientific apprehension of the world.

THE ROMANCE OF PSYCHICAL RESEARCH

For Frederic Myers, unlike Sidgwick or Wallace, psychical research constituted an endeavor to provide the foundation for a new religion. By religion, Myers understood "the sane and normal response of the human spirit to all that we know of cosmic law; that is, to the known phenomena of the universe, regarded as an intelligible whole." Since existing scientific knowledge was undermining traditional doctrines, the dawning religious synthesis Myers envisioned had to originate in genuinely new knowledge about nature. He expected psychical research to furnish data that would lead to "the discovery by scientific methods of a spiritual world" and eventually to a religion according to which neither the life nor the love of human beings could ever become extinct. It would be a religion

> which no longer depends on tradition and intuition only, but on reason also and on experiment; which is not locked away in an emotional compartment of our being, nor adapted to the genius of special races alone, but is oecumenical as Science is oecumenical, is evolutionary as Science is evolutionary, and rests on a permanent and provable relationship of the whole spiritual to the whole material world.[34]

Should psychical research fail in this task, Myers thought religion itself would pass away.

Myers regarded psychical research as a means of rescuing both religion and science from sinking "into mere obscurantism." Without the new data provided by the psychical researchers, religion could not adapt to the new age, and science could not address those ques-

33. Ibid., p. 280.
34. Ibid., p. 284; FM, *Fragments of Prose and Poetry*, p. 107; FM, *Human Personality*, 2 : 304.

tions that touched men's lives most deeply. As he told the Society for Psychical Research in 1900: "Our duty is not the founding of a new sect, nor even the establishment of a new science, but is rather the expansion of Science herself until she can satisfy those questions which the human heart will rightly ask, but to which Religion alone has thus far attempted an answer." [35] Myers thus proposed to deal with religious questions, which he considered normal to the human situation, by the methods and theories of science.

Myers recognized the peculiar nature of his venture when he commented, "The inquiry falls between the two stools of religion and science; it cannot claim support either from the 'religious world' or from the Royal Society." [36] His idea of religion was not that of Christians. His concept of science was not that of the exponents of scientific naturalism. In fact, his quest may best be understood historically as neither religious nor scientific but more nearly as romantic. Four elements of the romantic tradition dominated Myers's thought in regard to psychical research. They explain in large measure why he could expect from science the provision of a new religious epoch at a time when most men regarded science as the major solvent of religion. Those patterns of romantic thought that determined much of Myers's reasoning were the beliefs that the contemplation of nature could reveal a spiritual reality conterminous with the physical world, that this reality might be particularly evident in the rustic and the primitive, that the earth, man, and the universe are part of and influenced by great cosmic forces, and that human beings possess nondiscursive mental faculties which permit them to transcend the world of their senses.

Myers was steeped in the thought and emotions of the English romantic poets. He was particularly fond of Wordsworth, about whom he contributed a volume in the English Men of Letters series. Like Wordsworth, Myers approached nature in the fervent expectation that "the contemplation of Nature can be made a revealing agency, like Love or Prayer—an opening if indeed there be any opening, into the transcendental world." [37] He combined that Wordsworthian sentiment with Shelley's belief that scientific analysis represented simply another way to contemplate the natural order

35. FM, *Human Personality*, 2 : 80, 305.
36. Ibid., p. 278.
37. FM, *Wordsworth* (New York: Harper & Bros., 1881), p. 130.

and that such analysis was compatible with the apprehension of spiritual realities.[38] In doing so, Myers synthesized Wordsworth's vision with Shelley's method.

In his view of the origins of religion and of the manifestations of spiritual influences, Myers partook of both romantic antinomianism and romantic primitivism. He claimed to base his research on "the uniformitarian hypothesis" that "if a spiritual world exists, and if that world has at any epoch been manifest or even discoverable, then it ought to be manifest or discoverable now." He affirmed the possibility that the spirituality of the cosmos might reveal itself in the primitive intuitions of savage peoples, the religious experiences of men and women at revivals, or in the equally primitive and unsophisticated mutterings of the spirits speaking through mediums. Myers saw no reason why the search for the spiritual realm might not most profitably begin with an examination of the primitive and the unsophisticated. He argued that "the founders of religion have hitherto dealt in the same way with the invisible world as Thales or Anaximander dealt with the visible. They have attempted to begin at once with the highest generalizations." Men must become wary of the view "that even as there is something grand and noble in the object, there ought to be something correspondingly exalted in the means employed [to discover it]." [39] The evidence of telepathy or even hysteria, though not grand or spiritually exalted, might reveal facts of the profoundest religious significance. Just as Wordsworth had received spiritual insight from the life of Cumberland rustics, Myers perceived it in the peculiar and often trivial manifestations of telepathy and apparitions.

The romantic inheritance allowed Myers to interpret certain features of contemporary science in a religious manner. In the concepts of continuity, evolution, and conservation of energy, he saw evidence for the presence of vast cosmic forces ruling the universe and man. As he explained in an undated fragment published in *Human Personality,*

> The material world has taught us lessons of which our conception of the spiritual world stood in no less urgent need. The

38. A. N. Whitehead, *Science and the Modern World* (New York: Mentor Books, 1956), pp. 82–89.

39. FM, *Human Personality,* 1 : 7; FM, *Essays: Modern,* p. 226; FM, *Human Personality,* 2 : 258.

study of visible Nature has taught us Uniformity, Conservation, Evolution; and these transform themselves in their spiritual aspect into an absolute Catholicity, an inescapable Justice, an ever-ascending Ideal. . . . And now that Science herself begins to teach us to expand once more the planetary into the cosmic view, we find that principles built up by minute and persistent observation of material law will expand and exalt themselves also to spiritual operation, and will give to the soul's future the stability of their own infinitude, the buoyancy of their own limitless march and assumption into realms higher and hopes unknown.[40]

Through psychical research Myers hoped to discover new supplementary and complementary laws that would account for man's mental and spiritual evolution.[41] He fully expected his investigations to prove that the relationship of the material and spiritual worlds constituted "a great structural fact of the Universe, involving laws at least as persistent, as identical from age to age, as our known laws of Energy or of Motion." [42]

Current scientific theory particularly encouraged Myers's speculations about invisible forces and gave them a certain plausibility. The most important of these ideas was the concept of a cosmic ether, an imperceptible substance that according to most physicists filled apparently empty space and provided the medium for the transmission of light and other forms of energy.[43] It was accepted and employed by advocates of scientific naturalism, such as Tyndall. The ether was, like the idea of continuity, a rationally postulated concept that permitted the rational interpretation of a particular set of natural phenomena. Myers was familiar with the theory of the ether and also with the discovery of new forms of energy, such as X rays. He read the literature on these topics and profited from conversations with his good friend and fellow psychical researcher Oliver Lodge, principal of the University of Birmingham and a physicist who

40. FM, *Human Personality*, 2 : 308.

41. FM and Edmund Gurney, "Apparitions," *Nineteenth Century* 15 (1884) : 792.

42. FM, *Human Personality*, 2 : 288.

43. Mary Hesse, "Ether," *The Encyclopedia of Philosophy* (New York: Macmillan Co. and The Free Press, 1967), 3 : 66–69; W. D. Niven, ed., *The Scientific Papers of James Clerk Maxwell* (New York: Dover Publications, 1965), 2 : 763–75; J. Tyndall, *Heat: A Mode of Motion*, 4th ed. (New York: D. Appleton & Co., 1877), p. 258, and *New Fragments* (New York: D. Appleton & Co., 1892), pp. 78–93.

devoted much of his professional career to investigating the ether.[44] The theory of the cosmic ether and the newly perceived forms of energy allowed Myers to believe that the scientific method itself would eventually reveal an invisible world that influenced life on earth.

> A subtler ether than ever hung round the windless Olympus is now the subject of differential equations. And man . . . has tamed for his use and fixed for his illumination the very flash and bolt of Jove. There is no need to multiply instances. Science, while perpetually denying an unseen world, is perpetually revealing it.[45]

If this theory were true, there was little reason to doubt that one realm of being might not exist side by side with or interpenetrate another. There was no reason why a spiritual world might not co-exist with the material world or more important why man's mental personality might not actually exist separately from his physical organism.

At the heart of Myers's cosmological speculations lay the platonic, neoplatonic, and Wordsworthian idea of interpenetrating realms of being.[46] Once such realms were recognized, the various manifestations of psychic life could be explained. The first realm was physical nature; the second, the cosmic ether. Then by analogy Myers posited the existence of a third realm. Reasoning from the principle of continuity as had Wallace, he contended, "Within, beyond, the world of ether,—as a still profounder, still more generalised aspect of the Cosmos,—must lie, as I believe, the world of spiritual life." This was the world of the "metetherial environment" characterized by an infinity of stages.[47] Those psychic phenomena, such as hypnotism and apparitions, and human moral qualities, such as platonic love, that did not originate in matter or in the ether pertained to this

44. Oliver Lodge, *The Ether of Space* (London and New York: Harper & Bros., 1909) and *Past Years: An Autobiography* (New York: Scribner's, 1932); David B. Wilson, "The Thought of the Late Victorian Physicists: Oliver Lodge's Ethereal Body," *Victorian Studies* 15 (1971–1972) : 29–48.

45. FM, *Essays: Modern,* p. 228.

46. FM, *Wordsworth,* p. 136; FM, *Science and a Future Life with Other Essays* (London: Macmillan & Co., 1893), pp. 166–67; FM, "The Subliminal Conscious," *Proceedings of the Society for Psychical Research* (1892), 8 : 534.

47. FM, *Human Personality,* 1 : 215–16.

realm. Beyond the metetherial environment lay the "World Soul." [48] Of this many-tiered universe, the human personality was an integral part that participated in each realm.

Myers's concept of the human personality supported these essentially romantic cosmological speculations, which in turn supported his romantic idea of the nature of man. Alfred Wallace had posited a cosmic environment for man only after he found that he could not account for moral faculties by natural selection. Myers, on the other hand, set out to discover what in the end because of his determination he naturally did discover—that man is a cosmic creature whose destiny is "Spiritual Evolution." He intended that psychical research should allow him to "beat against the bars of our earthly prison-house" and force "a narrow opening through which we seem to breathe immortal air." To that end Myers actually searched for "the accidental discovery of some faculty within us which was not traceable to the actions of our terrene antecedents." [49] Such faculties had posed a problem for Wallace; they provided an opportunity for Myers to explore the nondiscursive elements of the human personality hidden in the "subliminal self."

THE SUBLIMINAL SELF

Frederic Myers was one of many late nineteenth-century philosophers and psychologists who investigated and speculated about the human unconscious. Contemporary researchers, such as Janet, Charcot, and Freud, sought to employ scientific knowledge of the unconscious to heal mental disease. Other men, including Myers, James, Flournoy, and Jung, without eschewing the medical implications of these investigations, were more nearly associated with earlier romantic writers who had seen in the nondiscursive functions of the mind a means of transcending the senses and of perceiving a nou-

48. The phrase "World Soul" appears relatively often in the works of FM's last ten years. He never defined what he meant by the term. His clearest statement occurred in the context of his review of William James's *The Principles of Psychology*. There FM wrote, "The *anima mundi*, or universal consciousness, can be best conceived by finite consciousnesses in the aspect of a universal memory, and that memory in the form of a universal *record* of past, present, and possibly even future events" (*Proceedings of the Society for Psychical Research* (1891–92), 7 : 119). See also ibid. (1895), 11 : 587–93.

49. FM, *Human Personality*, 2 : 281; FM, *Fragments of Prose and Poetry*, p. 80; FM, *Science and a Future Life*, p. 37.

menal reality.[50] Myers hoped this new knowledge of what he considered a spiritual nature in man might heal the *Weltschmerz* infecting contemporary intellectual life. As he wrote in January 1890,

> There is no fear lest the Cosmos itself be meaningless or incoherent; the question for us is whether we men are ever to have a chance of entering into its meaning, recognizing its coherence; or are we doomed to remain on the outside of all deep significance, and but to gaze for a moment on the enormous pageant as it sweeps by us with an unknown purport in obedience to an incognisable Power.

Myers employed his hypothesis of the subliminal self to set human beings into the very core of the meaning of the universe and to suggest that man is a creature who is "not a planetary or transitory being" but one who "persists as very man among cosmic and eternal things." [51]

Myers formally enunciated his theory of the subliminal self to the Society for Psychical Research in 1892.

> I suggest . . . that the stream of consciousness in which we habitually live is not the only consciousness which exists in connection with our organism. Our habitual or empirical consciousness may consist of a mere selection from a multitude of thoughts and sensations, of which some at least are equally conscious with those that we empirically know. I accord no primacy to my ordinary waking self, except that among my potential selves this one has shown itself the fittest to meet the needs of common life. I hold that it has established no further claim, and that it is perfectly possible that other thoughts, feelings, and memories, either isolated or in continuous connection, may now be actively conscious, as we say, "within me,"—in some kind of co-ordination with my organism, and forming some part of my total individuality. I conceive it possible that at some future time, and under changed conditions, I may recollect all; I may assume these various personalities under one single conscious-

50. Henri F. Ellenberger, *The Discovery of the Unconscious* (New York: Basic Books, 1970), pp. 110–330, 749–885.

51. FM, "A Defence of Phantasms of the Dead," *Proceedings of the Society for Psychical Research* (1889–90), 6 : 341; FM, *Human Personality*, 1 : 26.

ness, in which ultimate and complete consciousness the empirical consciousness which at this moment directs my hand may be
only one element out of many.

Normal or terrene consciousness was but one stream among many
that composed the total human personality and constituted the part
of the mind or personality that pertained to man's earthly requirements. Other streams of consciousness—"potential personalities, with
imperfectly known capacities of perception and action"—allowed
man to perceive and to participate in other realms of being.[52]

As Myers developed the idea of the subliminal self until the time
of his death in 1901, it came to include all those aspects of human
personality that did not fit into the traditional view of the rational,
discursive human mind. The latter Myers termed the "supraliminal
mind," whose sphere of activity was man's physical environment.
The subliminal self included all facets of the human personality
above and below this pragmatic supraliminal threshhold of consciousness. Myers considered the subliminal self as "half lumber-
room and half king's-treasury."[53] It included the disintegrative
streams of consciousness that were manifested in hysteria, the personality absorbing cosmic metetherial energy in sleep, and the
personality rising to new spiritual awareness in ecstasy and inspiration. Through these usually unconscious streams of personality,
man's relationship to the unseen constituted a structural fact of the
universe.

By this hypothesis Myers united three major ideas that he had
affirmed in the 1880s and had combined to solve his spiritual problems. These ideas were the independence of psychical from physical
life, personality interpreted as streams of consciousness, and the existence of a human soul participating in both a terrene and an extraterrene environment. He employed these to refute the hypothesis
of the physiological psychologists that "my organism is the real basis
of my personality; I am still but a colony of cells, and the unconscious or unknowable from which my thoughts and feelings draw
their unity is below my consciousness and not above it; it is my proto-

52. FM, "The Subliminal Consciousness," *Proceedings of the Society for Psychical
Research* (1891–92), 7 : 301, 308. See also FM, *Human Personality*, 1 : 11–15, and Gauld,
The Founders of Psychical Research, pp. 275–99.

53. FM, *Human Personality*, 1 : xxi, 11–15; 2 : 299.

plasmic substructure, not my transcendental goal." [54] Myers in his maturity never questioned that man had a transcendental goal. Through hypnotism, seances, and automatic writing he delved into the human personality to discover what he considered scientific evidence of that goal.

Myers used the analogy of men watching a chess game through a keyhole to compare his view of the human personality with that of the physiological psychologists. The latter, having witnessed only the movement of pawns, declared that the game was played with only pawns. Myers contended that the yet unmoved rooks, knights, bishops, queen, and king were also involved in the play.

> The chessboard in this parable is the Cosmos; the pawns are those human faculties which make for the preservation and development on this planet of the individual and the race; the pieces are faculties which may either be the mere by-products of terrene evolution, or on the other hand may form an essential part of the faculty with which the human germ or the human spirit is originally equipped, for the self-development in a cosmical, as opposed to a merely planetary, environment.

Reasoning from such analogies, Myers argued that "Thought and Consciousness are not, as the materialists hold them, a mere *epi-phenomenon*, an accidental and transitory accompaniment of more permanent energies, a light that flashes out from the furnace door but does none of the work,—but, on the other hand, are, and always have been, the central subject of the evolutionary process itself." [55] The psychic phenomenon that convinced Myers that mind could and did exist separately from the physical organism was telepathy or those occurrences "where there is reason to suppose that the mind of one human being has affected the mind of another, without speech uttered, or word written or sign made;—has affected it, that is to say, by other means than through the recognized channels of sense." [56] His efforts in the collection and examination of materials for *Phantasms of the Living* (1886) served to persuade Myers that such

---

54 FM, "Human Personality in the Light of Hypnotic Suggestion," *Proceedings of the Society for Psychical Research* (1886–87), 4 : 4.

55. FM, *Human Personality*, 1 : 94; FM, *Science and a Future Life*, p. 37.

56. FM, Introduction to *Phantasms of the Living*, by E. Gurney, FM, and F. Podmore (London: Trubner & Co., 1886), 1 : xxxv.

communication did take place.[57] This conviction gave him reason to believe that the immaterial personality survived bodily death and could participate in the nonphysical, extraterrene, metetherial environment.

Myers's endeavor to collect evidence for the separate existence of mind and body proved rich in results for psychology. William James explained, "Through him for the first time, psychologists are in possession of their full material, and mental phenomena are set down in an adequate inventory." It was primarily during this formative period of the eighties that Myers made the inventory that he published as appendixes to the main chapters of *Human Personality and Its Survival of Bodily Death*. Those materials accounted for more than half of the thirteen hundred pages of the work and constituted "an unparalleled collection of source material on the topics of somnambulism, hypnotism, hysteria, dual personality, and parapsychological phenomena." [58]

During the same decade Myers had also concluded that normal waking consciousness was but one facet of the total personality. His investigation of automatic writing had persuaded him there were levels of the mind beneath and above waking consciousness which could manifest themselves and which the psychologist must take into account.[59] Myers stood among the vanguard of intellectuals who taught men to see the human mind not as a rational entity but as a collectivity of irrational facets and manifestations. In 1885 he noted that writers had traditionally posited a normal, unitary mind in which mental disease represented an aberration from the norm. However, Myers argued,

> [I]t is rather sanity which needs to be accounted for; since the moral and physical being of each of us is built up from incoordination and incoherence, and the microcosm of man is but a micro-chaos held in some semblance of order by a lax and sway-

57. Gauld, *The Founders of Psychical Research*, pp. 153–85.

58. James, *Memories and Studies*, p. 153; FM, *Human Personality*, 1 : 298–700; 2 : 315–627; Ellenberger, *The Discovery of the Unconscious*, p. 788.

59. FM, "Automatic Writing," *Contemporary Review* 47 (1885): 233–49; FM, "Automatic Writing," *Proceedings of the Society for Psychical Research* (1885), 3 : 1–63; (1886–87), 4 : 209–61; (1888), 5 : 522–47. See also FM and E. Gurney, "Some Higher Aspects of Mesmerism," *Proceedings of the Society for Psychical Research* (1885), 3 : 401–23; and FM, "Human Personality in the Light of Hypnotic Suggestions," *Proceedings of the Society for Psychical Research* (1886–87), 4 : 1–24.

ing hand, the wild team which a Phaeton is driving, and which must needs soon plunge into the sea.

Samuel Butler and James Ward would suggest a similar view of mind, but without Myers's vivid metaphor which is reminiscent of those in Freud's later work. Myers thought that this concept of mind meant in turn that "we must face the idea of concurrent *streams of being,* flowing alongside but unmingled within us, and with either of which our active consciousness may, under appropriate circumstances, be identified." [60]

There was nothing particularly novel in Myers's belief in the presence, power, and influence of the unconscious mind.[61] Nor was there any special contemporary novelty in his view that these unconscious facets became "more conspicuous in various supernormal, abnormal, and morbid states." Myers's novelty resided in his own particular interpretation of the significance of the unconscious mind. He recognized that "hidden in the deep of our being is a rubbish-heap as well as a treasure-house;—degenerations and insanities as well as beginnings of higher development." He went so far as to assert "that we should now see the subliminal self no longer as a mere chain of eddies or backwaters, in some way secluded from the mainstream of man's being, but rather as itself the central and potent current, the most truly identifiable with the man himself." [62] The discovery of this rubbish-heap and backwater of the hidden self was not for Myers, as it was for Freud, a final blow to man's narcissism. Paradoxically, Myers regarded the abnormal facets of the mind as evidence of man's spirituality rather than of his irrationality. His romantic cosmology saved him from the latter conclusion. The apparently irrational and abnormal elements of the human personality pertained to other realms of being of which they were streams. Within the context of those nonterrene realms, the irrational might be perfectly rational.

The third idea that Myers embraced during the 1880s was the belief that each human being possessed a "soul." [63] He was never espe-

---

60. FM, "Automatic Writing," pp. 233–34 (FMT's emphasis).

61. Ellenberger, *The Discovery of the Unconscious,* pp. 254–350.

62. FM, "Further Notes on the Unconscious Self," *Journal of the Society for Psychical Research* 2 (1885): 131; FM, *Human Personality,* 1: 72, 297.

63. For the various shades of FM's opinion on the nature of the human soul, see the *Journal of the Society for Psychical Research* 2 (1885): 131; 4 (1887): 60–63, 78, 149;

cially comfortable with this concept and never developed it clearly. In the mid-eighties he wrote in terms of a transcendental ego, much like that suggested by James Ward in his article on "Psychology" in the *Encyclopaedia Britannica*.[64] However, after the appearance of William James's *Principles of Psychology*, Myers reaffirmed the stream of consciousness concept of personality. He never totally abandoned the concept of an ego but came to term it the "individuality" of the personality.[65] This concept served two functions. It suggested a binding unity to the various streams of consciousness. The individuality was the bed of personality over which and through which the streams flowed. He once wrote, "The mind is no walled plot which a diagram will figure; it is a landscape with lines which stretch out of view, and an ever-changing horizon." [66] Individuality was the landscape itself. Second, the idea of individuality preserved the autonomous existence of each personality and prevented it from becoming a subset of a universal mind or World Soul.

The subliminal self, which united these varied ideas and functions, was a genuinely bold and imaginative concept, especially within the context of English thought. Its plausibility and attraction can be seen in the men who believed it worthy of respect and consideration—William James, Oliver Lodge, F. C. S. Schiller, and Carl Jung—as well as in the critics whom it aroused—G. F. Stout, William McDougall, W. H. Mallock, and Ernest Jones.[67] In a sense, the theory of the subliminal self stood as the culmination of much that romantic writers had said about the human mind over the course of the century. It united into one concept the idea of the mind as non-

---

9 (1890), 291, and the *Proceedings of the Society for Psychical Research* (1886-87), 4 : 2-3, 260. See also Gauld, *The Founders of Psychical Research*, pp. 300-05.

64. *Encyclopaedia Britannica*, 9th ed., s.v. "Psychology" by James Ward.

65. FM, "Letter to the Editor," *Journal of the Society for Psychical Research* 4 (1887) : 60-61.

66. FM, *Human Personality*, 1 : 98.

67. William James, Oliver Lodge, T. Flournoy, and Walter Leaf respectively in *Proceedings of the Society for Psychical Research* (1903-04), 18 : 22-61; W. H. Mallock, "The Gospel of Mr. F. W. H. Myers," *Nineteenth Century* 53 (1903) : 628-44; Ernest Jones, *Papers on Psycho-Analysis* (New York: William Wood & Co., 1918), p. 122; C. G. Jung, "The Psychological Foundations of Belief in Spirits," *Proceedings of the Society for Psychical Research* (1921), 31 : 76; W. McDougall, "Critical Notice of F. W. H. Myers's *Human Personality* . . . ," *Mind*, n.s. 12 (1903) : 513-26; F. C. S. Schiller, "The Progress of Psychical Research," *Fortnightly Review* 83 (1905) : 60-73; G. F. Stout, "Mr. F. W. H. Myers's Human Personality . . . ," *Hibbert Journal* 2 (1903-1904) : 44-64.

discursive, irrational, imaginative, ecstatic, and divine. It set forth, with a large body of supporting empirical evidence, all those mental phenomena that most nineteenth-century scientific psychologists had attempted to ignore. For this reason William James could claim that "Frederic Myers will always be remembered in psychology as the pioneer who staked out a vast track of mental wilderness and planted the flag of genuine science upon it." [68]

Myers employed the subliminal self to set forth what W. H. Mallock condescendingly termed a "religio-scientific gospel." [69] It provided a conceptual framework in which the plethora of psychical phenomena might be coordinated. Hypnotism, sleep, hysteria, telepathy, automatic writing, and mediumistic messages were each a manifestation of a stream of subliminal consciousness intruding on the normal terrene consciousness.[70] It was this psychological aspect and function of the theory that sparked professional scientific interest.

Interestingly enough, it was just this unifying function that caused Alfred Wallace to reject the theory. Once again the subtle differences between Wallace and Myers emerge. For Wallace, psychic phenomena were evidence of the presence of spirits who aided and assured man's moral development. The spirits were the souls of the departed, and their antics, attempts to cheat, and trivial activities were inferior characteristics of the personalities they possessed prior to their physical deaths.[71] Myers's goal was far more complicated. He was less concerned with man's moral development than with his own assured spiritual existence and evolution. To find proof for these he felt he had to expand the "normal" personality to include the trash of the lumber room and the refined faculties of the king's treasury. Wallace wanted only the treasure because the whole point of his reasoning was to insure moral development. Myers accepted both because in doing so he could rationalize human personality as an entity existing simultaneously on several planes of being. Only such a view of man could assure him that the entire human personality was not annihi-

68. James, *Memories and Studies*, p. 170.

69. W. H. Mallock, "The Gospel of Mr. F. W. H. Myers," *Nineteenth Century* 53 (1903) : 633.

70. For a general overview of FM's intended use of the concept, see FM, *Human Personality*, 1 : 11–33.

71. Alfred Wallace, *Miracles and Modern Spiritualism*, rev. ed., with chapters on Apparitions and Phantasms (London: Nichols, 1901), pp. 262–64.

lated by bodily death. Immortality rather than morality was Myers's foremost concern.

The theory of the subliminal self allowed Myers to breach the walls of the prisonhouse of life in the New Nature that was circumscribed by the capacities of the physical senses. Through sleep, telepathy, hypnotism, and the like, man's distinctly human personality extended beyond the borders of the discursive understanding. Human perceptions were almost infinitely expanded. Man possessed the capacity to perceive spiritual—metetherial—realities. Moreover, human relationships, such as he had experienced with Annie Marshall, were not confined to physical or earthly boundaries. Human love became part of "the energy of integration which makes a Cosmos of the Sum of Things." [72] Moreover, man could enter into a relationship with the very source of his spiritual being. He could by the extraterrene faculties of his personality ascend to the World Soul. The streams of human consciousness were as many as the several realms of being. [73]

As a direct heritage from earlier romantic authors, Myers regarded the subliminal self as the path whereby creative and artistic imagination surfaced into normal consciousness. The inspiration of the artist, or of the mathematical genius for that matter, was the result of a subliminal inrush of creative energy. [74] The man of genius was not limited to such knowledge as he could obtain from his senses. His inspirations "spring from a source one step nearer to primitive reality than is that specialised consensus of faculties which natural selection has lifted above the threshold for the purposes of working-day existence." The subliminal source of artistic inspiration explained why "there may really be something at times *incommensurable* between the inspirations of genius and the results of conscious logical thought." [75] Significantly, Myers's chapter on genius and inspiration included no extended appendixes. He had drawn from his own poetic experience, that of his friend Robert Louis Stevenson, and the recorded experiences of other poets. [76]

Myers believed his analysis of subliminal human personality would "prove the preamble of all religions," that is, it would constitute

---

72. FM, *Human Personality*, 1 : 112.
73. Ibid., 1 : 118, 215–19; 2 : 186, 505–54.
74. Ibid., 1 70–120.
75. Ibid., 1 : 97, 98.
76. FM, *Fragments of Prose and Poetry*, pp. 84–85.

scientific proof of the existence of a spiritual world.[77] Mankind participated in realms of being other than the physical. Consequently, human immortality seemed highly probable. Death pertained only to the body; the personality extended to nonphysical realms. When applied to Christianity, Myers's ideas had surprising results. The resurrection of Christ became believable, but the unique features of the incarnation vanished. Christ had simply been one of many religious spirits from the metetherial environment who over the course of history had educated mankind in religious truth commensurate with the level of man's mental evolution. Therefore, while convinced that within a century everyone would believe in both Christ's resurrection and their own immortality, Myers felt that Christianity itself would be superseded by fresh spiritual knowledge discovered through psychical research and communicated largely through mediums.[78] Hence, though Christianity stood doomed, religion itself stood on the verge of new vitality.

Finally, Myers employed his idea of the subliminal self to describe man's cosmic situation. Since man's personality possessed streams in the various realms of being, he could absorb energy from each of them.

> There exists around us a spiritual universe, and that universe is in actual relation with the material. From the spiritual universe comes the energy which maintains the material; the energy which makes the life of each individual spirit. Our spirits are supported by a perpetual indrawal of this energy, and the vigor of that indrawal is perpetually changing, much as the vigor of our absorption of material nutriment changes from hour to hour.[79]

Sleep and prayer were modes of indrawing that vital spiritual metetherial energy. The availability of such energy meant that the human

77. FM, "On the Possibility of a Scientific Approach to the Problems Generally Classed as Religious," in *Papers Read before the Synthetic Society,* ed. Arthur J. Balfour (London: Spottiswood & Co., 1908), p. 193. See also FM, *Human Personality,* 2 : 284–307.

78. "I do not feel the smallest doubt that we survive death, & I am pretty confident that the whole scientific world will have accepted this before A.D. 2000" (FM to J. A. Symonds, 20 June 1890, J. A. Symonds Papers, University of Bristol Library, Bristol, England. See also FM, *Human Personality,* 2 : 288.

79. Quoted by William James in *The Varieties of Religious Experience* (New York: The Modern Library, 1929), p. 456.

soul could never become extinct. On another occasion he sought to
assert the eternal nature of the soul by declaring, "That which lies
at the root of each of us lies at the root of the Cosmos too. Our
struggle is the struggle of the Universe itself; and the very Godhead
finds fulfillment through our upward–striving souls." [80] Shades of
Hegel should not be read into this last statement. Myers's footnotes
and his journal indicate that the idea was taken from Plotinus.[81]
Indeed Myers's view of man and the cosmos owed much to the
platonic tradition for which in essence he attempted to provide
empirical verification and scientific rationalization.

However, as Myers attempted to provide a scientific basis for
platonic ideas, he inevitably ran into the problem of dualism. In his
determination to regard the various realms of being as interpene-
trable, he moved steadily toward a monistic view of the cosmos that
he concealed even from himself under the cover of verbiage such as
"transcendental energy." For example, in a letter of 21 June 1894,
he sought to explain to Oliver Lodge the relationship of matter,
living matter, and mind.

> It is selective molecular action [which] is the secret of life,—
> the mode in which transcendental energy habitually encounters
> matter. No wonder that when unembodied intelligences act on
> matter by other methods than that of direct incarnation, they
> should be found employing that very form of action [like] unto
> which in our own subliminal selves we are already familiar. . . .
> And as that selective molecular action which we call life involves
> a concentrated reaction in detail against the lapse of entrophy
> which is the death & dissolution of matter as spirit—so also it is
> the entrophic energy of the World-Soul which out of Chaos
> shapes Cosmos & order of Nature God.[82]

Myers rather wisely kept such speculations private, but they were
among the unwritten assumptions of his more guarded psychological
essays.

Ideas, such as those expressed to Lodge, as well as spiritual energy

---

80. FM, *Human Personality*, 2 : 277.

81. There are several references to Plotinus in FM's journals in the F. W. H. Myers
Papers. See also FM, *Human Personality*, 2 : 277, 288–91.

82. FM to Oliver Lodge, in Oliver Lodge Papers, 1400, Archives of the Society for
Psychical Research, London.

and the metetherial environment, illustrate an ironic feature of Myers's thought. For all the vestigial elements of Christianity and platonism present in his mind, Frederic Myers stood very much intimidated by scientific naturalism. When all had been said and done, Myers believed that the only truly eternal entities in the universe were matter and energy. If the human soul were to survive death, if the personality were never to be annihilated, and if human love were to last through the ages, it was because some form of matter and energy constituted that personality and those to whom it related. Man could be immortal, not because his soul resembled an immaterial God, but rather because it resembled enduring matter and energy. Myers did maintain his platonic and romantic vision, but the environment of scientific naturalism had rendered him incapable of believing in a spirituality genuinely distinct in nature from the physical world. In essence, he materialized the spiritual. It would perhaps be neither an exaggeration nor simply a play on words to suggest that as Carlyle set forth a "natural supernaturalism," Myers set forth a "supernatural naturalism."

A similar intimidation exerted by the concepts of matter and energy over the thought of religiously oriented men manifested itself in panpsychism or the view that matter and mind coexist in the same substance. George Romanes, Samuel Butler, and James Ward explored this alternative. Panpsychism represented a means of reconciling the mechanical appearance and operation of nature with the presence and influence of a mind or minds in nature. Whereas the psychical researcher or spiritualist saw mind as external to the physical world, the panpsychist saw mind as immanently present in physical nature.

George Romanes was not one of the major figures in this panpsychist tradition. However, he is a significant figure for the present study. Whereas Myers was a romantic who turned to science, Romanes was a scientist who turned to a rather romantic view of man and nature. Moreover, he was one of the very few men who left Christianity, served the cause of scientific naturalism, and then returned to a very nearly Christian position.

6

George John Romanes: From Faith to Faith

ONE MAN COME TO REPENTANCE

Everyone knows how the Victorians admired repentance. During the entire century English Christians directed their moral and financial resources toward saving souls on every continent and toward the moral and religious rehabilitation of England itself. The Gospel was printed, preached, and propagated as perhaps never before or since. Drunkards were reclaimed and prostitutes made honest women. Novels, tracts, and hymns traced the journey from early sin to degradation and then to repentance and salvation. During the second half of the century, however, the novels of William Hale White (Mark Rutherford) and Mrs. Humphry Ward and the lives of men such as Leslie Stephen and W. K. Clifford portrayed the new religious syndrome of faith dissolving into skepticism.[1] Anger, dismay, and frustration filled the minds of orthodox believers. Consequently, when one sinner of stature did repent, even though posthumously, conditionally, and undogmatically, the joy of the faithful became all the more sweet. They seized upon the incident as a sign of revitalization for beleaguered Christianity.

The year 1895 provided high Anglicans with one of those all too rare occasions for rejoicing. Late in that year there appeared in the religious bookstalls *Thoughts on Religion* by the late George John Romanes, followed early in 1896 by the *Life and Letters of George John Romanes*, written and edited by his wife.[2] These two books,

1. Noel Annan, *Sir Leslie Stephen: His Thought and Character in Relation to His Time* (London: MacGibbon & Kee, 1951); Owen Chadwick, *The Victorian Church* (London: Adam & Charles Black, 1970), 2 : 1–34; Basil Willey, *More Nineteenth Century Studies* (New York: Harper Torchbooks, 1966), pp. 106–247.

2. George John Romanes, *Thoughts on Religion*, ed. Charles Gore (Chicago: The Open Court Publishing Co., 1895); Ethel Romanes, *The Life and Letters of George John Romanes written and edited by his wife* (London: Longmans, Green, & Co., 1896). Unless otherwise noted, all references are to this edition of the biography. George John Romanes hereafter cited in footnotes as GJR.

long ago relegated to the musty lumber room of late Victoriana, contained a welcome message for religiously minded contemporaries: a scientist, a skeptic, and the author of a rationalist attack on evidence for the existence of God had returned to religious faith.

George Romanes died on 23 May 1894. Shortly before his death he had turned over most of his unpublished scientific manuscripts to C. Lloyd Morgan, his chief literary executor. His other remaining papers included a set of very fragmentary notes on religion. Romanes had requested that Charles Gore, the Canon of Westminster and editor of *Lux Mundi,* examine these and decide what might best be done with them.[3] Significantly, Romanes left no positive instructions that the manuscript be published.

The religious notes represented the beginning of a projected book, *A Candid Examination of Religion.* It would have voiced modifications in the opinions that Romanes had stated in his agnostic work, *A Candid Examination of Theism,* published in 1878. When printed as *Thoughts on Religion* these notes amounted to slightly less than ninety-one pages and revealed nothing more than that Romanes had come to believe in the possible validity of religious sentiments as a means to transcendental knowledge. While making friendly gestures toward Christian doctrines, Romanes affirmed the truth of none of them.[4] In a carefully worded preface, Gore acknowledged that these religious musings represented only "a tendency of one 'seeking after God if haply he might feel after Him and find Him,' and not a position of settled orthodoxy." He explained that they contained "many things which could not come from a settled believer." However, the fragments did represent a considerable re-evaluation of Romanes's earlier position. Gore concluded his remarks by saying, "It will surprise no one to learn that the writer of these 'Thoughts' returned before his death to that full, deliberate communion with the Church of Jesus Christ which he had for so many years been conscientiously compelled to forego." [5]

One suspects that Gore agreed to edit the volume primarily to

3. Gore, Preface to GJR, *Thoughts on Religion,* pp. 5–6.

4. In addition to the notes written primarily in 1893, Gore also included two earlier essays on "The Influence of Science upon Religion," which GJR had composed sometime prior to 1889.

5. Gore, Preface to GJR, *Thoughts on Religion,* p. 6; Gore, Concluding Note by the Editor in *Thoughts on Religion,* p. 196.

forestall Mrs. Romanes from doing so herself.[6] Ethel Romanes was a devout Christian and the author of several devotional works.[7] In the *Life and Letters of George John Romanes* she assumed a position considerably less equivocal than that of Gore. Determined to prove that her husband had absolutely returned to Christian faith, Mrs. Romanes quoted him as declaring a few days before his death, "It is Christianity or nothing." [8]

There is no doubt both Gore and Mrs. Romanes were sincere and essentially honest; nevertheless a certain aura of opportunism surrounds their books. Employing the lingering evangelical belief that a man on or near the point of death will reveal what he truly believes about God and his own soul, they sought to rehabilitate Romanes's character and reputation within religious circles.[9] They appropriated the painful spiritual odyssey of an intelligent and sensitive man to serve a religion in which, at best, he held but a tenuous faith. Both writers sought to transform the life of a man who had always avoided

6. Charles Gore was one of the most distinguished churchmen of his day. He was also a highly intelligent theologian. His introduction and commentary on GJR's fragmentary notes are fair and cautious. However, two factors render his conduct in this affair somewhat suspect. First, GJR had intended to publish his projected book anonymously. Gore thought that, given its incomplete nature and the death of its author, GJR's name should be placed on the title page. No doubt Gore attached GJR's name to the book out of genuine consideration for Mrs. Romanes's feelings. This action was straightforward enough. However, if the notes had been published anonymously, no attention would have been paid to them. They became interesting and significant only because the name of a one-time naturalistic thinker was associated with them. The conclusion that the public would hopefully draw was obvious. As published, the notes possessed none of the character of a thought experiment that GJR had intended. Second, in regard to the two essays on "The Influence of Science on Religion," Gore stated that he published them "with more hesitation" (p. 6) than the incomplete notes. Here Gore's own reasoning is unclear. The two essays were more complete than the notes and subject to far less misconstruing. Yet those essays were much more cautious about the validity of religion. It would seem that Gore was hesitant about the essays because they might cast doubt on GJR's final more positive view of religious knowledge.

7. Among Ethel Romanes's books were *Thoughts on the Collects for the Trinity Season*, 2 vols. (London: Longmans, Green, & Co., 1899); *Thoughts on the Gospels* (Oxford: A. R. Mowbray, 1899); *Thoughts on Holy Communion* (London and Oxford: Mowbray & Co., 1903); *Meditations on Portions of St. John's Gospel* (London: Mowbray & Co., 1912).

8. E. Romanes, *Life and Letters of GJR*, p. 349. "Presently he added, 'I as yet have not that real inward assurance; it is with me as that text says, "I am not able to look up," but I feel the service this morning is a means to grace' " (Ibid., p. 349).

9. Geoffrey Best, "Evangelicalism and the Victorians," *The Victorian Crisis of Faith*, ed. Anthony Symondson (London: Society for Promoting Christian Knowledge, 1970), pp. 54–55.

dogma of any form into a prop for the faltering cause of dogmatic Christianity.

The *Saturday Review* recognized the effort for exactly what it was—an example of "the militant evangelism of the High Church party." Certain religious magazines seized upon the books with considerable zeal and tissue-thin honesty. *The Sunday Magazine* considered one of the great lessons of *Thoughts on Religion* to be "that the full acceptance of all the proved conclusions of science, *in her proper sphere,* need not bar our way to the confession of Christ— that we may hold the scientific view of the origin and development of the visible world, and yet at the same time cry: 'Lord, to whom shall we go? Thou hast the words of Eternal Life.' " Only a highly selective reading of *Thoughts on Religion* could substantiate so confident a conclusion. The *Quarterly Review* offered a more thoughtful evaluation, choosing to see in Romanes's thinking a sign of better times ahead. It asserted that his "mental history" represented "a current of recent thought so strong that, with obvious reservations, it may be called the movement of the age. He represented its earlier—we hope that he also foreshadowed its later— progress." [10] This was a fair but overly optimistic judgment. Although Romanes's posthumous fragments did represent one more contribution to the growing doubt about the adequacy of scientific naturalism, they were not symptomatic of a general return to traditional Christianity.

Voices of dissent soon rose from the naturalistic camp. Edward Clodd dismissed Romanes's thoughts and conversion as the product of a deteriorating mind and Mrs. Romanes's harassment.[11] Paul Carus, editor of *Monist,* read *Thoughts on Religion* with more care than had the reviewers for the religious journals. He concluded,

10. *Saturday Review* 81 (1896): 181. W. Garrett Horder, "From Unbelief to Faith," *The Sunday Magazine,* 2nd series, 25 (1896): 197. This conclusion was indeed possible. However, the article did not point out the conditional or hypothetical mode of all of GJR's statements in regard to Christianity. This article emphasized his return to Christ, something which *Thoughts on Religion* did not actually reveal. "Through Scientific Doubt to Faith," *Quarterly Review* 183 (1896): 286. This was generally a very sensitive and perceptive article, but the writer was perfectly willing to employ GJR's life as an object lesson for the age.

11. E. Clodd, *Memories* (London: Chapman & Hall, 1916), p. 38. Mrs. Romanes denied that her husband's final illness accounted for his return to religious awareness. E. Romanes, *Life and Letters of GJR,* new ed. (London: Longmans, Green, & Co., 1896), p. v.

"Concerning Professor Romanes's progress from a position of unbelief to one of belief, we are unable to discover any evidence of great consequence." But even Carus could not resist at least one sentence of condemnation, declaring, "As Abraham went out to sacrifice his only son Isaac, so Romanes seriously tried to slaughter his reason on the altar of faith." [12] The ire of naturalistic writers could be as unfair as the zeal of the religious when directed toward the backsliding of a former comrade.

George Romanes was a most unlikely figure to emerge even posthumously as a rebel against scientific naturalism. Darwin himself had sought out Romanes in 1874 after reading one of the younger man's letters in *Nature*. They became friends and correspondents; Romanes preserved all of his letters from Darwin in a bound volume in his office.[13] Darwin consulted Romanes on matters of animal psychology and entrusted him with an unpublished manuscript on instinct.[14] Hoping to continue Darwin's studies of animal intelligence, Romanes intended to trace the natural evolution of mind in nature from primitive origins to man as Darwin had traced the natural evolution of organisms. In 1886 the *Times* declared, "Mr. George Romanes appears to be the biological investigator upon whom in England the mantle of Mr. Darwin has most conspicuously descended." [15]

Though hardly the heir of Darwin's mantle, Romanes did make significant contemporary contributions in three areas of scientific research.[16] Commencing in 1875, he wrote a number of key physiological papers on the nervous systems of the medusae and of other

12. Paul Carus, "The Late Professor Romanes' Thoughts on Religion," *Monist* 5 (1894–95) : 392, 398. Carus himself was deeply interested in new religious alternatives and would not have been hostile to one that he might have discerned in GJR's notes.

13. Paul Carus, "Professor George John Romanes," *The Open Court* 8 (1894) : 411.

14. This manuscript was published as an appendix to GJR, *Mental Evolution in Animals* (New York: D. Appleton & Co., 1884), pp. 353–84.

15. *Times* (London), 16 August 1886, p. 8.

16. For details of his scientific career, in addition to the *Life and Letters of GJR*, see E. R. Lankester, "George John Romanes," *Nature* 50 (1894) : 108–09; C. Lloyd Morgan, "George John Romanes," *Dictionary of National Biography*, ed. Leslie Stephen and Sidney Lee (London: Oxford University Press, 1950), 17 : 177–80; Richard French, "Some Concepts of Nerve Structure and Function in Great Britain, 1875–1885: Background to Sir Charles Sherrington and the Synapse Concept," *Medical History* 14 (1970) : 154–65; Richard French, "Darwin and the Physiologists, or the Medusa and Modern Cardiology," *Journal of the History of Biology* 3 (1970) : 253–74; Philip G. Fothergill, *Historical Aspects of Organic Evolution* (London: Hollis & Carter, 1952), pp. 139–40, 148–50.

sea animals. In 1875 and 1881 these were designated as the Croonian Lecture of the Royal Society, a distinction then bestowed on the outstanding biological paper of the year. From investigating the physiology of primitive nervous systems, Romanes moved to a more general examination of psychology. In 1881 he published *Animal Intelligence,* which was followed in 1883 by *Mental Evolution in Animals* and by *Mental Evolution in Man* in 1888. His three volumes constituted the first attempt to place comparative psychology on a formal scientific basis and formed the connecting link between Charles Darwin and C. Lloyd Morgan in the development of this branch of psychology.[17] Finally, in 1886 Romanes entered the revised debate on Darwinism by suggesting a theory of physiological selection that supplemented natural selection. He also embraced a position of moderate Lamarckianism in regard to the inheritance of acquired characteristics that he considered consistent with Darwin's final opinions.

Romanes's service to British science, like that of the leaders of scientific naturalism, extended beyond the laboratory. He was honorary secretary of the Linnean Society, where Darwin, Hooker, and Huxley had sponsored his membership.[18] He served on the Council of University College of the University of London. Romanes was a founder, secretary, and treasurer of the Physiological Society and a member of the Royal Society. He was appointed Rosebery Lecturer at Edinburgh and Fullerian Professor at the Royal Institution. He wrote public letters in defense of vivisection and delivered popular lectures on science throughout Great Britain. In short, Romanes was one of those men through whose activity the ideas of scientific naturalism filtered beyond the world of the scientists into the realm of the average, educated citizen.

Between 1875 and 1885 Romanes was numbered among the advocates of scientific naturalism. As will be seen, Samuel Butler considered him one of the most arrogant men of science.[19] Moreover, Romanes followed the pattern of Huxley and Tyndall by venturing

17. "Romanes' book on animal intelligence is the first comparative psychology that was ever written" (E. Boring, *History of Experimental Psychology* [New York: The Century Co., 1929], p. 463). L. S. Hearnshaw, *A Short History of British Psychology 1840–1940* (New York: Barnes & Noble, 1964), pp. 92–96.

18. E. Romanes, *Life and Letters of GJR,* p. 38. GJR was elected to the Royal Society in 1879.

19. Butler believed GJR had included part of his own life-and-habit theory in *Mental Evolution in Animals.* See p. 176 of this book.

into the area of philosophy and theology. In 1878, under the pseudonym "Physicus," he published *A Candid Examination of Theism*,
in which he denied the validity of the traditional arguments for
natural religion.[20] So far as its methods and reasoning were concerned, the volume was a splendid, if not sparkling, example of
naturalistic thought. Few who read it would have imagined that its
author might ever abandon the presuppositions of scientific naturalism or that seventeen years later he would be heralded as a convert
to Christianity. However, *A Candid Examination of Theism* represented only one strand in a highly complex fabric of unbelief.

THE FABRIC OF UNBELIEF

George Romanes was born in 1848 in Kingston, Canada, where his
father was a clergyman and professor of Greek at the university.
Shortly thereafter, his father came into an inheritance, and the
family returned to England. After receiving a private education,
Romanes entered Gonville and Caius College, Cambridge, in 1867.
He wanted to become a clergyman, but for unknown reasons his
family dissuaded him from that calling. Consequently, in 1870 he
ceased reading for a classical tripos and began to study for the natural
science examination of that year. He completed the examination
with no particular distinction, but remained in Cambridge to study
medicine and physiology with Michael Foster, who also trained
James Ward. In 1874 Romanes moved to London to study with
Professor Burdon Sanderson of the University of London.

Before leaving Cambridge, Romanes found occasion to combine
his several interests by entering the Burney Prize Essay competition
for 1873. The topic for discussion was the relationship of prayer and
general scientific law—a question that had been debated in the press
for a decade. To his own surprise and that of his college, Romanes,
trained neither as philosopher nor as metaphysician, won.[21] No
doubt this early amateur success spurred Romanes's confidence in his
talent for theological and philosophical reasoning.

In the Burney Prize Essay, *Christian Prayer and General Laws*,
Romanes adopted a position more nearly deistic than Christian.[22]

20. GJR, *A Candid Examination of Theism by Physicus* (Boston: Houghton, Osgood,
& Co., 1878).

21. E. Romanes, *Life and Letters of GJR*, pp. 2–13.

22. GJR, *Christian Prayer and General Laws being the Burney Prize Essay for the
year 1873, with an Appendix, The Physical Efficiency of Prayer* (London: Macmillan &
Co., 1874).

The entire tediously reasoned book represented what he termed an "elaborate exposition of the argument from ignorance." Romanes contended that religious apologists should not attempt to explain the manner in which God might answer prayer for that knowledge lay beyond the ken of human beings. There was no reason to believe that God could not employ natural laws to answer prayer. Eschewing miracles, Romanes argued, "It becomes impossible for human intelligence to predicate the number and kinds of the special results which it is possible for the Final Directive Influence to produce, through the purposive combination of Natural Laws." He then countered naturalistic writers, such as Tyndall, who had argued that natural law forbade the possibility of answers to prayer. Romanes declared that philosophy, by which he meant naturalistic philosophy, must "above all things abstain from the folly of asserting what the Unknown God can or cannot do—what He does or does not desire:—so shall she cease to stultify herself, and to mislead the less thoughtful of her children." [23] The essay, though clearly favoring the possibility of answered prayer, revealed neither zeal for orthodoxy nor firm adherence to naturalistic opinion. Rather, it sought to fend off the dogmatic claims of both positions.

Romanes published *Christian Prayer and General Laws* in 1874. By this time he had decided to pursue a career in natural science rather than in medicine. During these same months he also reexamined his religious convictions in the light of his vocational choice and decided that he was no longer a believing Christian. This particular instance of self-evaluation was characteristic of Romanes. He constantly experimented with his ideas, testing his opinions against new ideas that he encountered. In fact, Romanes was somewhat chameleon-like in his tendancy to gauge his opinions to those of the intellectual circle with whom he was involved at the moment. For example, he wrote *Christian Prayer and General Laws* while among his theistic undergraduate mentors. He composed *A Candid Examination of Theism* after deciding to devote his life to science and when he was becoming assimilated into the Darwin circle. Finally, he penned the notes that became *Thoughts on Religion* after he had become close friends with several high Anglican clergymen at Oxford.[24] Romanes was not a sycophant, but he was clearly a man of unsettled intellectual convictions who throughout life kept

23. GJR, *Christian Prayer and General Laws*, pp. 121, 165, 133.
24. E. Romanes, *Life and Letters of GJR*, pp. 13–15, 78–88, 248–52, 271–73.

hoping to discover a single set of principles that would satisfy all conditions. In the late 1870s he saw such principles in the methods of science.

Romanes wrote *A Candid Examination of Theism* in 1876 but did not publish it until 1878 when he was well established within the scientific community. Under the pseudonym "Physicus," Romanes asserted without equivocation that the scientific method was the very best instrument for the pursuit of truth about all questions.

> If it is retorted that the question to be dealt with [the existence of God] is of so ultimate a character that even the scientific methods are here untrustworthy, I reply that they are nevertheless the *best* methods available, and hence that the retort is without pertinence: the question is still to be regarded as a scientific one, although we may perceive that neither an affirmative nor a negative answer can be given to it with any approach to a full demonstration.[25]

Reasoning from this premise, Romanes subjected the arguments for theism to careful criticism.

Employing Spencer's matter-and-force analysis of nature, Romanes dismissed the theistic arguments based on the existence of the human mind, design, and teleology. The existence of the human mind provided no evidence of a greater mind since all mind was merely a product of matter and force. Spencer's theory of cosmic or nebular evolution permitted Romanes to discard the argument from design.[26] He asserted, "Science, by establishing the doctrine of the persistence of force and the indestructibility of matter, has effectually disproved the hypothesis that the presence of Law in nature is of itself sufficient to prove the existence of an intelligent Law-giver." Indeed, these laws had proved the whole hypothesis of mind and purpose in nature to be "certainly superfluous."[27]

Romanes also criticized arguments based on what he termed "metaphysical teleology," by which he meant any form of transcendental reasoning. The example to which he addressed himself was Spencer's Unknowable. Romanes contended that the evidence for

25. GJR, *A Candid Examination of Theism*, pp. x–xi.

26. Throughout the essay, Spencer was the prime influence. GJR made few references to Darwin. GJR considered evolution itself, not the mechanism of evolution, destructive to the theistic position.

27. GJR, *A Candid Examination of Theism*, pp. 75–76, 64.

such reasoning was not drawn from empirical experience but was subjective in nature and could possess no objective, hence no scientific, validity.

> Let no man think that he has any argumentative right to expect that the mere subjective habit or tone of his own mind should exert any influence on that of his fellow; but rather let him always remember that the only legitimate weapons of his intellectual warfare are those the *material* of which is derived from the external world, and only the *form* of which is due to the forging process of his own mind.

The proper attitude for the rational mind to assume in regard to subjective arguments was that of "pure scepticism." [28] Romanes would later develop this stance into what he called "pure" agnosticism and employ it against the negativity of the adherents of scientific naturalism.[29]

If the intellectual tone of the book was confident, the emotional tone was less so. Romanes did not enjoy being an unbeliever. He saw his loss of faith as a direct result of the general collapse of natural theology and yearned for the serenity of the previous generation. He reflected,

> [I]f it had been my lot to have lived in the last generation, I should certainly have rested in these "sublime conceptions" [of Baden Powell] as in an argument supreme and irrefutable. I should have felt that the progress of physical knowledge could never exert any other influence on Theism than that of ever tending more and more to confirm that magnificent belief, by continuously expanding our human thoughts into progressively advancing conceptions, ever grander and yet more grand, of that tremendous Origin of Things—the Mind of God. Such would have been my hope—such would have been my prayer. But now, how changed! [30]

George Romanes was one of the very few men whose loss of faith in the truth of religion can be directly ascribed to the influence of

28. Ibid., pp. 72, 101, 112.

29. GJR, *Mind and Motion and Monism*, ed. C. Lloyd Morgan (London: Longmans, Green, & Co., 1895), pp. 35–38.

30. GJR, *A Candid Examination of Theism*, pp. 51–52.

scientific naturalism.[31] The higher criticism of the Scriptures may have undermined his adherence to dogmatic Christianity, although this is not certain; but it was the dogmas of contemporary science that led him to the reluctant but nevertheless firm conclusion that he dwelled in a godless universe.

A sense of utter cosmic abandon permeated Romanes's conclusion to *A Candid Examination of Theism.*

> And now, in conclusion, I feel it is desirable to state that any antecedent bias with regard to Theism which I individually possess is unquestionably on the side of traditional beliefs. It is therefore with the utmost sorrow that I find myself compelled to accept the conclusions here worked out; and nothing would have induced me to publish them, save the strength of my conviction that it is the duty of every member of society to give his fellows the benefit of his labors for whatever they may be worth. . . . And forasmuch as I am far from being able to agree with those who affirm that the twilight doctrine of the "new faith" is a desirable substitute for the waning splendour of "the old," I am not ashamed to confess that with this virtual negation of God the universe to me has lost its soul of loveliness; and although from henceforth the precept to "work while it is day" will doubtless but gain an intensified force from the terribly intensified meaning of the words that "the night cometh when no man can work," yet when at times I think, as at times I must, of the appalling contrast between the hallowed glory of that creed which once was mine, and the lonely mystery of existence as now I find it,—at such times I shall ever feel it impossible to avoid the sharpest pang of which my nature is susceptible.[32]

Such was hardly the declaration of an ebullient agnostic who found the fulfillment of his aspirations within the New Nature created by science. It was rather an undesired conclusion forced upon the writer by the weight of the evidence. Romanes could and did follow the ideas and methods of scientific naturalism to the letter, but, like Henry Sidgwick, he could live neither happily nor contentedly in a godless cosmos.

31. Chadwick, *The Victorian Church,* 2 : 14–15.
32. GJR, *A Candid Examination of Theism,* pp. 113–14.

Romanes had insisted that his religious opinions meet the test of conforming to scientific method. After writing *A Candid Examination of Theism,* he demanded that the ideas of naturalism provide an adequate guide and inspiration for men dwelling in a universe robbed of "its soul of loveliness." [33] It was not long before Romanes's skepticism in regard to the adequacy of naturalism surfaced.

A few months after the publication of *A Candid Examination of Theism,* Huxley invited Romanes to join the Association of Liberal Thinkers which at first Romanes understood to be a group that would directly and aggressively combat "contemporary superstition." Romanes replied in a spirit of deep social and emotional conservatism that always prevented him from fervently embracing the secular society of the New Nature. In a letter he told Huxley that he could not in good conscience enter into the projected attack.

> For, rightly or wrongly, I am of [the] opinion that all changes in popular beliefs which are calculated to the influence of personal conduct ought to be made gradually, and that the old landmarks in the territory of religious belief are now being hurried away at a rate which scarcely seems to call for any organized effort to ensure their more rapid destruction.
>
> I know it may be thought that in abstaining, for any such prudential motives, from taking part in the destruction of error, I am actuated by the spirit of Jesuitism—that as an honest man I ought to promote & leave the consequences to take care of themselves. I can only reply—This I shall be fully prepared to do at whatever time it is made clear to me that, in the absence of theistic or optimistic standards, Truth must in all things be better than Expediency. But meanwhile and in the matter of religious belief, I think that the more gradually Truth is allowed to dawn upon the masses the better will it be for humanity.[34]

The sentiments of the letter were less far removed from those of *A Candid Examination of Theism* than might be supposed. There he had limited the propagation of new truth to such endeavors as were

33. Ibid., p. 114.

34. GJR to Huxley, 3 January 1879, Huxley Papers, 25.206, Imperial College of Science and Technology, London. For Huxley's reply to the first letter, see Leonard Huxley, *The Life and Letters of Thomas Henry Huxley* (New York: D. Appleton & Co., 1902), 2 : 3.

"unbiased and sincere." [35] His own book fit that description since it was anonymous and had not attacked the Bible or baited the clergy. It had been a work of intelligent skepticism rather than of secular agnosticism in service to the New Nature. Huxley's association would have been sincere, but not unbiased. Moreover, Romanes had received Huxley's invitation only a few weeks prior to his marriage. He was no doubt already aware that his bride-to-be would not approve of his participation in such a society.

Huxley immediately wrote to assure Romanes that the new group would not be so aggressive as the latter had feared. Still Romanes refused to join. This time he voiced a doubt about the ability of naturalistic thinkers to provide adequate alternatives to the traditional ideas they sought to displace.

> Of course I have no doubt that in the long run Truth, however hideous, must prevail & I have as little doubt that as it does so mankind will make the best of it, whatever it may be; but these considerations do not touch the question as to how far it is desirable that painful truths (or probabilities) should be rendered more painful by their rapid promulgation.
>
> If I were a theist I should regard this view as closely bordering on blasphemy; but as an agnostic I regard it as logic. And I think that the only reason why we have got into the habit of what—I may term Truthworship, in *all* things is because in *some* things we find such worship to pay. But the fact that Truth is of the first importance in things physical is no pledge that it must be equally desirable in things hyperphysical; & I can only too well imagine the possibility that the realization of the prayer of Culture—"Light, more Light"—, may be a less desirable thing than the realization of the prayer of Religion—"Take not thy holy spirit from us." Even though this spirit be but "the spirit of superstition," it still believes there is a God where the influence of light may only reveal a Mummy.[36]

The note reveals the most serious rent in the fabric of Romanes's unbelief. If he was to be an agnostic in matters of religious dogma, he would also be an agnostic in regard to the dogmatic certainty of naturalistic opinions.

35. GJR, *A Candid Examination of Theism*, p. 113.
36. GJR to Huxley, 5 January 1879, Huxley Papers, 25.208.

Besides a general distrust of dogmatism, two other factors lay behind these remarkable letters. In the first place, Romanes was generally a social and political conservative and by no means sure that naturalistic ethical systems could restrain the strivings of mankind's lower yearnings. Consequently, his social practices compromised his intellectual convictions. Unlike Henry Sidgwick, Romanes attended church regularly, led evening prayers, and was very fond of reading long sermons to his family and servants. He permitted his children to be reared and educated according to orthodox beliefs.[37] In 1889 Romanes even delivered an address at Toynbee Hall on the "Ethical Teaching of Christ" in which he declared, "The originality of Christ's teaching might in some quarters be overrated, but the achievement . . . [is] impossible to overrate. It is only before the presence of Christ that the dry bones of ethical abstraction have sprung into life. The very essence of the new religion consists in re-establishing more closely than ever the bonds between morality and religion." [38]

Nevertheless, during these years of external religious conformity Romanes did not hold Christian convictions. In 1891 he wrote to the missionary–biologist Thomas Gulick that he could not be a Christian. In the first place, Romanes said, "Now that we know what is 'man's place in nature,' the doctrine of God having become Man has surely been rendered much more incredible than it was in earlier times, when it was not unreasonably believed that this earth was the center of the universe, and human thought, as it were, the measure of all things." Moreover, evolution had made sin and evil "imaginary." "Considered objectively," Romanes continued, "they are but the necessary result—or, rather, an integral part—of the evolution itself; for all that they mean is, that moral growth entails the passage of morality through ascending degrees of development." Romanes also reminded Gulick that Darwinism had undermined the foundations of Pauline theology: "The 'first man' having been politely removed, there is no longer any logical justification (according to this theology) for the 'second man.' " [39]

Another factor in 1879 also prevented Romanes from joining

37. E. Romanes, *Life and Letters of GJR*, pp. 156–58.
38. Ibid., pp. 226–27.
39. GJR to J. T. Gulick, 19 May 1891, *Correspondence of G. J. Romanes and J. T. Gulick*, pp. 163–65. Typescript in possession of the Linnean Society, London.

Huxley's proposed offensive against contemporary superstition. At that time George Romanes was deeply interested in at least one form of such "superstition"—spiritualism. It is not certain when Romanes began to investigate spiritualistic phenomena, but for a brief period in the mid-seventies he stood convinced of the validity of what he had witnessed. He then discovered fraud on the part of the medium and in 1876 wrote to Darwin, "I do hope next winter to settle for myself the simple issue between Ghost *versus* Goose." [40] As late as 1880, Romanes continued to investigate psychical phenomena. That year he sent an anonymous letter to *Nature* requesting materials for investigation. A brief correspondence with Alfred Wallace ensued in which Romanes told Wallace:

> If I could obtain any definite evidence of Mind unassociated with any observable organization, the fact would be to me nothing less than a revelation. . . . And altho. I might say to others "come and see," my chief end would have been attained if I could say—"I have found that of which the prophets (to wit, Crookes, Wallace, Varley, & the rest) have spoken." [41]

Romanes never believed that he had found the necessary evidence. Surprisingly, he did not join the Society for Psychical Research, which proposed an organized effort in the very direction that Romanes had suggested in 1880. However, as late as 1889, he did send an account of a psychical incident to the society. Mrs. Romanes reported that "he could never assure himself that there was absolutely nothing in spiritualism." [42] This quietly persistent interest probably did much to prevent Romanes from embracing the negativism of scientific naturalism, though he ultimately moved to a view of mind as intrinsically related to matter rather than as existing in disassociation from it.

Romanes's interest in psychical phenomena coincided with a final test or experiment to which he submitted naturalistic ideas—the facing of death. Though less preoccupied with the issue of immor-

40. ARW, *My Life*, 2: 336–38; GJR to C. Darwin, n.d., in E. Romanes, *Life and Letters of GJR*, p. 46.

41. *Nature* 21 (1880) : 348. See also E. Romanes, *Life and Letters of GJR*, p. 97. GJR to ARW, 20 February 1880, A. R. Wallace Papers, British Museum, add. MSS. 46439. See also ARW, *My Life*, 2 : 331.

42. *Journal of the Society for Psychical Research* 4 (1890) : 212–13; E. Romanes, *Life and Letters of GJR*, pp. 48–49.

tality than Frederic Myers, Romanes was deeply concerned about the fact of death and the manner in which men, especially himself, faced it. On one occasion he sent out a questionnaire to ascertain human feelings on the subject.[43]

The two years of his final illness, when he had to discontinue his experiments and when he wrote his religious fragments, afforded Romanes all too much time to ponder the problem of death. In 1892, in a most peculiar letter to Huxley, Romanes discussed his recent stroke, which he termed his "dress rehearsal." "But I have derived one benefit from my full dress rehearsal of the final act . . . ; and this is the certain knowledge of being at any time able to repeat the last words of Darwin—'I am not the least afraid to die.'" These were not the words of a man who had abandoned the ultimate concerns of religion nor of a man who could dwell in the New Nature free of ontological anxiety. Indeed, a day before writing the note to Huxley, Romanes had penned a similar letter to Francis Darwin but had prefaced his boast with the confession, "I do think I make a decently good Stoic, but confess that in times like this Christians have the pull." [44] At some point in the closing weeks of his life, that ontological anxiety won out in his dying mind. Romanes confronted the total impotence and futility of scientific naturalism in the face of natural death. As naturalism failed its final and most crucial test, George Romanes cast off his threadbare cloak of unbelief.

Faith was not, however, a last-minute deathbed alternative for Romanes. For almost ten years he had been slowly edging away from the naturalistic concept of truth toward one that acknowledged the validity of faith and intuition as a means to transcendental knowledge. In doing so he had largely unraveled his fabric of unbelief already severely rent by ethical concerns, spiritualistic interests, and ontological anxieties.

The Pure Agnostic

Throughout the 1870s George Romanes had rigidly adhered to the naturalistic view that men could perceive the truth solely through the objective scientific method to the exclusion of feeling,

43. E. Romanes, *Life and Letters of GJR*, pp. 188–89.
44. GJR to Huxley, 9 October 1893, Huxley Papers, 25.265; GJR to F. Darwin, 8 October 1893, in E. Romanes, *Life and Letters of GJR*, pp. 317–18.

instinct, and sentiment. Even in his analysis of prayer, he had "abstained as much as possible from mingling with it the element of *feeling.*" In 1881, addressing an opponent's objection that evolution degraded man by relating him to monkeys, Romanes replied, "Although I cannot affect your sentiments in this matter, I may be permitted to point out that, as they are only sentiments, they are quite worthless as arguments or guides to truth." [45]

Romanes gradually modified this stance. By the time of his death he had come to believe that emotions, instinct, imagination, and faith, as well as scientific reason, might reveal knowledge about reality and man's spiritual condition. Romanes probably set out on this new course after his investigations of spiritualism provided him with no empirical evidence of a spiritual reality. He was also spurred to further reaction against the naturalistic idea of truth by what he considered the illegitimate, dogmatic negativism of certain agnostics and by the hesitancy of professional scientists to break with accepted modes of thought and to consider new speculative theories.

In 1885 Romanes delivered the Rede Lecture at Cambridge. In the course of this address, he defined the concept of pure agnosticism that he employed against both dogmatic religion and dogmatic naturalism. He told his audience, "If it be true that the voice of science must thus of necessity speak the language of agnosticism, at least let us see to it that the language is pure; let us not tolerate any barbarisms introduced from the side of aggressive dogma." [46] The "aggressive dogma" to which Romanes referred was that of W. K. Clifford, one of the most articulate naturalistic writers. Clifford had suggested that the agnostic should simply disregard the question of the existence of God. Romanes argued that the pure agnostic could not in good conscience ignore the question because the existence of God remained a rational though empirically unverifiable possibility.

Romanes was attempting to make honest men of the agnostic advocates of scientific naturalism. They could have either agnosticism or dogmatic negation, but they could not have both. Scientists overstepped the boundaries of their proper intellectual sphere when they either advocated or denied religious doctrine.

My whole contention from first to last has been that men of science, as such, have no business either "to run with the hare

45. GJR, *Christian Prayer and General Laws*, p. 121; GJR, "Scientific Evidence of Organic Evolution," *Fortnightly Review* 36 (1881) : 758.
46. GJR, *Mind and Motion and Monism*, p. 37.

of religion" or "to hunt with the hounds of antitheistic negation." . . . Or, to drop the not too happy metaphor, even if a man of science is profoundly interested in the great questions of religion, he should recognize that they have no more bearing upon his professional occupation than have the questions of politics, literature, art, or any other department of rational thinking.[47]

Romanes had directed this particular remark, made in 1886, toward St. George Jackson Mivart, a Roman Catholic critic of Darwin. However, Romanes increasingly turned his pure agnostic criticism against naturalistic authors.

For George Romanes, the agnostic author of *A Candid Examination of Theism,* speculation in regard to ultimate questions could not receive scientific verification. For George Romanes, the pure agnostic of the 1880s, it could not receive scientific negation. Transcendental hypothesis was as likely to be correct as it was to be false. To disregard such speculations or to employ agnosticism as an instrument to forestall contemplation of speculative possibilities was to risk losing the opportunity for discovering truth.

The reluctance of his fellow scientists to consider new scientific theories particularly increased Romanes's suspicion of the negativism of naturalistic thought. Romanes believed that natural selection had become a scientific dogma within England. He fully accepted the concept but thought that it required supplementary theories, such as Darwin himself had advocated. Dogmatic adherence to natural selection seemed to account for the lack of enthusiasm for his own supplemental theory of physiological selection.[48] Romanes considered the

47. GJR, "Mr. Mivart on the Rights of Reason," *Fortnightly Review* 45 (1886) : 333.

48. The simplest explanation of physiological selection was that given by C. Lloyd Morgan: "The suggestion is briefly as follows. It was part of the body of biological doctrine that when a group of animals or plants belonging to any species is isolated by geographical barriers, that group tends, under the influence of its specialized environment, to develop characters different from those of the main body of the species from which it is isolated. Eventually the divergence of characters may proceed so far as to render the isolated group reciprocally sterile with the original species, and thus to render it not only morphologically but also physiologically a distinct species. Romanes, in his Linnean paper, suggested that reciprocal sterility between individuals not otherwise isolated may be the primary event, the cause and not the effect; and that in this way a physiological barrier may be set up between two groups of the individuals originally belonging to one species and inhabiting the same geographical area. The essential feature of the suggestion is that this physiological barrier may be primary and not secondary. The title of the paper was unfortunate. 'Physiological Isolation' would have indicated the author's contention more accurately than 'Physiological

only difference between the scientific obstructionists of Darwin's day and those of his own to be that

> the latter have grown up in a Darwinian environment, and so . . . have more or less thoughtlessly adopted some form of Darwinian creed. But this scientific creed is not a whit less dogmatic and intolerant than was the more theological one which it has supplanted; and while it usually incorporates the main elements of Darwin's teaching, it still more usually comprises gross perversions of their consequences.[49]

Such dogmatism represented a hindrance to new discovery for it prevented free scientific exploration.

Romanes believed one of Darwin's great contributions to thought was his example of the fertility of a carefully speculating mind.

> Darwin has shown that next only to the importance of clearly distinguishing between facts and theories on the one hand, and of clearly recognizing the relation between them on the other, is the importance of not being scared by the Bugbear of Speculation. The spirit of speculation is the same as the spirit of science, namely, . . . a desire to know the causes of things.[50]

Romanes considered himself as being particularly suited by both temperament and social circumstances to pursue a similar life of scientific speculation tempered by close examination of the facts.

This self-image drew Romanes into conflict with the growing professionalism of late Victorian scientists. He believed the more professionally oriented of the critics of physiological selection were working on a "treadmill." (T. S. Kuhn would say they were pursuing "normal science.") Romanes saw himself in a very different situa-

---

Selection,' and would perhaps have more effectually guarded him from the attacks of those who charged him with the intention of substituting a new doctrine of the origin of species for that which was associated with the name of Darwin" (*Dictionary of National Biography*, s.v. "George John Romanes"). See also, E. Romanes, *Life and Letters of GJR*, pp. 169–84, 211–22, 246–53; GJR, "Physiological Selection," *Nineteenth Century* 21 (1887) : 59–80; "Mr. Wallace on Physiological Selection," *Monist* 1 (1890–1891) : 1–20; *Darwin and After Darwin* (Chicago: The Open Court Publishing Co., 1897), vol. 3; Vernon Kellogg, *Darwinism Today* (New York: Henry Holt & Co., 1907), pp. 45–51.

49. GJR, *Darwin and After Darwin* (Chicago: The Open Court Publishing Co., 1892), 1 : 11–12.

50. Ibid., p. 6.

tion. In 1890 he wrote to Thisleton–Dyer to complain about a letter Ray Lankester was about to publish in *Nature:*

> Nor am I really "hard" upon my friends of the "treadmill." I believe that they are doing excellent work, as long as they stick to their mill—driving the machinery of scientific progress to better efforts than I can in my less laborious life. But when this life enables me—as it has—to soak myself in Darwinian litera-ture for so many years, I cannot help feeling the arrogance of those more professional naturalists who, with many other occupations and without half the study or thought which I have given to this particular subject, seek to ride rough shod *à la* Duke of Argyll with all the four hoofs of dogmatism.[51]

The professional men of science actually closed themselves off from the possible discovery of new truth about nature just as the more vocal agnostics refused to consider new truths in philosophy. His resentment of their narrowness and his profound desire for at least the possibility of a spiritual truth perceivable by man increasingly led Romanes toward a more positive view of the imagination, emo-tions, and intuitions as faculties of knowledge.

Romanes first probed the role of nondiscursive mental faculties in poetry written for his own pleasure. As a poet, he displayed no hesitation in pondering ontological questions that as a man of science he should by his own view have spurned. Though much of his verse was religious, he denied to both Huxley and Paul Carus that it implied any return to orthodoxy.[52] However, his poems dis-played a marked inclination to question the adequacy of discursive reason as the sole means of attaining knowledge. For example, in a long memorial poem, "To Charles Darwin," written in 1882 or 1883, Romanes raised the hope of immortality and commented:

> To Reason's eye those words may not be proved,
> Which were but sounds to touch the list'ning heart;
> Yet why, among the senses of the soul,

51. T. S. Kuhn, *The Structure of Scientific Revolutions* (Chicago: The University of Chicago Press, 1969), pp. 23–24; GJR to Thistleton–Dyer, 26 March 1890, Linnean Society, London. The reference to the Duke of Argyll is to the Scottish peer who as a self-styled naturalist had written a number of books attacking Darwin's theory.

52. GJR to Huxley, 31 October 1892, Huxley Papers, 25.244; P. Carus, "Professor George John Romanes," *The Open Court* 8 (1894) : 411.

Should I alone attend the seeing part,
And not draw all my knowledge from the whole?
I am a man, and but as man I know:
Let Instinct speak where Reason fails to show.[53]

In 1889, during an address to the Aristotelian Society, Romanes expressed publicly the view of truth implicit in his private poetry. The question under discussion was "Is there evidence of Design in Nature?" Romanes argued that the answer to this question turned upon the issue of causation. Scientific method could deal with causation only in terms of succession of phenomena. Romanes, however, suggested possible ontological explanations for the succession of phenomena that scientists termed causation. By even broaching the problem of ontology he had left the bounds of naturalistic thought. He posed two alternative ontological explanations: the presence of a divine being and physical mechanism. Romanes claimed that science, philosophy, and religion could offer no aid in choosing between these two possible interpretations of causation. Rather the issue

can only be determined in those mysterious depths of human personality, which lie beyond the reach of human investigation, but where it is certain that through processes as yet unknown to us, by causes—if they be causes—as yet unrevealed to us, there results for each individual mind either the presence or the absence of an indissoluble persuasion that "God is."

Romanes indicated that in his own case the "internal persuasion, or antecedent belief, is but extremely vague." Consequently, he perceived no evidence of design in Nature but rather the operation of a physical mechanism. However, this personal feeling did not hinder him from understanding that to someone possessing the necessary inherent antecedent belief, the evidence for design in nature would be very strong and possibly true so far as a pure agnostic might know. He concluded his paper with a declaration that totally rejected the naturalistic view of truth: "The question 'Is there evidence of Design in Nature?' has been referred from the lower courts of objective fact to the supreme courts of subjective personality; and there

53. GJR, *Poems 1879–1889*, for private circulation (London: Harrison & Sons, 1889), p. 114. It should be noted that about the time GJR was writing this poem, he told the Harvard biologist Asa Gray that he no longer held all the arguments he had stated in *A Candid Examination of Theism* (GJR to Asa Gray, 16 May 1883, in E. Romanes, *Life and Letters of GJR*, p. 154).

it stands to be described by each man for himself at the tribunal of his own judgment." [54]

By the late 1880s Romanes clearly considered discursive reason as only one of man's mental faculties. He saw the emotions and the will as distinct parts of the human mind. When he finished *Mental Evolution in Man,* Romanes intended to write other volumes on the human will and on the religious and moral instincts.[55] He did not live to complete that work. However, the psychology that he undoubtedly would have outlined was implicit in *Thoughts on Religion.*

In those incomplete notes on religion Romanes interpreted faith as the activity of the mind in which all human mental faculties participated in concert to open vistas of knowledge closed to reason alone.

> For reason is not the only attribute of man, nor is it the only faculty which he habitually employs for the ascertainment of truth. Moral and spiritual faculties are of no less importance in their respective spheres even of everyday life; faith, trust, taste, etc., are as needful in ascertaining truth as to character, beauty, etc., as is reason. Indeed we may take it that reason is concerned in ascertaining truth only where *causation* is concerned; the appropriate organs for its ascertainment where anything else is concerned belong to the moral and spiritual region.

Objective criteria were not wholly applicable in cases where faith guided man. If faith provided a man with what he believed to be knowledge, he must act upon that knowledge. In so acting, "He is morally right even if mentally deluded." [56]

Romanes based his trust of this nondiscursive activity of the mind on two considerations. First he noted, as would James Ward and Samuel Butler, that reason was never the sole guide for human action.

> Reason is very far indeed from being the sole guide of judgment that it is usually taken to be—so far, indeed, that, save in matters approaching down-right demonstration . . . it is usu-

54. "Is there Evidence of Design in Nature?: A Symposium," *Proceedings of the Aristotelian Society* 1, no. 3 (1889–90): 75–76. See *A Candid Examination of Theism,* p. 112, for the subtle contrast in tone between GJR's earlier and later statements of the skeptical dilemma.

55. GJR, *Mental Evolution in Man* (New York: D. Appleton & Co., 1889), pp. vi–vii.

56. GJR, *Thoughts on Religion,* pp. 118, 150.

ally hampered by custom, prejudice, dislike, etc., to a degree that would astonish the most sober philosopher could he lay bare to himself all the mental processes whereby the complex act of assent or dissent is eventually determined.

No doubt Romanes had in mind his personal experience with the intransigence of professional scientists in regard to his evolutionary theory. Secondly, he believed that the objective evidence from lives of men living with and without faith bore witness to the efficacy of faith. Such evidence demonstrated that the "nature of man without God" is "thoroughly miserable, as is well shown by Pascal." On the other hand, the testimony of those who possessed faith suggested that "it differs from all other happiness not only in degree but in kind." [57]

Romanes argued that a pure agnostic could not deny that the emotions and will in concert with the reason in the act of faith might lead men to a valid knowledge of transcendental truth.

> There are two opposite casts of mind—the mechanical (scientific, etc.) and the spiritual (artistic, religious, etc.). These may alternate even in the same individual. An "agnostic" has no hesitation . . . that the former only is worthy of trust. But a *pure* agnostic must know better, as he will perceive that there is nothing to choose between the two in point of trustworthiness. Indeed, if choice has to be made, the mystic might claim higher authority for his direct intuitions.

Such intuitions originated in the whole man and involved more effort than unbelief. Romanes declared, "Unbelief is usually due to indolence, often to prejudice, and never a thing to be proud of." [58] Unbelief by its very nature could not ascertain knowledge. The enduring truths of the universe were open only to the man willing to employ his whole being through faith. In this respect, Romanes's dealing with the nature of truth is symptomatic of all the other figures in this study, but especially of Butler and Ward. Their search for an intellectual synthesis between religion and science stemmed less from a desire for some modicum of religious comfort than from the desire to restore a new and higher unity to the various aspects

57. Ibid., p. 145 (A footnote to this passage refers to Newman's *Grammar of Assent*, Pascal's *Pensées*, and Dean Church's *Human Life and its Conditions*); ibid., p. 160, 162.
58. Ibid., pp. 119, 154.

of human nature that naturalistic writers either reduced to matter and energy or left fragmented by their analysis.

This organic unity of human nature required a cosmos very different from that associated with scientific naturalism. To achieve this alternative cosmology two paths were open. The first, which had been followed by Sidgwick, Wallace, and Myers, consisted of discovering in physical nature empirical data not encompassed by the theories of scientific naturalism. The second, which was pursued in a crude manner by Romanes and much more successfully by Butler and Ward, consisted of postulating the existence of a non-mechanical *Urbild,* or noumenal reality, of which "prime" or mechanical nature was in some manner a product or manifestation.[59] From speculations regarding that *Urbild,* Romanes suggested a view of nature possessing the possibility of spiritual life.

The aim of Romanes's speculation was the achievement of a plausible religious or spiritual synthesis that was neither Christian nor secular. In 1892 he explained to Huxley that there was no point to a religion which simply reverenced an abstraction, such as Humanity.

> Thus strictly or liberally speaking, one cannot construct a religion for men or for anybody else, by making a composite photograph of philosophical concepts—albeit these be derived from the best thinking in that department of thought. For in the measure that belief in personality is excluded, the resulting system, whatever it may be, is a mere matter of logical definition, not religious.

Romanes shunned such "god making" as an attempt "to sham" a full confession of agnosticism.[60] However, as a pure agnostic he could and did speculate upon the metaphysical conditions necessary for the possible validity of mankind's religious sentiments.

In his pursuit of this spiritual realm, Romanes had to abandon many of the basic assumptions that had undergirded *A Candid Examination of Theism.* His flirtation with spiritualism had already

59. The concepts of the *Urbild* and Prime Nature are taken from E. D. Hirsch, Jr., *Wordsworth and Schelling: A Typological Study of Romanticism* (New Haven: Yale University Press, 1960), pp. 55–61. None of the men in the present study employ such terms, but these terms suggest the view of nature that each man in his own way sought to develop.

60. GJR to Huxley, 7 December 1892, Huxley Papers, 25.246.

displayed his willingness to consider alternatives to the naturalistic interpretation of the cosmos. In 1882 he abandoned the materialistic hypothesis in regard to psychological phenomena and philosophy generally, explaining,

> [O]f however much service the theory of materialism may be made up to a certain point, it can never be accepted by any competent mind as a final explanation of the facts with which it has to deal. Unquestionable as its use may be as a fundamental hypothesis in physiology and medicine, it is wholly inadequate as a hypothesis in philosophy.[61]

His desire for "a final explanation of the facts" was indicative of a mental temper that would never rest content within the confines of naturalistic thought. He was determined to ask questions that the adherents of naturalism wanted to ignore.

In the 1885 Rede Lecture, Romanes enunciated a monistic theory of the universe. Obviously monism may be interpreted either materialistically or idealistically (Romanes termed the latter spiritualism). However, Romanes based his monism on a single neutral substance of which both matter and mind were modes or manifestations.

> If we unite in a higher synthesis the elements both of spiritualism and of materialism, we obtain a product which satisfies every fact of feeling on the one hand, and of observation on the other. . . . We have only to suppose that the antithesis between mind and motion—subject and object—is itself phenomenal or apparent: not absolute or real. We have only to suppose that the seeming duality is relative to our modes of apprehension; and, therefore, that any change taking place in the mind, and any corresponding change taking place in the brain, are really not two changes, but one change.

Such monism supposed "only one stream of causation." Matter and mind depended upon the particular apprehension of that single monistic substance. Romanes had essentially outlined what James

---

61. GJR, "The Fallacy of Materialism," *Nineteenth Century* 12 (1882): 872–73. See also, Philip Howard Gray, "Prerequisite to an Analysis of Behaviorism: The Conscious Automaton Theory from Spalding to William James," *Journal of the History of the Behavioral Sciences* 4 (1968): 374–75.

Ward would later term "neutral" monism.[62] Naturalistic authors often advocated such a neutral monism but then slipped into materialism when they gave a practical explanation of some phenomenon. Romanes was determined to keep his monism as neutral as his agnosticism was pure.

For this reason he turned the guns of pure agnosticism on the monistic "mind-stuff" theory of W. K. Clifford. The latter had argued that mind was the product of a particular arrangement of matter and that mind could not exist apart from that arrangement since men have no empirical evidence of such a separate existence. Clifford also claimed that while each particle of "mind-stuff" possessed mind, there did not exist any single overall mind in the universe. Mind dissolved and ceased to exist whenever the necessary arrangement of matter was disturbed.[63] Romanes replied that a pure agnostic would see no reason why mind and matter might not exist in another form somewhere else in the universe. Absence of experience with another manifestation of mind or absence of proof of a universal mind did not constitute proof of their nonexistence. Pure agnostics could not exclude the possibility that the monistic substance was mental or that it displayed personality. Neither could the pure agnostic affirm such opinions.[64] Naturalistic thinkers did not approve of this lecture. Huxley considered it "a bid for orthodoxy." [65]

The next year Romanes published an article entitled "The World as Eject" in which he suggested the possibility of an integrating mind in nature. He argued that according to the principle of continuity it was reasonable to project qualities of subjectivity into the cosmos as a whole—to view nature ejectively. Although man cannot know the nature of that cosmic mind, he must assume that it totally transcends the human mind and is thus a "Superconscious." Romanes believed it improbable that the human mind was the "highest manifestation of subjectivity in this universe of infinite objectivity." Throughout the universe there existed "unquestionable evidence of some one integrating principle, whereby all its many and complex

62. GJR, *Mind and Motion and Monism*, pp. 27–28; James Ward, *Naturalism and Agnosticism* (London: A. & C. Black, 1899), 2 : 206.

63. GJR, *Mind and Motion and Monism*, pp. 32–33. See W. K. Clifford, *Lectures and Essays*, ed. L. Stephen and F. Pollock (London: Macmillan & Co., 1901), 2 : 1–51.

64. GJR, *Mind and Motion and Monism*, pp. 34–37.

65. Quoted in "In Memoriam—G. J. Romanes," *Proceedings of the Aristotelian Society* 3, no. 1 (1895–96) : 177.

parts are correlated with one another in such wise that the result is universal order." [66]

In the years after 1886 the Superconscious, which Romanes later termed God, appeared more prominently in his metaphysical speculations. In an essay written before 1889 but probably after 1886 Romanes actually embraced a tenuous theism. Reversing his position in *A Candid Examination of Theism,* he noted that in his skeptical volume he had failed "to perceive that even if Mr. Spencer's theory [of matter and force] were conceded fully to explain all the facts of causality, it would in no wise tend to explain the cosmos in which these facts occur." Romanes argued that a *"causa causarum"* must be posited. He found himself thus "driven upon the theory of Theism as furnishing the only nameable explanation of this universal order." However, he denied that men could have any conception of the nature of that *causa causarum.*[67] Romanes's God, or Superconscious, closely resembled Spencer's Unknowable, supplied with a tenuous personality.

In *Thoughts on Religion* Romanes speculated on the nature of that cause and of its relationship to man and nature. He there argued that the conflict of religion and science had arisen from the mutual acceptance of the "highly dubious hypothesis" that *"if there be a personal God, He is not immediately concerned with natural causation."* This mutually accepted proposition accounted for the separation of the "natural" and the "supernatural." In his projected *Candid Examination of Religion* Romanes planned to refute that hypothesis. He outlined the reasoning he intended to follow to prove the possibility of the union of personality with immanence so as to escape the abstract god-making that he criticized in his letter to Huxley. He expected to demonstrate the following propositions:

> Namely, (A) That if there be a personal God, no reason can be assigned why He should not be immanent in nature, or why all causation should not be the immediate expression of His will.

66. GJR, *Mind and Motion and Monism,* pp. 107, 108.

67. GJR, *Thoughts on Religion,* p. 73 (This essay was one of the two entitled "The Influence of Science Upon Religion" that Gore published with the notes on religion. These essays had been written prior to 1889 for *Nineteenth Century* but were never published. Gore decided not to publish a fragment of a third essay in the series); ibid., pp. 71, 75, 76.

(B) That every available reason points to the inference that He probably is so. (C) That if He is so, and if His will is self-consistent, all natural causation must needs appear to us 'mechanical.' Therefore, (D) That is no argument against the divine origin of a thing, event, etc., to prove it due to natural causation.[68]

He hoped that in the future a "true religion" might rest on a view of divine immanence.[69] He believed this concept of God and his idea of the world as eject would avoid the reductionism of the naturalistic writers. In 1886 he had explained that "by regarding physical causation as everywhere but the objective phenomenal aspect of an ejective or ontological reality . . . [monism] furnishes a logical basis for a theory of things which is at the same time natural and spiritual." [70] In this manner Romanes pointed toward a reconciliation of the subjective and objective perceptions of the world. Man's subjective feelings, emotions, and intuitions were part of this Superconscious immanent in all things. They could therefore grant to man valid knowledge of that transcendental reality. Faith based on will, emotions, and intuitions thus brought man closer to the root of all existing things.

George Romanes's musings on the possibility of a religious interpretation of man and nature did not embrace Christian theology. There was no creation, no incarnation, no sin, no redemption, no absolute difference between the nature of the Superconscious and of man. However, he did believe that he had legitimized religious sentiments, such as were associated with Christianity. He also believed that Christianity remained the highest expression of those sentiments. "Only to a man wholly destitute of spiritual perception can it be that Christianity should fail to appear the greatest exhibition of the beautiful, the sublime, and of all else that appeals to our spiritual nature, which has ever been known upon our earth." [71] As a pure agnostic, Romanes explained that he could not deny the doctrines of the Incarnation and Trinity. However, as a pure agnostic he could not and did not affirm them.

On the other hand, while neither accepting nor affirming any

68. Ibid., p. 127 (GJR's emphasis); ibid., p. 128.
69. Ibid., p. 129.
70. GJR, *Mind and Motion and Monism*, p. 115.
71. GJR, *Thoughts on Religion*, p. 171.

dogmas, Romanes did affirm the "experiment of faith." "Thus viewed it would seem that the experiment of faith is not a 'fool's experiment;' but, on the contrary, so that there is enough *prima facie* evidence to arrest serious attention, such an experimental trial would seem to be the rational duty of a pure agnostic." [72] Had death been stayed, Romanes might have set out upon that experiment. His final reconciliation with the Anglican church was his first and last step in that direction. It was an act of pure agnosticism rather than one of renewed dogmatism. It marked the failure of scientific naturalism to meet the test of life and death.

In 1873, twenty-one years before Romanes's death, there had appeared a curious religious work entitled *The Fair Haven*. The book consisted of two parts. The first was a "Memoir of the Late John Pickard Owen" written by his brother. The memoir recorded Owen's abandoning Christianity and his painful return to that faith after passing through skepticism and Catholicism before settling into the Broad Church party. The second section of the book, which Owen had written before his death, consisted of an apology for Christianity against the higher criticism. The form and content of *The Fair Haven* were strikingly similar to Romanes's *Thoughts on Religion* and *The Life and Letters of George John Romanes*. There was, however, one crucial difference. *The Fair Haven* was from beginning to end a carefully constructed and finely executed hoax intended as a satire of contemporary Christianity.[73] The author of this imaginative work was Samuel Butler, who a year earlier had achieved certain literary notoriety with his novel *Erewhon*.

Over the years a number of parallels and interrelations developed between the novelist who wrote *The Fair Haven* and the scientist who in large measure enacted the drama in real life. Both Romanes and Butler studied for the ministry but then abandoned Christianity and turned to science as a guide to life. At different moments in their lives both men enjoyed the friendship of Charles Darwin. In this regard, Romanes became the man that Butler might have become had the latter been willing to apply himself to scientific theory. Each man became disillusioned with the naturalistic theory of truth and with professional scientists. Here Butler became the man

72. Ibid., pp. 178–79.
73. Samuel Butler, *The Fair Haven* (1873) (London: Jonathan Cape, 1923).

Romanes might have become had the latter possessed Butler's infinite capacity for heaping scorn on Victorian culture. Paradoxically, at the time of Butler's disillusionment, Romanes remained in the naturalistic ranks and was one of Butler's chief opponents. He considered Butler an ill-informed and scurrilous critic of Darwin. Butler considered Romanes a plagiarizer of one of his own books. Yet after a few years both eventually embraced panpsychism, suggested an immanent view of God, and criticized reason as an instrument for achieving knowledge. But at the point in their lives when they finally might have been able to agree on more issues than they disagreed, they simply ignored each other. Viewed together, their lives illustrate how two men of almost diametrically opposed character and temperament—one accepted practically all contemporary values and cultural institutions and one rejected practically all those values and institutions—might discover scientific naturalism to be an inadequate and unsatisfactory interpretation of life.

7

Samuel Butler: The Man of Temper

An Ironic Subject

In 1902 an acquaintance observed of Samuel Butler, "His is, indeed, one of those personalities which find no adequate expression in modern life." This is a curious judgment about a man whose published works fill more than twenty volumes and whose carefully self-annotated correspondence and notebooks amount to more than sixteen folio volumes. He once confided to his sister, "What a lot I have written about my books—but then my books are to me much the most important thing in life. They in fact are 'me' much more than anything else is." [1] Yet those books, as well as his paintings and musical compositions, never quite succeeded in expressing Butler's personality. He recognized that fact. His numerous writings were less an expression of his personality than a protest against modern life, in which a man like himself—and in this respect Butler considered himself everyman—could not achieve adequate or authentic expression.

Butler wrote in 1865 that "loss of faith in the general right-mindedness and clear-headedness of one's age is a much more serious thing than loss of faith in a personal Deity." [2] He sustained that general loss of faith in every intellectual guide available in Victorian society. Through his own encounters with the religious, intellectual, scientific, and social norms of the day, Butler came to regard all norms as nothing more than expedient conventions whereby men

---

1. Harry Quilter, *What's What* (London: Sonnenschein & Co., 1902), p. 311; Samuel Butler to May Butler, 1 February 1884, in *The Correspondence of Samuel Butler with His Sister May*, ed. Daniel F. Howard (Berkeley: University of California Press, 1962), p. 116. Samuel Butler hereafter cited in footnotes as SB.

2. SB "Precaution in Free Thought" (1865), in *A First Year in Canterbury Settlement and Other Early Essays* (London: Jonathan Cape, 1923), p. 240. Unless otherwise noted all citations to SB's books are from *The Shrewsbury Edition of the Works of Samuel Butler*, ed. H. F. Jones and A. T. Bartholomew (London: Jonathan Cape, 1923-26).

organized and directed their lives. The conventions and the systems of thought employed to justify them had no counterpart in reality. Conventions were by no means necessarily evil; indeed life required them. However, they became evil and incompatible with the authentic expression of life when confused with reality or when regarded as the unchanging expression of an underlying reality. Butler detected the illicit use of conventions in every stratum of Victorian life. His parents believed their evangelical morality expressed the will of God. Artists and literary critics thought their rules of composition were determined by some unerring standard. The men of science seemed to argue that scientific theories described the unchanging constitution of nature. Butler contended all such determined patterns of thought and life separated men from any genuine relationship to the underlying reality of things, which he usually termed the "unseen kingdom" or "unseen world." [3]

During his undergraduate years Butler had deplored the constraints of authoritative rules imposed by self-proclaimed experts. Rules might hinder an instinctive perception of truth.

> I incline to believe that as irons support the rickety child, whilst they impede the healthy one, so rules, for the most part, are but useful to the weaker among us. Our greatest masters in language, whether prose or verse, in painting, music, architecture, or the like, have been those who preceded the rule and whose excellence gave rise thereto; men who preceded, I should rather say, not the rule, but the discovery of the rule, men whose intuitive perception led them to the right practice.[4]

Throughout his life Butler sought to vindicate intuitive perception of truth whether in the realm of religion, science, or social behavior. He wanted to probe the very source of rules, norms, or conventions and to understand the basis of their pervasive authority. This pursuit transformed him into one of the most subversive writers of his age.

Butler was unique among English unbelievers. Nietzsche once remarked, "In England one must rehabilitate oneself after every

3. These phrases occur repeatedly in SB's notebooks. See H. F. Jones, ed., *The Note-Books of Samuel Butler* (London: Fifield, 1912), pp. 168, 320; A. T. Bartholomew, ed., *Further Extracts from the Note-Books of Samuel Butler* (London: Jonathan Cape, 1934), pp. 214, 274, 322.

4. SB, "On English Composition and Other Matters" (1858), in *A First Year in Canterbury Settlement*, pp. 3-4.

little emancipation from theology by showing in a veritably awe-inspiring manner what a moral fanatic one is. That is the penance they pay there." Samuel Butler refused to pay such penance. He regarded Christian theology as simply one facet of the total system of conventions that restricted life in English society. The home, the family, the universities, and the doctrines of science were likewise hollow, graceless, and constricting conventions separating men from the unseen kingdom. It was this total inadequacy of contemporary life that he portrayed so indelibly in *The Way of All Flesh*. The misery of young Ernest Pontifex was not the fault of insensitive parents. Those parents were merely the archetypes of all Victorian authority figures who restricted men's lives by imposing rules upon them. As the narrator Overton observed, "Surely it was the tower of Siloam that was naught rather than those who stood under it; it was the system rather than the people, that was at fault." [5] The system was always the real target of Butler's attack. He protested a system that required men and women to submit themselves to the authoritative pronouncements of clergy, professors, scientists, and other self-proclaimed experts whose doctrines, ideas, and theories could neither rise above the level of expedient convention nor set forth knowledge of real, unchanging truth.

Butler's Edwardian and post–World War I admirers thought his rebellion the mark of genius.[6] Edmund Gosse, on the other hand, deemed it the characteristic of an "inspired 'crank.'" [7] Both judgments were perhaps beside the point. Butler more nearly resembled the ironic subject whom Kierkegaard described in his master's thesis. Kierkegaard argued that there exist moments in history when mankind's perception of the world ("actuality" is Kierkegaard's term) undergoes a total change. Old interpretations became invalid for numerous people. During these moments some individuals, the prophets, suggest the direction of the future course of thought. Others, the tragic heroes, attempt to forge the future reality. There

5. F. Nietzsche, *Twilight of the Idols* in *The Portable Nietzsche*, ed. Walter Kaufman (New York: The Viking Press, 1967), p. 515; SB, *The Way of All Flesh*, ed. D. F. Howard (London: Methuen & Co., 1965), p. 240.

6. For accounts of the fortunes of SB's posthumous reputation, see L. E. Holt, "Samuel Butler's Rise to Fame," *Publications of the Modern Language Association* 57 (September 1942) : 867–78, and *Samuel Butler* (New York: Grosset & Dunlap, 1964), pp. 149–52.

7. Edmund Gosse, *Aspects and Impressions* (New York: Scribner's, 1922), p. 60.

is, however, a third response different from both prophecy and tragedy—that of irony.

> For the ironic subject the given actuality has completely lost its validity; it has become for him an imperfect form which everywhere constrains. . . . He it is who has come to render judgment. The ironist is in one sense prophetic, to be sure, for he constantly points to something future; but what it is he knows not. . . . The ironist . . . has advanced beyond the reach of his age and opened a front against it. That which shall come is hidden from him, concealed behind his back, but the actuality he hostilely opposes is the one he shall destroy.[8]

The ironic subject has intellectually severed himself from bondage and commitment to the substantial forms of thought and action through which his society expresses itself—its institutions, its authorities, its values, its goals, its gods. For him these forms stand in contradiction to the authentic expression of life. The ironist seeks to reveal the inadequacies of these modes of thought, expression, and action and to make them reveal their own inadequacy. He exalts in a state of subjective iconoclastic freedom wherein he seeks to destroy and subvert the present conventional reality rather than to create a new one.

Regarding Butler as an ironic subject points up a paradoxical feature of his personal frustration and his posthumous fame. His contempt for contemporary thought and mores pointed to the general repudiation of "Victorianism" that distinguished the early decades of the twentieth century when later men and women saw in Butler a kindred spirit. Yet his personal hatred for and attack against religion, science, and contemporary social morality originated in a long but futile attempt to achieve success and acclaim through conformity with those institutions and values. Butler desired fame and reputation, but resented the narrowness of the path that might have led to the fulfillment of those ambitions. Consequently, thwarted in his own attempt to forge a satisfactory identity within Victorian society, he set about to purge what he had come to consider the corrupt state and illicit constrictions of English thought and morals. In this role he fancied himself as "the *enfant terrible*

---

8. Søren Kierkegaard, *The Concept of Irony with Constant Reference to Socrates*, trans. Lee M. Capel (Bloomington: Indiana University Press, 1968), pp. 277–79.

of literature and science. If I cannot, and I know I cannot, get the literary and scientific big-wigs to give me a shilling, I can, and I know I can, heave bricks into the middle of them." [9] The bricks that Butler heaved had been baked—he would probably have said "half-baked"—in the kilns of Victorian religion and scientific naturalism. They were the bricks with which most Victorian intellectuals had constructed their mental homes. Butler had tried to build with them. However, after his house twice collapsed over him, he went in search of better materials, never forgiving the cheating brick merchants who had swindled him.

BETRAYED BY FALSE GODS

By the close of the 1870s Samuel Butler had discovered what he considered the untenability and the blatant dishonesty of both Christianity and scientific naturalism.[10] His two journeys toward unbelief and general disillusionment consisted of similar stages and eventually illustrated Nietzsche's thesis that "the untenability of one interpretation of the world, upon which a tremendous amount of energy has been lavished, awakens the suspicion that *all* interpretations of the world are false." [11] Butler first became disenchanted with the doctrines and practices of Christians and scientists. Conviction that supporters of each set of ideas had falsified their histories soon followed. Finally, he regarded both as supporting and sustaining hypocritical professions. From these experiences he emerged an ironic subject intent upon revealing the inadequacy of the Christian and scientific world views and the deceit of the men who espoused them.

While reading for Holy Orders in 1859, Butler realized that he could not agree with the articles of the Anglican church that explained baptismal regeneration. As he wrote to his most unsympathetic father:

9. Jones, *The Note-Books of Samuel Butler*, p. 183. For an explanation of the curious editing of the published notebooks, consult L. E. Holt, "The Note-Books of Samuel Butler," *Publications of the Modern Language Association* 60 (December 1945) : 1165–79.

10. See Joseph Fort, *Samuel Butler (1835–1902), Etude d'une Charactère et d'une Intelligence* (Bordeaux: J. Biere, 1934), pp. 353–55, for a general characterization of the processes involved in SB's modification of opinion. This is the best study of SB.

11. Nietzsche, *The Will to Power*, trans. and ed. Walter Kaufman and R. J. Hollingdale (New York: Random House, 1967), p. 7.

Believing for my own part that a man can, by making use of
the ordinary means of grace, attain a condition in which he can
say, "I do not offend *knowingly* in any one thing either habitu-
ally or otherwise and believe that whereas once on a time I was
full of sin I have now been cleansed from all sin and am Holy
even as Christ was holy upon earth." . . . Nay more, that unless a man can at some time before his death say such words as
these he is not incorporate with Christ and cannot be saved.[12]

Canon Butler attempted to steer his son away from this somewhat
Pelagian position but to no avail. The younger man persisted in his
opinion. That Butler's initial protest against religious orthodoxy
arose over this particular point of doctrine foreshadowed what
would become a characteristic hostility to all forms of determinism,
whether of Augustinian original sin or of Darwinian natural selection. Both were fatal to man's instinctive capacity for dealing with
his moral and physical circumstances—an ability Butler denoted by
the term "cunning."[13] Indeed, one might say that his later Lamarckianism amounted to biological Pelagianism.

Butler's intellectual heresy soon received practical confirmation.
Among the students in his London Sunday school class, he could
discern no perceptible difference in the moral character of those who
had received regeneration through baptism and those who had not.
With this discovery Butler decided his entry into the ministry (never
zealously contemplated) was impossible. The well-known Butler
family quarrel over his vocation ensued and was resolved by his
emigration to New Zealand as a sheep farmer.[14]

In September 1859 Butler left England a wavering Christian and
arrived in New Zealand a few months later a wavering unbeliever.[15]
The first night of the voyage he did not say his prayers. During the
trip he read Gibbon's *Decline and Fall of the Roman Empire*. The

12. SB to his father, 9 May 1859, in *The Family Letters of Samuel Butler*, ed. Arnold
Silver (Stanford, Calif.: Stanford University Press, 1962), pp. 73–74. SB had already
begun to discuss alternative careers when he raised this doctrinal objection. However, he appears to have been perfectly sincere in questioning the article.

13. SB, *Luck or Cunning?* (1885) (London: Jonathan Cape, 1924), pp. 79–80; Jones,
The Note-Books of Samuel Butler, pp. 319–20.

14. H. F. Jones, *Samuel Butler, Author of Erewhon (1835–1902): A Memoir* (London:
Macmillan & Co., 1919), 1 : 59–61 (hereafter cited as Jones, *Memoir*); Silver, *The Family
Letters of Samuel Butler*, pp. 64–90.

15. Jones, *Memoir*, 1 : 71–74.

wiles of the satirical chapters on the early church claimed yet another Christian soul. For a second time, Butler discovered that
orthodox Christianity was not what it claimed to be or, rather, to
have been.

An encounter with the higher criticism soon reinforced his disillusionment with Christian history. Though it is not certain, Butler
probably read Strauss. Before long he had abandoned the final
vestiges of his Christian faith. In August 1862 he declared, "For the
present I renounce Christianity altogether." [16] Perhaps not content
with absorbing the thought of Strauss, Butler turned to his own
examination of the Bible with special emphasis on the resurrection.
There in the wilds of New Zealand, surrounded by thousands of
sheep, Samuel Butler concluded that Jesus not only had never risen
from the dead, but also had never even died. He had swooned on
the cross, had been removed by his friends, had recovered his health,
and then had returned to his disciples. Butler later published the
theory in a pamphlet and incorporated it into his satire of unbelief,
The Fair Haven.[17] This action illustrated Butler's inability to think
about any issue that especially interested him without expanding on
it and making his own insights available to the public.

Just as he was in the process of separating himself from Christianity and the social mores of English society in favor of the higher
criticism and frontier customs, Butler read the *Origin of Species*.
Several years later he told J. B. Yeats that the *Origin* had destroyed
his belief in a personal God.[18] Of equal importance, the book convinced him of the occurrence of evolution. Previously Butler apparently believed that organic species, morals, and artistic rules
existed *sub species aeternitatis*. Afterwards, he viewed all of them as
existing in a permanent state of flux and considered nothing in the
world as fixed or permanent. Like many other people of the day,
Butler confused the ideas of evolution and natural selection.[19] Not
until 1876 did he come to understand that they were separate concepts.

In 1864 Butler sold his holdings in New Zealand for a consider-

16. SB to an unnamed correspondent, 14 August 1862, in ibid., p. 98.
17. Ibid., pp. 98–99; SB, *The Evidence for the Resurrection of Jesus Christ by the
Four Evangelists Critically Examined* (Privately printed, London: 1865).
18. J.B. Yeats, *Essays Irish and American* (New York: Macmillan Co., 1918), p. 17.
19. Philip G. Fothergill, *Historical Aspects of Organic Evolution* (London: Hollis &
Carter, 1952), pp. 116–22.

able profit and returned to England to try his fortunes at studying art. Before departing New Zealand, he had defended Darwin in the *Christchurch Press* and had written the essays that became the basis for *Erewhon,* which he published in 1872.[20] His attempt to become an artist proved futile. The success of *Erewhon* was shortlived, and in 1873 *The Fair Haven* was a total failure.[21] Butler simply could not establish himself in the artistic and literary fields. Consequently, he became highly suspicious of all professional authority. The social and intellectual respect accorded to members of the artistic, literary, and religious professions stood as a constant reminder of his own failure to forge an identity for himself within Victorian society.

During these same trying years, Butler retained considerable respect for men of science. In 1865 he had asked a friend, "What is knighthood or decoration in comparison with the *bona fide* applause of the real leaders of science?" [22] Until the mid-seventies Butler appears to have believed that science, unlike art, literature, or religion, constituted an objective description of the external world. The scientists actually pursued the truth that artists, literary men, and priests confused with their own expedient rules and doctrines. Not until he formulated a speculative scientific theory of his own did Butler recognize the similarly conventional nature of scientific thought.

While still enamored with science, Butler also fancied that the

---

20. SB, "Darwin on the Origin of Species: A Dialogue," *Christchurch Press,* 20 December 1862, reprinted in *A First Year in Canterbury Settlement,* pp. 188–97. Other letters to the *Press* followed this dialogue; see pp. 198–207.

21. *Erewhon* sold very well for as long as the public did not know the identity of the author. Sales dropped sharply when SB's authorship became known. *The Fair Haven* never sold well. SB was criticized for not making its satirical purpose properly clear. In response to such criticism, he wrote: "A writer cannot write for everybody; he must assume a certain amount of apprehensiveness on the part of his readers, and is justified in leaving children and stupid people out of his calculations. Satire, to be satire, *must* have a hidden meaning. If this is so hidden that reasonably careful readers fail to see it, it has no point, and ceases to be satire. If, again, it obtrudes itself even upon the least reflecting, it fails not less completely. I endeavoured to steer as evenly as I could between these two dangers" (*Spectator,* 22 November 1873, p. 1470). SB may have steered too perfectly, for some clergymen thought his fabricated history of J. P. Owen was true and recommended its study to wavering souls. See SB, *The Fair Haven* (London: Jonathan Cape, 1923), pp. xvii–xxii.

22. SB to Dr. Haast, 12 November 1865, in Samuel Butler Papers, British Museum, add. MSS. 44027, pp. 122–23.

adherents of scientific naturalism might assist a young man who sought to unmask the dishonesty of religion and the conventional nature of current morality. Therefore, he moved to inculcate himself with the leaders of scientific naturalism. Between 1865 and 1877, Butler sent most of his essays and all his books to Charles Darwin for the latter's perusal, pleasure, and praise. This correspondence and his two visits with Darwin were part of an effort at self-advancement.[23] He had published his early essays in a New Zealand newspaper and in George Holyoake's secularist *Reasoner,* an organ of working-class and lower-middle-class opinion. Admission to the Darwin circle or perhaps even moderate praise from its members would aid his literary career as a freethinker.

Butler was correct in perceiving that an amateur writer might succeed as an author of naturalistic articles and books. Neither Leslie Stephen nor W. K. Clifford had been trained to write their criticism of religion. Nor had professional scientists, such as Huxley and Tyndall, been educated to compose philosophical essays. Butler's mistake was to suppose that since the naturalistic coterie permitted amateurs to criticize religion and philosophy, they would also allow an amateur to set forth a scientific theory. Butler attempted to contribute such a theory in 1877. The frustrations occasioned by this venture caused his loss of faith in scientific naturalism.

Hoping to shore up investments that he had mismanaged after returning to England, Butler visited Canada in 1874. There he formulated his life-and-habit theory. The idea was quite simple: hereditary traits and habits, including physiological activity, were transmitted through inherited organic memory.[24] Heredity was a lively question in the 1870s. Failure to understand its nature posed one of the chief stumbling blocks to the acceptance of natural selection.[25] If Butler's speculation was correct, his fame would be achieved. With a record of artistic, literary, and financial failure behind him, he was clutching for something at which he could suddenly and strikingly succeed. On returning to England from Canada, he set to work on a book about his theory.

Only at that time did Butler realize that science closely resembled

23. Jones, *Memoir,* 1 : 123–25, 156–58, 165.

24. Ibid., pp. 212–13, 232–34, 265.

25. Loren Eiseley, *Darwin's Century: Evolution and the Men Who Discovered It* (Garden City, N.Y.: Doubleday, 1961), pp. 205–33.

the other professions with which he had become disenchanted. He made this discovery through W. B. Carpenter, an important English physiologist and leading exponent of the unconscious activity of the mind. There is a certain irony in the fact that it was Carpenter who turned Butler's wrath on science. Carpenter was a theist who was not identified with the adherents of naturalism and who entertained considerable doubt about natural selection.[26] He appears to have refused permission for Butler to quote from one of his books. Also, from the introduction to *Life and Habit,* it would appear that Carpenter had told Butler or Butler had surmised from certain of the physiologist's books that the life-and-habit theory would not pass muster among professional scientists and that untrained men should not speculate on technical issues.[27]

Having come to anticipate criticism from men such as Carpenter, Butler modified the purpose of *Life and Habit* in the midst of composition.[28] Besides presenting his own theory of heredity, Butler also sought "to place distrust of science upon a scientific basis." [29] He intended to register a protest against the same facet of modern intellectual life that later troubled Henry Sidgwick—cultural domination by scientific experts. For his own self-preservation Butler needed to establish the right of a nonscientifically trained writer to publish a "scientific" treatise that could receive serious attention. Just as he had believed that by ordinary grace a Christian could avoid sin, Butler now subscribed to the belief that ordinary common sense represented a more perfect form of knowledge than the theories of professionals.

Butler hoped to prove that scientific theories were just as much expedient conventions as were opinions in morality or religion. If he could sustain that argument, then his theory would be as legitimate as that of any man of science. Butler opened his attack by redefining knowledge. Rather than an objective description of an external reality, knowledge was an activity or a means to an end.

26. J. Estlin Carpenter, "Memorial Sketch," in W. B. Carpenter, *Nature and Man: Essays Scientific and Philosophical* (London: K. Paul, Trench & Co., 1888), pp. 1–152.

27. F. Darwin to SB, September or October 1877, in Samuel Butler Papers, British Museum, add. MSS. 44028, p. 98. Francis Darwin mentioned SB's having approached Carpenter on the matter of using quotations.

28. Jones, *Memoir,* 1 : 257–60; SB, *Unconscious Memory* (1880) (London: Jonathan Cape, 1924), pp. 13–27.

29. Jones, *Memoir,* 1 : 266.

To know meant the ability to do or to act effectively. Human beings knew those things that they could do most facilely. What they knew best they did by unconscious habit. Butler contended, "The older the habit the longer the practice, the longer the practice the more knowledge—or, the less uncertainty; the less uncertainty the less power of conscious self-analysis and control.[30] His favorite examples of perfected knowledge were the physiological activities of the body and mastered skills such as language and musical ability. Conscious or discursive knowledge by the very fact of its consciousness remained in a state of trial and error.

In opposition to the naturalistic ideal of reasoned truth, he declared: "Knowledge is in an inchoate state as long as it is capable of logical treatment; it must be transmuted into that sense or instinct which rises altogether above the sphere in which words can have being at all, otherwise it is not yet incarnate." He pilloried the concept of empirical proof that stood at the core of naturalistic thought. Discursive proof and discursive knowledge testified to their own inadequacy.

> For power to prove implies a sense of the need of proof, and things which the majority of mankind find practically important are in ninety-nine cases out of a hundred above proof. The need of proof becomes as obsolete in the case of assured knowledge, as the practice of fortifying towns in the middle of an old and long settled country.

That a discursive theory of science upheld during one decade was often replaced by another during the next decade illustrated the folly of embracing discursively proved knowledge as the truth. Real knowledge and real truth, as Butler presented them in the opening chapters of *Life and Habit*, belonged "to the nice sensible people who know what's what rather than to the professorial classes."[31] True science permitted the active, subjective getting along in the world. It was never a body of objective truth. Common sense or antinomian insight were as likely—probably more likely—to be correct than the theories of science. Butler's epistemology was highly suggestive of William James's pragmatism and John Dewey's instrumentalism.

During the same months that Butler recognized the conventional

30. SB, *Life and Habit* (1877) (London: Jonathan Cape, 1923), p. 11.
31. Ibid., pp. 25, 29.

nature of scientific theory, he found his discovery borne out in regard to evolution. When he had finished *Life and Habit,* he received from Edward Clodd a copy of St. George Mivart's *Genesis of Species.*[32] For the first time, Butler became aware that evolution and natural selection were not synonymous. He immediately rejected natural selection in favor of the immanent, teleological evolution advocated by Mivart without, however, accepting Mivart's theism. Butler regarded immanent evolution as equivalent to the active common sense of the species.[33] As in the case of original sin, Butler chose freedom over determinism.

Butler's rejection of natural selection did not occasion his break with Darwin.[34] That all too famous quarrel arose in 1879 and revolved about Darwin's historical sketch of the development of evolutionary theory rather than about natural selection.[35] After reading Buffon, Erasmus Darwin, and Lamarck, Butler became convinced that Charles Darwin took too much credit for the discovery of evolution. The real credit for the theory of evolution should go to the earlier writers. As Butler later wrote of Darwin, "The ground of complaint against him is that he muddied the water after he had drawn it, and tacitly claimed to be the rightful owner of the spring, on the score of the damage he had effected." [36] In his rejection of scientific naturalism on the grounds of the dishonesty of its ad-

32. Jones, *Memoir,* 2 : 433–34. For Mivart's theory, consult Jacob W. Gruber, *A Conscience in Conflict: The Life of St. George Jackson Mivart* (New York: Temple University Publications by Columbia University Press, 1960), pp. 52–70.

33. Edward Clodd related SB's fate in this manner: "And yet when Butler wrote *Life and Habit* as a serious contribution to the doctrine of Evolution, he resented the attitude of the readers of *Erewhon* and *The Fair Haven,* when he was asked 'Where was the joke?' And he protested 'that there was no joke,' the more did his readers laugh and say, 'Oh no, we're not such fools as all that, we know it's your fun'" (*Memories* [London: Chapman & Hall, 1916], p. 263). See also R. A. Streitfield's Introduction to *The Fair Haven,* p. xiii.

34. SB to F. Darwin, 25 November 1877, and F. Darwin to SB, 28 December 1877, in Jones, *Memoir,* 1 : 257–61, 263–64.

35. The SB–Darwin quarrel has been generously recorded for posterity. SB presented his case in *Evolution, Old and New* (1879) (London: Jonathan Cape, 1924) and in *Unconscious Memory,* pp. 28–56. H. F. Jones and Francis Darwin published all the relevant letters in *Charles Darwin and Samuel Butler: A Step toward Reconciliation* (London: A. C. Fifield, 1911). Jones discussed this pamphlet and reprinted some letters in *Memoir,* 2 : 424–28, 446–67. Nora Barlow published other materials in Charles Darwin, *Autobiography (1809–1882),* (London: Harcourt, 1959), pp. 167–219. The best discussion of the quarrel is found in Basil Willey, *Darwin and Butler: Two Versions of Evolution* (London: Chatto & Windus, 1960).

36. SB, *Unconscious Memory,* p. 39.

herents, Butler's reading of the pre-Darwinian evolutionists played the same role as had his previous reading of Gibbon in his break with Christianity.

A second, less well-known incident occurred in 1884 and did even more to confirm Butler's conviction of the duplicity of professional scientists. In 1883 George John Romanes had published *Mental Evolution in Animals* in which he suggested that certain instincts were modes of inherited memory.[37] This theory closely resembled what Butler had proposed in *Life and Habit* and had seen rejected on the grounds that its author was not a professional man of science. Romanes had already made an enemy of Butler by his savage review of *Evolution Old and New* and *Unconscious Memory,* which contained Butler's denunciation of Darwin.[38] Early in 1884 the *Athenaeum* reviewer of *Mental Evolution in Animals* accused Romanes of having taken his theory of inherited memory from Butler. Moreover, the reviewer pointed out that Romanes provided an incorrect reference for his theory. Romanes, still fighting within the ranks of scientific naturalism, protested his innocence, corrected the reference, and suggested that Butler's theory was nothing but foolishness. The journal maintained its original charge, arguing that no matter where Romanes might have found a reference to inherited memory, the theory had enjoyed no currency until Butler had published *Life and Habit.* Ray Lankester and Herbert Spencer then entered the fray to suggest other sources for the theory, to depreciate Romanes's originality, and to dismiss Butler.[39] These letters did nothing to aid Romanes, but they gave Butler the ironic pleasure of seeing his own theory bantered about while the professional men of science displayed their lack of candor to the world.[40]

Butler's experience with the arrogance of professional scientists, their unnecessary adherence to a rigidly deterministic evolution, and their dishonesty in regard to the history of that theory convinced him that they represented nothing more than successors to the cheating priests of Christianity. The professional defense of Darwin,

37. GJR, *Mental Evolution in Animals* (New York: D. Appleton and Co., 1884), pp. 113–16.

38. *Nature* 23 (27 January 1881) : 285–87.

39. *Athenaeum,* 1 March 1884 (p. 283); 8 March (pp. 312–13); 15 March (pp. 348–49); 22 March (p. 380); 29 March (pp. 411–12); and 5 April (p. 446). See also SB, *Luck or Cunning?,* pp. 37–53.

40. SB believed these letters proved that the world of science had accepted his theory, albeit without acknowledgment. Jones, *Memoir,* 1 : 408–10.

natural selection, and scientific expertise reenacted the clergy's defense of the Scriptures after the emergence of the higher criticism. The latter defense had been the target of *The Fair Haven*.[41]

Butler's perception of the similarity between the clergy and the adherents of scientific naturalism represented one of his most penetrating insights into the nature of his culture. He understood that the conflict of religion and science was in reality a struggle for the cultural domination of England. He once remarked, "When people talk about reconciling religion and science they do not mean what they say; they mean reconciling statements made by one set of professional men with those made by another set whose interests lie in the opposite direction—and with no recognized president of the court to keep them within due bounds that is not always easy." [42] Butler recognized that for all their differences, the clergy and the scientists agreed that men with access to true knowledge should dominate society. However, for Butler, who rejected both the truth of revelation and the truth of scientific analysis, neither group could legitimately guide their fellow men.

With his usual uncanny wit and perception, Butler turned the naturalistic analysis of religion against its proponents. The naturalistic writers had persistently contended that scientific theory must replace the religious interpretation of nature and that both religion and science originated in the primitive impulse to understand the external world. Butler agreed that the man of science was indeed the successor to the priest. "He is but medicine-man, augur, priest, in its latest development; useful it may be, but requiring to be well watched by those who value freedom. Wait till he has become more powerful, and note the vagaries which his conceit of knowledge will indulge in." Already he saw them attempting to secure their position in society in a permanent fashion as had the clergy. "It would end in college fellowships with all their worst abuses over again, and silly people would leave money to science as they used to leave it to religion—with the same results." [43] If and when the scientists succeeded, there would be no room left for common sense. Men would once more be locked into a pattern of conventional and expedient thought that its self-serving exponents set forth as eternal truth.

The specter of encroaching scientific domination of modes of

41. SB, *The Fair Haven*, pp. 153–54; *Luck or Cunning?*, pp. 218–19.
42. SB, *Luck or Cunning?*, p. 193.
43. SB, *Life and Habit*, p. 35; SB, Manuscript Note-Books, Williams College, 2 : 6.

thought and perception led Butler to speak more favorably of organized religion. Being realistic enough to know that neither profession would be abolished, he thought that each might counterbalance
and check the worst abuses of the other. He also hoped that his
criticism of science and Christianity might reconcile the adherents of
each to "common modesty, accuracy, and straightforwardness." [44]
Once both the clergy and the men of science had recognized the
limits of their knowledge, the intellectual climate would be such
that other men might be able to forge new, more modest, and more
tempered approaches to life—approaches that might not separate
men from the unseen kingdom as had the formalized doctrines of
Christianity and science.

The Attack against Intellectualism

To disarm the professional scientists and clergy and to diminish
their pernicious influence, Butler perceived that he must strike at
their point of crucial agreement. This was the belief that men could
achieve and act upon some form of certain knowledge. While differing as to the means of acquiring that knowledge, they agreed that
once it had been obtained, men could employ it to make reasonable
decisions and to pursue rational actions. Butler denied these propositions. No group of professional men possessed any corner on the
truth, for the simple reason that human beings were incapable of
acquiring, communicating, or acting upon either discursive or revealed knowledge. As he told a correspondent in 1887, "A perfectly
neat system free from any error which has to be distributed as a
tuner distributes his 'wolf' . . . can no more be found than the
circle can be squared. We have to look for the most convenient practical distribution of an initial error that is bound up with the very
fact of our existing consciously at all." [45] Butler played the role of
the ironic subject seeking to persuade his contemporaries that what
they claimed to be truth was in reality taste and what they claimed
to be reasonable actions were actually fortunate judgments based on
illusion. His skepticism was reminiscent of Hume and his relativism
foreshadowed later pragmatists and linguistic skeptics.[46]

44. SB to Dr. Dudgeon, 20 August 1894, in Jones, *Memoir*, 2 : 191.

45. SB to Mr. Opperheim, 28 June 1887, Samuel Butler Papers, British Museum, add.
MSS. 44032, p. 77.

46. L. E. Holt, *Samuel Butler*, p. 152; C. E. M. Joad, *Samuel Butler, 1835–1902*
(London: Leonard Parsons, 1924), pp. 139–45; John Passmore, *A Hundred Years of
Philosophy* (London: Penguin Books, 1968), p. 567.

A correct understanding of man's conscious experience in an evolving or changing world, Butler argued, must begin with a dismissal of the conventional procedures of logical analysis.

> [W]e must begin by flying in the face of every rule that professors of the art of thinking have drawn up for our instruction. These rules may be good enough as servants, but we have let them become the worst of masters, forgetting that philosophy is made for man, not man for philosophy. Logic has been the true Tower of Babel, which we have thought to build so that we might climb up into the heavens, and have no more miracle, but see God and live—nor has confusion of tongues failed to follow on our presumption.

It was little wonder that logic had ended in confusion of tongues. Logic could employ only words, concepts, feelings, and perceptions, which were themselves conventional expediencies. All of these stood at several removes from the unseen kingdom with which "professional truth-tellers" so often confused them.[47]

The problem of communication fascinated Butler as it has numerous philosophers in the twentieth century. Exploring it in terms of painting, music, and writing, he usually reached pessimistic conclusions. "Communication of all kinds," he once suggested, "is like painting—a compromise with impossibilities." Even if communication were possible, language was too frail a vehicle to convey knowledge of either objective or subjective experience. Butler stood at one with Alfred North Whitehead in being "impressed by the inadequacy of language to express our conscious thought, and by the inadequacy of our conscious thought to express our subconscious." At one particularly bleak moment of linguistic despair, Butler scrawled in his notebook, "We want words to do more than they can. We try to do with them what comes to very much like trying to mend a watch with a pickaxe or to paint a miniature with a mop; we expect them to help us to grip and dissect that which in ultimate essence is as ungrippable as shadow." Language, he told the readers of *Life and Habit,* was merely a convention which at best "is but a kind of 'patter,' the only way, it is true, in many cases, of expressing our ideas to one another, but still a very bad way, and not for one moment comparable to the unspoken speech which we may sometimes have recourse to." Words were for Butler mere "creatures of

47. SB, *Luck or Cunning?*, p. 23; Jones, *The Note-Books of Samuel Butler,* p. 222.

our convenience" possessing no "claim to be the actual ideas themselves concerning which we are conversing." [48]

Ideas or concepts were also conventional and no more corresponded to reality than did the words by which men expressed them. In the early 1880s Butler commented, "Men strive after fixed immutable arrangements of ideas much as the French strive after a written constitution, and with much the same result." [49] Concepts with which men interpret their experience were utterly relative arrangements that conformed to ever-changing personal needs and requirements. Butler does not appear to have been thinking in terms of Kantian categories, although he had read some Kant. Rather, he was suggesting, as James Ward would suggest more formally, that subjective factors rather than the objective nature of perceived reality determine human conceptions, and perhaps even human perceptions, of the world.

The clearest discussion of the relativity of concepts (Butler is never perfectly lucid on the topic) is found in his lecture "On the Genesis of Feeling," delivered to a workingman's institute in 1887.[50] Butler explained to his audience that every man, depending upon his profession or particular interests, interpreted the world differently. Consequently, he said, "There are not more stars in heaven than there are worlds of thought within this our own planet, and each one of them, though conducted on the same general principles, requires a modification in the ideas and conceptions of him or her who for the time being enters it." [51]

Butler explained that the particular manner of conceiving an object at any one moment represented "nothing but an arbitrary artificial and conventional connection with the object which it serves to bring before the mind." For example, everyone has an idea of what a stone is. However, that particular image of a stone becomes quite modified if we conceive it as a mass of vibrating molecules.

48. Bartholomew, *Further Extracts from the Note-Books of Samuel Butler*, p. 24; A. N. Whitehead, *Dialogues of Alfred North Whitehead*, ed. Lucien Price (Boston: Little, Brown & Co., 1954), p. 368; Jones, *The Note-Books of Samuel Butler*, p. 94; SB, *Life and Habit*, pp. 67–68.

49. SB, *Collected Essays* (London: Jonathan Cape, 1925), 1 : 164. This statement is taken from a collection of fragments entitled "Life and Habit, Vol. 2," which SB intended to turn into a second volume of *Life and Habit* but did not do so. These notes are an especially good source for books that SB read between 1877 and 1885.

50. Ibid., pp. 185–210.

51. Ibid., p. 189.

But the thing about which we happen to be thinking has not changed. It is we who have seen fit to adopt a new set of ideas in lieu of old ones which we have discarded as inconvenient. And this shows plainly enough, that the ideas we attach to objects have reference to our own convenience rather than the thing itself, and that we can take this or that idea and apply it to this or that object, in whatever manner we find to fit in most comfortably with the arrangements we have already made in respect of our other ideas. If, then, we can modify them at will in later stages, where they come under our ken and can be detected in the act of varying, there is the strongest presumption that will, effort, and deliberation have been essential factors in the formation of the idea from its earliest inception to its most matured form.[52]

All concepts represented varieties of subjectivity and even when set forth by men of science remained conventional arrangements. Things never determined thoughts. In denying that any thought was genuinely disinterested or devoid of the influence of subjective interest, Butler very nearly approximated the existentialist view that all thinking must of necessity be passionate thinking.

Butler did not conclude his analysis when he had reduced the rational concepts of human beings to creatures of subjective convenience. He then considered subjective feelings and denied that they had any necessary correspondence to the objects that aroused them.

What applies to ideas must, as I have already insisted, inevitably apply to the feelings upon which ideas are based, and we should hold that even our most well defined and hereditarily instinctive feelings were in the outset formed, not so much in involuntary, self adjusting, mimetic correspondence with the objects that give rise to them, as by long and arduous development of an originally conventional arrangement of sensation and perception—symbols—caught hold of in the first instance as the only things we could grasp, and applied with as little rhyme or reason as children learning to speak often apply the strange and uncouth sounds which are all they can then utter.[53]

52. Ibid., pp. 200, 204.
53. Ibid., p. 205.

Butler thus turned against the romantic tradition that had considered feelings more indicative of reality than concepts of the discursive understanding. Both human ideas and feelings were expedient, convenient arrangements of sensations and perceptions that through hereditary memory had developed over the generations. They bore no necessary relationship to the reality of things or to the unseen kingdom which lay behind them.

The final basis for Butler's view of the relativity of human knowledge and action was his theory of hereditary memory, which he had expounded in *Life and Habit*.[54] Within his memory each man carried the accumulated experience of all the past generations of his ancestors. He directly perpetuated the personality transmitted through his ancestors and contributed to the further development of that personality through his own experiences. The instinctive actions of children and adults, as well as the unconscious physiological activities of their bodies, were memories from the lives of their ancestors awakened by the association of ideas. Inherited memory equipped men to deal with most of the problems that they would confront during their lives.

Butler's theory resembles Plato's doctrine of reminiscence tied to the currents of contemporary psysiological thought. When a man appeared to be learning, he was actually only remembering. Only when he confronted some situation where direct memory or rearrangements of the elements of his memory failed, did he really learn. However, such learning was not an act of discursive reason or understanding; it was rather an act of blind or illusory faith based upon a necessarily illusory perception of the situation. The person could view the new situation only in terms of the inherited memories that he possessed. However, in an evolving universe, no new situation could exactly resemble a past situation that was retained in the memory.[55]

This theory allowed Butler to strike directly at the enlightenment tradition of reason as the interpreter of life. Scientific naturalism stemmed from that tradition. Butler contended that men not only lacked knowledge of reality but also possessed only an illusory per-

54. This theory had been discussed prior to SB by Edward Herring. SB scrupulously gave credit to Herring. See *Unconscious Memory*, pp. 59–68. Also consult Joad, *Samuel Butler*, pp. 35–45.

55. SB, *Unconscious Memory*, pp. 178–90.

ception of the world of sensations. Even if men limited themselves
to the realm of sense experience, as did the adherents of scientific
naturalism, they still dealt only with illusion.

> We do not sufficiently realize the part which illusion has played
> in our development. One of the prime requisites for evolution
> is a certain power for adaptation to varying circumstances, that
> is to say, of plasticity, bodily and mental. But the power of
> adaptation is mainly dependent on the power of thinking certain
> new things sufficiently like certain others to which we have
> been accustomed for us not to be too much incommoded by
> the change—upon the power, in fact, of mistaking the new for
> the old.

All perceptions that result in action were necessarily illusory perceptions. Butler commented, "Mr. Locke has been greatly praised for
his essay upon human understanding. An essay on human misunderstanding should be no less interesting and important." If at any
given moment men really knew what the world was like, they would
stand paralyzed by the correct conviction that they did not possess
knowledge to deal with it. However, their illusion that the present
exactly resembled the past allowed them to act, to adapt themselves,
and to evolve. Butler explained in *Unconscious Memory:*

> [A]ction is taken in the dark, which sometimes succeeds and
> becomes a fertile source of further combinations; or we are
> brought to a dead stop. All action is random in respect of any
> of the minute actions which compose it that are not done in
> consequence of memory, real or supposed. So that random, or
> action taken in the dark, or illusion, lies at the very root of
> progress.[56]

The illusory development was the result not of reason but of cunning action that represented a form of faith.

The cunning action of living things, whereby they successfully
adapted to their changing environment, was a point of connection
between them and the unseen kingdom.

> Action is the connecting link between the physical and psychical
> worlds; it is a kind of mean proportional between body and

56. SB, *Alps and Sanctuaries* (1881) (London: Jonathan Cape, 1924), p. 26; ibid., p.
27; SB, *Unconscious Memory*, p. 183.

mind; it is the invisible immaterial opinion that belongs to the spiritual world, taking material shape, coming among us, and revealing itself to us in the only way in which we can understand anything about it.[57]

Action originated in the inexplicable core of existing things and among human beings was stimulated by a sense of need, desire, or will. Scientific explanation abstracted action so as to dismiss the very origin of the act. Scientific knowledge and discursive understanding came after the initial illusory action and were post facto explanations or justifications. Butler despised these explanations of action because by their very nature they excluded the influence of the invisible world that touched men who were acting.

Butler not only displayed the strains of Lamarckian thought but also closely approached a position outlined earlier in the century by Ravaisson. In 1838 the latter had written,

Up to that point [the examination of internal consciousness], nature is for us a spectacle that we view only externally. We observe only the exterior action of things; we do not see the disposition any more than the power. In consciousness, on the contrary, it is the same being who acts and who sees the act, or rather the act and the view are mingled. The author of the drama, the actor, the spectator are one. Thus, it is here only that one can hope to ascertain the principle of action.[58]

While no evidence suggests any direct influence of Ravaisson on Butler's thought, the affinity of their ideas and especially their introspective examination of mental activity demonstrate the Euro-

57. SB, *Collected Essays*, 1 : 197. Compare with Whitehead's comment: "Most of what we think or say with our conscious minds and speech is shallow and superficial. Only at rare moments does the deeper and vaster world come through into the conscious thought or expression; they are the memorable moments of our lives, when we feel—when we know—we are being used as instruments of a greater force than ourselves for purposes higher and wider than our own" (Price, *Dialogues of Alfred North Whitehead*, pp. 368–69).

58. Jusque-là, la nature est pour nous un spectacle que nous ne voyons que du dehors. Nous ne voyons des choses que l'extériorité de l'acte; nous ne voyons pas la disposition, non plus que la puissance. Dans la conscience, au contraire, c'est le même être qui agit et qui voit l'act, ou plutôt l'acte et la vue de l'acte se confondent. L'auteur, le drame, l'acteur, le spectateur, ne font qu'un. C'est donc ici seulement qu'on peut espérer de surprendre le principe de l'acte (Felix Ravaisson, *De L'Habitude*, nouvelle edition (Paris: Librairie Felix Alcan, 1927), p. 17).

pean context of Butler's protest against discursive reasoning and the reduction of life to abstract mechanistic explanations.

So much attention has been devoted to Butler's disputes with English writers that his position as a European thinker has been obscured. Its recognition renders Butler a less perplexing figure. Although his most familiar books lampooned English society and religion, his less well-known works included lengthy translations of French and German writers, as well as Homer, and criticism of minor Italian artists. It was not by chance that his ideas bore resemblance to those espoused by Nietzsche and Bergson. They had been nurtured on the same Greek classics, had studied many of the same French and German voluntarist and biological authors, and had rebelled against similar bourgeois mores. However unique Butler may appear in the English setting, his thought and many of its sources were at one with the numerous continental writers of the late romantic tradition who were asserting the primacy of subjective perception and motivation.

For Butler, subjective faith rather than reason guided human beings as they acted to fulfill their inner desires.[59] Reason formulated explanations for action initiated by faith, the pre-reflective basis for all living action. By faith rather than by discursive understanding human beings dealt with the conditions of their existence. For too long men had followed a "will-o'-the-wisp" in their desire for "a single spot of absolutely unassailable ground" based on reason. Butler contended, "We have been penny-wise in the matter of risk, and prove pound-foolish in the end; we have tried to get rid of faith altogether as involving uncertainty, and, behold, when our faith was dead, our reason was dead also." [60] Henry Sidgwick had reached a similar conclusion during his mental crisis of 1887. James Ward would turn such an insight into one of the key features of his psychology. This view of the intrinsic interdependence of reason and instinctive faith liberated Butler from the professional truth-tellers who interpreted life by dead doctrines or abstract formulae.

In light of the illusory nature of all forms of truth and the impossibility of separating reason and faith, Butler once posed the ques-

59. For SB's ponderings on reason and faith, see *Collected Essays*, 1 : 101–83, and *Alps and Sanctuaries*, pp. 87–88.
60. SB, *Collected Essays*, 1 : 152.

tion of who could act as guides to life. "Who are these now?" he demanded. "The clergy? Hardly. Men of science? Still less. The ordinary 'good fellow', in the best of the more common interpretations of the words, he is the only one worth considering." Butler discovered in the common sense of "the ordinary good fellow" the guidance that Wallace sought from the spirits, Myers from a certainty of immortality, Sidgwick from philosophy, and Romanes from a combination of science and religion. Once the nature of truth was recognized, men could never again docilely follow professional intellectual or spiritual guides. Each man must come to the conclusion that dawned upon Ernest Pontifex in his jail cell, where he had been imprisoned on a false charge of assault. The bewildered young man realized that there were no perfect rules for discerning truth or guiding life. He finally understood that

> the rules which governed them were sometimes so subtle, that mistakes always had and always would be made; it was just this that made it impossible to reduce life to an exact science. There was a rough-and-ready rule-of-thumb test of truth, and a number of rules as regards exceptions which could be mastered without much trouble, yet there was a residue of cases in which decision was difficult—so difficult that a man had better follow his instinct than attempt to decide them by any process of reasoning. Instinct then is the ultimate court of appeal. And what is instinct? It is a mode of faith in the evidence of things not actually seen. And so my hero returned almost to the point from which he had started originally, namely that the just shall live by faith.[61]

The inherited experiences of numberless generations that each man carried within himself was his surest guide. To follow that guide was an act of objectively uncertain faith in the futurity residing in man himself and ultimately in the universe. It was a Pelagian faith that rejected original sin. Rather than bearing within himself the seeds of his self-condemnation, man carried within his being his own salvation wrought by the cunning faith of ages past and by his own present faith.

Butler asked the men of professional religion and science to adopt this faith and the intellectual modesty it nurtured. So long as they

61. Bartholomew, *Further Extracts from the Note-Books of Samuel Butler*, p. 26; SB, *The Way of All Flesh*, p. 246.

expressed themselves modestly and in recognition that they possessed no final truth, professional men might aid their fellow human beings' passage through life. That men could speak only through conventions was no reason for them to cease speaking, but it was good reason for them to cease speaking dogmatically. In place of absolute truth all men should aim "at the greatest coming-togetherness or convenience of all our ideas and practices; that is to say, at their most harmonious working with one another." Men who so guided their own and others' lives provided examples of the "man of temper." This creature "will be certain in spite of uncertainty, and at the same time uncertain in spite of certainty; reasonable in spite of his resting mainly upon faith rather than reason, and full of faith even when appealing most strongly to reason." [62]

Toward a Comfortable Nihilism

It was as a man of temper that Butler traversed the passage between "the Scylla of Atheism and the Charybdis of Christianity" into a metaphysical calm of comfortable nihilism.[63] His speculations tended toward nihilism because he denied the validity and meaningfulness of the Christian and scientific interpretations of reality and by implication all logical, abstract systems. However, his nihilism was tempered, comfortable, and comforting. It was tempered in that Butler did not deny that meaning existed in the universe, but rather that human beings could perceive or communicate that meaning. This view was comfortable because in the absence of absolute truth about the world, men were free to devise their own norms whereby they might personally liberate themselves from the conventions of determinism and death associated with both Christianity and scientific naturalism. This tempered nihilism was comforting because it saved Butler from self-condemnation for his failure to make his way in Victorian society and afforded him a means of subjective liberation from its inhibiting and life-smothering social and intellectual modes of thought. As an old acquaintance wrote, "Butler's emancipated intellect had won for his soul and sense a freedom which he wished to share with others; he had as it were acquired a freedom to be on good terms with himself." [64]

62. Jones, *The Note-Books of Samuel Butler*, p. 310; SB, *Alps and Sanctuaries*, p. 88 (see also *Collected Essays*, 1 : 127–28); SB, *Alps and Sanctuaries*, p. 88.
63. Bartholomew, *Further Extracts from the Note-Books of Samuel Butler*, p. 268.
64. J. B. Yeats, *Essays Irish and American*, p. 13.

In an unpublished fragment from his notebook, copied in 1896 but probably written in 1884 or 1885, Butler reflected:

> Substance, feeling, motion, or if the reader prefers to omit the first two commas, substance feeling motion—that is the ultimate three-in-one of our life; or rather it would be, if there did not lie behind them something still more incomprehensible—that is none of them but enters into them all—a something which is as the spirit of God walking upon the face of the waters.

The conviction of the presence of that haunting "something still more incomprehensible" saved Butler from complete nihilism. He never claimed to know what the "something" was, but he considered it the source of all life, all memory, and all existence. Belief in this "something" exacerbated his hostility to both Christianity and scientific naturalism. The church had attempted to incarcerate the presence in creeds and doctrines; the leaders of naturalism had ignored it. Butler always considered the latter course the more reprehensible. As Ernest Pontifex concluded, "The spirit behind the church is true though her letter—true once—is now true no longer. The spirit behind the Huxleys and Tyndalls is as lying as its letter." [65] To ignore the existence of the "something still more incomprehensible" amounted to blasphemy.[66]

Though Butler was not an existentialist, his musings over the nature of man's existence and of the "something" behind that existence were often suggestive of ideas later associated with existentialism. Moral, intellectual, physical, and metaphysical essences were absent from his world of thought. Existence itself preceded all conventions whether they were physical laws, moral rules, or intellectual concepts. Conventions originated in the existential needs and desires of existing consciousnesses—entities that Butler never attempted to define. Objective reality and man's perception of that reality were the products of the development or the striving of these conscious-

65. SB, Manuscript Note-Books, Williams College, 2 : 196 (this passage was cut from *Luck or Cunning?* and thus was probably written about 1884); SB, *The Way of All Flesh*, p. 334.

66. "I begin to understand what Christ meant when he said that blasphemy against the Holy Ghost was unforgiveable, while speaking against the Son of Man might be forgiven. He must have meant that a man may be pardoned for being unable to believe in the Christian mythology, but that if he made light of that spirit which the common conscience of all men, whatever their particular creed, recognizes as divine, there was no hope for him. No more there is" (Jones, *The Note-Books of Samuel Butler,* p. 348).

nesses to fulfill their needs and desires. Although by memory each living entity carried much of its nature into the universe, only in action with existing circumstances did its essence emerge as the result of the combination of inheritance and cunning. Moreover, there was nothing in Butler's writings to suggest that he believed the presence behind reality itself had any essence. In fact most of what he said in regard to that "something" would lead one to think that it simply created its own essence as did every existing being. Finally, Butler's general attack upon the confusion of convention and reality reflected his desire to probe existence itself and to peer behind the rules and laws of life to their very source. Butler stood among those men of existential passion who, in the words of Paul Tillich, have sought "to protect us from the annihilation of the 'creative Source' by an 'objective world' which was created out of that 'Source' but which is now swallowing it like a monstrous mechanism." [67] Butler was determined to oppose "the present mindless, mechanical, materialistic view of nature" that confused allegedly objective reality with the unseen kingdom.[68]

Butler discovered a comfortable manner of viewing the universe—one that acknowledged the presence of the unseen kingdom through Lamarckian evolution, a near-pantheist view of God, and panpsychism. Through each of these he assumed an ironic stance toward contemporary religion and scientific naturalism. As he explained in 1886 in regard to *Luck or Cunning?*:

> Orthodox the book is not, religious I do verily believe and hope it is: . . . and though I know very well that churchmen will not like it, I am sure they will like it much better than they like the opinions now most generally accepted, and that they will like it much better than men of science will.

Butler's repudiation of the validity of abstract logical systems allowed him to play fast and free in combining ideas that clergymen and scientists usually regarded as contradictory or mutually self-exclusive.

> I know that contradiction in terms lurks within much that I have said, but the texture of the world is a warp and woof of contradiction in terms; of continuity in discontinuity, and dis-

67. Paul Tillich, *Theology of Culture* (New York: Oxford University Press, 1968), p. 96.

68. SB to Mrs. A. Tylor, 17 October 1886, in Jones, *Memoir*, 2 : 41.

continuity in continuity; of unity in diversity, and of diversity in unity. As in the development of a fugue, where, when the subject and counter subject have been enounced, there must henceforth be nothing new, and yet all must be new, so throughout organic life—which is as a fugue developed to a great length from a very simple subject.[69]

Butler was an amateur musician and often employed musical metaphors. He believed that logical analysis of a single naked fact could tell no more about it than the analysis of a single tone, abstracted from a chord and from the preceding and following chords, could explain the nature and function of that sound. In the cosmic fugue Butler heard the verbally inexpressible but harmonious development of subject and counter-subject—creation and evolution, God and nature, mind and matter, life and death. The elements in each pair were so intrinsically related that neither could exist without the other.[70]

Once having realized the conventional nature of scientific theory, Butler rejected natural selection as a life-suffocating convention that foreclosed the possibility of a "cunning" life. He turned to the Lamarckian alternative just as he had chosen Pelagianism over the determinism of original sin. Butler's biological and moral Lamarckianism illustrates one of the neglected features of late nineteenth-century thought. While Darwin did apparently persuade the world that evolution had occurred, he did not convince it or eventually even himself that natural selection had been the sole evolutionary mechanism. In the post-1859 evolutionary debates, Lamarckianism, or what was so termed, probably enjoyed as many adherents and almost as much influence on popular thought as natural selection. This alternative to the mechanism suggested by Darwin and Wallace was associated with the tenets that organs or modes of action develop through a sense of perceived need and through persistent use and that characteristics so acquired can be inherited.

In the late editions of the *Origin of Species* Darwin himself edged toward inheritance of acquired characteristics in regard to certain

69. Ibid., p. 41; SB, *Luck or Cunning?*, p. 234.

70. SB's metaphysical musings fit into those of a group of men writing in the 1860s and 1870s who sought to reconcile mechanism with the existence of mind in nature. See James Hinton, *Life in Nature* (London: Smith, Elder, & Co., 1862); J. J. Murphy, *Habit and Intelligence* (London: Macmillan & Co., 1869); and J. A. Picton, *The Mystery of Matter* (London: Macmillan & Co., 1873).

issues. George Romanes went so far as to criticize Wallace for term-
ing strict adherence to natural selection "Darwinism." It is also
significant that Butler incurred the wrath of professional scientists
for questioning Darwin's integrity rather than for questioning his
theory. Many of the next generation of English biologists, including
Francis Darwin, were neo-Lamarckians. Spencer, Peirce, Nietzsche,
Bergson, Shaw, and Freud bear as many or more traces of Lamarckian ideas as of Darwinian traits. Moreover, voluntarists and twentieth-century existentialist thinkers hold an essentially Lamarckian
position. However much Lamarck's and Butler's biology may now
stand discredited, the substance of Butler's thought was by no
means wholly outside a contemporary intellectual mainstream.[71]

Butler embraced Lamarckianism because it seemed to set the
origin of evolution at the core of existence itself. In *Life and Habit*
he had argued that all conscious and unconscious knowledge or
facile action, if traced to its source, would lead to

> little more than a sound of "going", as it were, in the brain, a
> flitting to and fro of something barely recognizable as the desire
> to will or know at all—much less as the desire to know or will
> definitely this or that. Finally, they retreat beyond our ken into
> the repose—the inorganic kingdom—of as yet unawakened in-
> terest.[72]

In the awakening of such inarticulate interest lay the origin of the
evolving conventions of organic life. All existing organic forms had
resulted from primal psychic activity that fulfilled this interest and
primitive will.

71. G. Cannon, *Lamarck and Modern Genetics* (Manchester: Manchester University Press, 1959); C. C. Gillispie, "Lamarck and Darwin in the History of Science," in *Forerunners of Darwin*, ed. B. Glass, O. Temkin, W. L. Strauss, Jr. (Baltimore: The Johns Hopkins Press, 1967), pp. 265–91; M. J. S. Hodge, "Lamarck's Science of Living Bodies," *British Journal for the History of Science* 5 (1970–1971): 323–52; John C. Greene, *The Death of Adam* (New York: Mentor Books, 1961), pp. 160–67; Loren Eiseley, *Darwin's Century*, pp. 48–52, 200–01, 217, 252; Peter J. Vorzimmer, *Charles Darwin: The Years of Controversy, The Origin of Species and Its Critics, 1859–1882* (Philadelphia: Temple University Press, 1970), pp. 27–40, 254–61; "Inaugural Address by Francis Darwin," *Nature* 78 (1908): 416–24; Vernon L. Kellogg, *Darwinism Today* (New York: H. Holt & Co., 1907), pp. 262–74; Walter Kaufman, *Nietzsche: Philosopher, Psychologist, Antichrist*, 3rd ed. (New York: The Viking Press, 1968), pp. 293–95; Philip R. Rief, *Freud: The Mind of the Moralist* (Garden City, N.Y.: Doubleday, 1961), pp. 218–22; Philip P. Wiener, *Evolution and the Founders of Pragmatism* (New York: Harper Torchbooks, 1965), p. 78.
72. SB, *Life and Habit*, pp. 15–16.

Once again Butler unwittingly echoed the ideas of Ravaisson and foreshadowed those of later French voluntarist writers. In a similar vein, Ravaisson had contended,

> Voluntary movement has not only its matter and substance but also its origin and source in desire. Desire is a primordial instinct, in which the purpose of action is mixed with the actor, the idea with the realization, the thought with the burst of spontaneity. It is the condition of nature; it is *nature* itself.[73]

For both writers, such a concept of action spelled the collapse of either purposeless or wholly deterministic development. Nature to its very core was cunning. Through Lamarckianism and a general voluntarism Butler envisioned a world without fixed entities in which all living things, at least in part, created their own essence from the circumstances of their existence. Such evolution was self-determining action in touch with the unseen kingdom.

Evolution that stemmed from the fulfillment of primitive desire was teleological. While there existed no overall organic design, each successive step originated in a microteleological impulse. Inherited memory assured that each purposive step would become cumulative and that a succession of deterministic cycles would not ensue.

> If there had been no such memory, the amoeba of one generation would have exactly resembled the amoeba of the preceding, and a perfect cycle would have been established; the modifying effects of an additional memory in each generation have made the cycle into a spiral, and into a spiral whose eccentricities, in the outset hardly perceptible, are becoming greater and greater with increasing longevity and more complex social and mechanical inventions.[74]

This memory was not supernatural; it inhered in nature. Nature would not be nature without it. This ever-present memory and the

---

73. Le mouvement volontaire n'a donc pas seulement sa matière, sa substance, mais son origine et sa source dans le désir. Le désir est un instinct primordial, dans lequel le but de l'acte est confondu avec l'acte, l'idée avec la réalisation, la pensée avec l'élan de la spontanéité; c'est l'état de nature, c'est la *nature* même (Ravaisson, *De L'Habitude*, p. 43).

74. SB, *Unconscious Memory*, p. 192.

teleological impulses behind evolutionary change assured Butler of a progressive, noncyclical evolution in the same way that the presence of spirits assured Wallace of man's continued spiritual progress and that faith in God assured James Ward that man might fulfill his ideals.

Butler believed this concept of evolution proved the process to be creative and nature to be nonmechanical. In *Luck or Cunning?* Butler quoted Claude Bernard's statement, *"Rien ne nait, rien ne se crée, tout se continue. La nature ne nous offre le spectacle d'aucune création, elle est d'une éternelle continuation."* Considering this view as only one side of the situation, Butler contended that Bernard might just as well have said, *"Rien ne se continue, tout nait, tout se crée. La nature ne nous offre le spectacle d'aucune continuation. Elle est d'une éternelle création;* for change is no less patent a fact than continuity, and, indeed, the two stand or fall together." [75] As each organism incorrectly perceived its present condition in terms of inherited memory and applied that memory, creation occurred. Once assimilated into the memory, these creative actions came to appear as natural law. They were never perfectly uniform or eternal for in the future the same kind of evolutionary modification would change them.

Only the achievement of this view of evolution provided for a satisfactory idea of God.[76] *God,* like all other words or concepts, was a convention, but a highly useful one.

> What can approach more nearly to a rendering of that which cannot be rendered—the idea of an essence omnipresent in all things at all times everywhere in sky and earth and sea; ever changing, yet the same yesterday, to-day, and forever; the ineffable contradiction in terms whose presence none can either ever enter, or ever escape? Or rather, what convention would have been more apt if it had not been lost sight of as a convention and come to be regarded as an idea in actual correspondence with a more or less knowable reality? A convention was converted into a fetish, and now that its worthlessness as a fetish is being generally felt, its great value as a hieroglyph or convention is in danger of being lost sight of.

75. SB, *Luck or Cunning?*, p. 22.
76. SB, *Collected Essays,* 1 : 39–40.

Butler hoped once more to render God into a valuable symbol that would confound both the fetishism of Christianity and the negativism of scientific naturalism. As a convention, God should express "our sense that there is an unseen world with which we in some mysterious way come into contact, though the writs of our thoughts do not run within it—used in this way, the idea and the word have been found enduringly convenient." [77] The convention of God reminded men of the unseen source of their life. Lamarckian evolution, based on primal psychic need, explained how God immanently permeated all living things.

Butler devoted his fullest attention to the problem of God in 1879 when he published a series of essays in the *Examiner* on "God the Known and God the Unknown." No single work by Butler has been more misunderstood, misinterpreted, and misconstrued by his admirers. This unfortunate situation came about because the essays, when republished after his death, were read in a totally different intellectual context from that in which Butler had composed them.[78] He wrote the articles when the protoplasmic theory of life was widely discussed in books, journals, and lectures. Naturalistic authors employed the theory to uphold a materialistic philosophy and to prove the absence of any necessity for a divine or supernatural source of life.[79]

During the 1870s Butler accepted the protoplasmic theory and believed that life and mind existed only where protoplasm was present. However, in 1879, totally disillusioned with both the clergy and the scientists, he wrote these essays to suggest to the consterna-

---

77. SB, *Luck or Cunning?*, pp. 115, 235.

78. SB, *God the Known and God the Unknown* (1879) (London: A. C. Fifield, 1909). These essays were first published as a single work thirty years after they had been written. The reviewers read the articles as an example of a humanistic, liberal theology. This was particularly the case when they were reprinted in the United States by Yale University Press, in 1917. For example, see Moreby Acklom, "Samuel Butler the Third: A Theological Rebel," *The Constructive Quarterly* 5 (1917): 194–95, and Felix Grendon, "Samuel Butler's God," *North American Review* 20 (1918): 277–88. Later scholars, however, who could have had easy access to SB's other books, particularly *Luck or Cunning?*, in which he explained the circumstances of the essays, also appear to be unaware of the protoplasmic atmosphere of the 1870s. See Clara Stillman, *Samuel Butler: A Mid-Victorian Modern* (New York: Viking Press, 1932), pp. 206–12; Holt, *Samuel Butler*, pp. 116–17, and T. A. Goudge, "Samuel Butler," *The Encyclopedia of Philosophy* (New York: Macmillan Co. and The Free Press, 1967), 1 : 435.

79. Gerald L. Geison, "The Protoplasmic Theory of Life and the Vitalist-Mechanical Debate," *Isis* 60 (1969) : 273–92.

tion of the materialists that their protoplasmic theory might provide a very useful concept of God. The articles were a characteristically ironic gesture. As he later explained his strategy:

> I pointed out another consequence, which, again, was cruelly the reverse of what the promoters of the protoplasm movement might be supposed anxious to arrive at, in a series of articles which appeared in the *Examiner* during the summer of 1879, and showed that if protoplasm were held to be the sole seat of life, then this unity of the substance vivifying all, both animals and plants, must be held as uniting them into a single corporation or body. . . . This came practically to saying that protoplasm was God Almighty, who, of all the forms open to Him, had chosen this singularly unattractive one as the channel through which to make Himself manifest in the flesh by taking our nature upon Him, and animating us with His own Spirit.[80]

Butler believed his argument would prove equally painful to the clergy since the last thing they wanted was a material God.

Butler contended the pantheist's God possessed body but no personality and the theist's God, a personality but no body. The truly knowable God, possessing both personality and body, must exist in "a single God-impregnate substance" that was "the parent from which all living forms have sprung." This God was "one spirit, and one form capable of such modification as its directing spirit shall think fit; one soul and one body, one God and one Life." [81] Such a God was the living spirit of the animal and vegetable world. Protoplasm itself was God—possessing both body and personality.[82]

In accordance with his life-and-habit theory, Butler considered the best indication of personality to be memory and the best indication of memory to be the ability to do things unconsciously. The unconscious operations and development of the organic world provided evidence of such a personality and memory.

> The memories which all living forms prove by their actions that they possess—the memories of their common identity with a single person in whom they meet—this is incontestable proof of

80. SB, *Luck or Cunning?*, p. 111. See also SB, *Collected Essays*, 1 : 176.
81. SB, "God the Known and God the Unknown," in *Collected Essays*, 1 : 30.
82. Ibid., pp. 30–31.

> their being animated by a common soul. . . . It is in this Per-
> son that we may see the Body of God—and in the evolution of
> this Person, the mystery of His Incarnation.[83]

Each living form was but one part of the greater body of God in the
same manner that each living cell is the living part of the larger
living organism.

Butler suggested that his God—organic nature—operated by what
appeared to be uniform laws because throughout His body He was
remembering actions acquired in His earlier existence. Moreover,
this Known God might Himself be but one element in the life of a
greater organism—the Unknown God. If the Known God were
evolving into this higher entity, the final effect of His evolution
would be a creative and indeterminate spiral rather than a determined cycle.

Not only was the Known God one such as the materialist hoped
to escape, but He was a better God than the theist hoped to keep.
Unlike the far-off transcendent God of the theologian who occupied
the position of an oriental despot, the Known God could be truly
loved and meaningfully worshipped.

> [W]e enthrone Him upon the wings of birds, on the petals of
> flowers, on the faces of our friends, and upon whatever we most
> delight in of all that lives upon the earth. We then can not only
> love Him, but we can do that without which love has neither
> power nor sweetness, but is a phantom only, an impersonal
> person, a vain stretching forth of arms towards something that
> can never fill them—we can express our love and have it ex-
> pressed to us in return. And this not in the uprearing of stone
> temples—for the Lord dwelleth in temples made with other
> organs than hands—nor yet in the cleansing of our hearts, but
> in the caress bestowed upon horse and dog, and kisses upon the
> lips of those we love.[84]

Such a God the man of temper could worship in every act of his life
and dwell with in perfect convenience and harmony.[85]

These essays were all in fun, a spoof against the men of science. Or

83. Ibid., p. 35.
84. Ibid., pp. 37–38.
85. SB suggested that men know three realms of life—that below the highly
organized level, the organized level culminating in man, and the life of the Known
God, which is the collectivity of all organic life. He then argued that the Known God

were they? The purpose of the articles was certainly ironic and satirical. The actual content less so. Butler did want to revivify the convention of God. The concept of God developed in the essays would serve that function for the time being.[86] In *Erewhon Revisited* Butler approved the Sayings of the Sunchild that represented his final comment on the deity and a departure from the 1879 essays. The Sunchild spoke of God as "the baseless basis of all thoughts, things and deeds" that lived in every atom of the universe. He was "God to us only so long as we cannot see Him." This God provided the instinct of the universe, and his conscious life reached its earthly maturity in man alone. Indeed, God depended upon man, "as man cannot live without God in the world, so neither can God live in this world without mankind." [87] Butler's final thought represented an attempt to suggest the presence of a limited God who required the free cooperation of man in the evolution of the world. This view of God closely resembled the concept of Myers's World Soul, Romanes's Superconscious, and the God described by James Ward in *The Realm of Ends*.

Butler had been compelled to extend the presence of God from the organic world alone to the entire universe because less than a year after completing *God the Known and God the Unknown,* he decided the protoplasmic theory was invalid. In 1880 he embraced a panpsychic view of nature whereby he regarded life and mind as present in all existing things.[88] In 1880, nearing the conclusion of *Unconscious Memory,* he advised his readers "to see every atom in the universe as living and able to feel and to remember, but in a humble way." He declared that man "must have life eternal, as well as matter eternal; and the life and the matter must be joined together inseparably as body and soul to one another." [89] This idea extended the presence of mind and God throughout nature. Logically, Butler should probably have become a pantheist. Yet since logic was rarely

---

himself might be but one element of an even greater life or organism—The Unknown God. If the Known God were evolving into this higher entity, the final effect of His evolution would be creative. SB did not develop his concept of the Unknown God any further (ibid., pp. 46–50).

86. Jones, *Memoir,* 1 : 407; SB, *Luck or Cunning?,* pp. 114–15, 234–35.

87. SB, *Erewhon Revisited* (1901) (London: Jonathan Cape, 1925), pp. 150–51.

88. SB, *Collected Essays,* 1 : 35–36; *Evolution Old and New,* pp. 321–52; Jones, *Memoir,* 1 : 302–03; R. F. Rattray, "The Philosophy of Samuel Butler," *Mind* 23 (1914) : 371–85; Paul Edwards, "Panpsychism," *Encyclopedia of Philosophy,* 6 : 22–31.

89. SB, *Unconscious Memory,* p. 194.

a concern for him, he still abjured pantheism but never explained exactly how.[90]

Panpsychism attracted Butler because it allowed him to avoid psychophysical parallelism and epiphenomenalism as well as an adventitious mind directing nature.[91] The former ideas smacked of the determinism of materialism and the latter of the determinism of theology. Panpsychism permitted him to conceive matter and mind in a perfectly intimate union. "Mind is not a thing or, if it be, we know nothing about it; it is a function of matter. Matter is not a thing or, if it be, we know nothing about it; it is a function of mind." Yet Butler recognized, at least occasionally, that mind and matter probably inhered in a third substance and that a monistic determinism still hung over him. However, he interpreted his panpsychism to combine the monism of substance with a pluralism of ends.

> Complex mind involves complex matter and vice versa. On the whole I think it would be most convenient to endow all atoms with a something of consciousness and volition, and to hold them to be *pro tanto,* living. We must suppose them able to remember and forget, i.e. to retain certain vibrations that have been once established—gradually to lose them and to receive others instead. We must suppose some more intelligent, versatile and of greater associative power than others.[92]

90. Jones wrote, "He often spoke of his religion as 'a modest Pantheism,' and, if he had rewritten the articles, I think the re-casting would have been confined to showing in what way his idea of Pantheism differed from that usually underlying the word; and to his pointing out that, although we cannot see the bowl and the water as part of the goldfish, yet that their material is not without intelligence, and that God, who is Life, is in everything" (*Memoir,* 1 : 303).

91. There are at least three possible sources for SB's modification of opinion. First, he had read Diderot and had become acquainted with the philosopher's view of life as residing in matter. Second, he may have come to this conclusion from reading books by the English aural surgeon James Hinton, who suggested that no genuine division separated the organic and the inorganic worlds. Hinton argued that only the limitations of human perception accounted for the traditional separation of the two realms. SB had read Hinton's *Life in Nature.* A passage in SB's notebook suggests this influence. A final possible source was the poetry of Walt Whitman, whom SB admired. He once considered using a line of Whitman's poetry on the activity of all nature as an epigraph. Whichever of these was the source of his new opinion, it is important to realize that SB was not alone in his panpsychical convictions nor a pioneer in their discussion. See Jones, *Memoir,* 1 : 268–70, 333; SB, *Collected Essays,* 1 : 158; Jones, *The Note-Books of Samuel Butler,* p. 179.

92. Jones, *The Note-Books of Samuel Butler,* pp. 67, 73.

Butler would seem to be saying that life can never be reduced to atoms and energy. The vibrations retained by individual atoms would seem to be akin to the vibrations of a musical chord and susceptible to the influence of other chords and tones. Its uniqueness was not in its substance but in its mode of vibration. A universe composed of such matter was capable of learning and retaining what it had learned. Its evolution could be progressive, cumulative, and self-determining.

What Butler's ideas lacked in philosophical rigor they made up for by the convenience they afforded him in confronting life and death.[93] Death represented the most telling argument against a universe of mind, purpose, and creative evolution. Butler did not, however, despair. His universe was essentially a Stoic one, just as his morality was essentially Epicurean. All parts of the cosmos were in one manner or another alive and partook of the Divine. In such a universe Butler saw the possibility of immortality and even a mode of resurrection.

He conceived a threefold immortality. First, men are immortal through the memory they have passed to their offspring. Second, immortality may be achieved by men whose lives, thoughts, and deeds come to live in and inspire the lives of other men.[94] Finally, Butler declared that there could be no death in a universe of creative life. The living matter of our bodies reentered the universe at large. However, since that matter had gained new qualities by participating in our organism, it came to enrich the quality of the universe. Though our personal consciousness was dissolved, its constituent parts lived in the ever-evolving grandeur of the living universe and might again in the future enter into a human consciousness. As Butler confidently penned in his notebook, "Life is the gathering of waves to a head, at death they break into a million fragments each one of which, however, is absorbed at once into the sea of life and helps to form a later generation which comes rolling on till it too breaks." [95]

Indeed, for Butler death represented nothing more than "the most inexorable of all conventions" of human existence.[96] Life and death

93. SB pondered death throughhout his life and in his books. See *Life and Habit*, pp. 44, 76–79; *Unconscious Memory*, pp. 138–39, 162–63; *Luck or Cunning?*, pp. 56–58, 127–29; Jones, *The Note-Books of Samuel Butler*, pp. 358–59.
94. Jones, *The Note-Books of Samuel Butler*, pp. 13–15.
95. Ibid., p. 15.
96. SB, *Life and Habit*, p. 44.

were but "the extreme modes of something which is partly both and wholly neither." Death possessed no more ultimate reality or authority for Butler than any other human convention that simplified human existence.

> If there is one thing which advancing knowledge makes clearer than another, it is that death is swallowed up in life, and life in death; so that if the last enemy that shall be subdued is death, then indeed is our salvation nearer than we thought, for in strictness there is neither life nor death, nor thought nor thing, except as figures of speech, and as the approximations which strike us for the time as most convenient.

That death was nothing more than a chord in the "infinite harmonics of life" was the final conclusion of Samuel Butler's journey between religion and science.[97] By asserting the conventional nature of all human experience, he disembarked into a comfortable nihilism that affirmed man's inalienable relationship to the unseen kingdom and the source of his existence.

Butler pursued his ideas with little philosophic rigor and even less system. Except for his novels, his books were of patchwork construction. Systematic or logical development stood at odds with his message. Only by comparing his various statements written in different places and at different moments of his life does the full dimension of his analysis emerge. While Butler came upon his insights haphazardly and usually at the expense of those contemporaries whom he hated, another English writer, James Ward, was carefully and systematically reasoning his way to conclusions strikingly similar to Butler's. Paradoxically, while Butler's ideas and style made him anathema to the intellectual establishment, Ward's philosophy earned him a respected position within English and transatlantic intellectual circles. Yet that achievement came relatively late in Ward's life and in fact only after he had left one life behind him.

97. SB, *Luck or Cunning?*, pp. 57, 58, 59.

8

James Ward: Psychologist of Faith and Freedom

ONE AGAINST THE DEVIL

One night late in 1870 shouts emanated from the room of a visitor to Spring Hill College, a Congregationalist school near Birmingham. Cries of struggle climaxed as raps from a broken chair leg reverberated against the door. Students, awakened by the din, hastened to the room and discovered the dazed inhabitant trembling with a smashed knuckle and a bruised foot acquired in his encounter with an intruder. The harried combatant was twenty-seven-year-old James Ward, a former Spring Hill student who had recently returned from study in Germany and who was about to accept a pastorate in Cambridge. His opponent in this nocturnal melee had been the devil.[1]

Forty-four years after the bout at Spring Hill College, James Ward, Professor of Mental Philosophy and Logic at Cambridge University, stood before a group of friends and admirers gathered to witness the presentation of his portrait to the university. Responding to the honor, Ward told his audience:

> I do not say that without this expression of your approval and goodwill I should have felt self-condemned. I believe in philosophy, though Cambridge as a whole doesn't or didn't. I know that philosophy can bake no bread, but I know too that man does not live by bread alone, and I believe that philosophy ministers to higher needs than science ever can. So I have worked loyally and whole-heartedly in the service of this ancient queen of the sciences, though I have had to share the contempt till lately accorded to her in this place.[2]

1. Olwen Ward Campbell, "Memoir," in James Ward, *Essays in Philosophy*, ed. W. R. Sorley and G. F. Stout (Cambridge: Cambridge University Press, 1927), pp. 38–39. Hereafter cited as Campbell, "Memoir." James Ward hereafter cited in footnotes as JW.
2. Ibid., p. 92.

In the duration between the struggle with the devil and this confession of faith in philosophy, James Ward had abandoned the nonconformist ministry and the Christian faith. He had turned away from a promising career in physiology and led a new departure in English psychology. Almost single-handedly he had destroyed the philosophical pretensions of Victorian scientific naturalism and had attempted to set forth a metaphysics that originated in empirical experience and pointed to a distant apprehension of God. The mature James Ward, who conversed with Russell, Moore, McTaggart, Broad, and Whitehead, wrestled no less zealously with the devil of naturalism than he had with the devil of Spring Hill College. The former devil symbolized a barrier to man's realization of his higher self; the latter a determinism that prevented man from fulfilling the will of God.

Like Mark Rutherford, James Ward embodied "the Puritan spirit adrift in the Age of Agnosticism." [3] He was born 27 January 1843 into one of those nonconformist households representative of the stark piety that Matthew Arnold derided for fostering "churches without great men, and without furtherance for the higher life of humanity." Ward's childhood was typical of the midcentury nonconformist life, marked by active weeks ending with the gloomy Sabbath of preaching, prayers, and cold supper. The two primary interests of these puritan descendants—"the concern for making money, and the concern for saving . . . souls"—figured prominently in Ward's early years.[4] His father futilely pursued the former only to declare bankruptcy on more than one occasion. The latter was the younger Ward's special province.

Arminianism had been growing among Congregationalists during the nineteenth century.[5] While relieving them of the tensions surrounding the doctrine of predestination, the new view nevertheless introduced the constant question of whether one's self, friends, and family had truly affirmed faith in Christ. Uncertainty of faith replaced uncertainty of election. While in his early twenties Ward expressed such anxiety about an aunt suffering from a terminal illness.

3. Basil Willey, *More Nineteenth Century Studies* (New York: Harper Torchbooks, 1966), pp. 186–87. For the general background of English Congregationalism, see R. W. Dale, *History of English Congregationalism*, 2nd ed. (London: Hodder & Stoughton, 1907).

4. Matthew Arnold, *Culture and Anarchy*, ed. J. Dover Wilson (Cambridge: Cambridge University Press, 1961), pp. 29, 157.

5. Dale, *History of English Congregationalism*, pp. 699–709.

I saw Aunt S. on Saturday for a little while. Her mind is very dark and she is in no way fit to die, though indeed she is sinking fast and cannot last long. Her one word for God is the Almighty; of the work of Christ she knows nothing; her only business she supposes is to be patient and "pray to the Almighty to take" her; she does not think she is condemned because she has no fear. Real sorrow for sin she has none, she does not trust Christ, she does not love God, at least as far as I can see. A despairing look gleamed from her eyes once or twice when I endeavoured to point out the lost state of all without Christ and referred to him as the Rock of Ages.[6]

While working as an architect in the early 1860s, this devout nephew continued to labor for the salvation of souls by teaching Sunday school. In 1863 his zeal for Christ got the better of him, and Ward decided to enter the ministry.

His delighted family prepared to make the necessary financial sacrifice to send him to Spring Hill College.[7] As with so many other men studying for the Christian ministry during those years, it was to be Ward's faith, as well as family savings, that was sacrificed. His faith altered slowly but steadily during the years at Spring Hill. Liberal influences had entered the college during the 1860s. Therefore, Ward received more sympathy from his mentors than had Mark Rutherford at a different school; but the demise of belief was no less certain.[8] The deciding factors were the higher criticism and unspecified philosophical doubts about immortality. Ward replaced his orthodoxy with a liberal religious ideal that seems to have owed much to Matthew Arnold.[9]

Doctrinal difficulties did not, however, dissuade Ward from his calling. Like Arnold, he seems to have felt for a time that the minister must lead the congregation toward a new conception of the faith. His personal capacity for "warmth," "imagination," and "sermonizing tact enough for a preacher" disturbed Ward more than his want of orthodoxy. In 1867 he told his father:

6. Campbell, "Memoir," p. 18.

7. Spring Hill College in 1890 transferred to Oxford and became part of Mansfield College. See *The Congregational Year Book 1863* (London: Jackson, Walford, & Hodder, 1863), p. 280, and R. W. Dale, "The History of Spring Hill College," in *Mansfield College, Oxford: Its Origin and Opening* (London: J. Clarke & Co., 1890), pp. 3–28.

8. Willey, *More Nineteenth Century Studies*, pp. 186–247.

9. Campbell, "Memoir," pp. 11, 25, 42–43.

I shall never get on as a minister, for I shall never make popular sermons. Some here stigmatized my sermon as an "essay." One good fellow said he should like to read it three times before he gave an opinion. *Oh how I long to know what my work in life is to be!* I must try to be a College Tutor; I should like it very well in some respects, though it is a higher work to be a successful minister.[10]

A reader of Ward's later books and articles can sympathize with the students who heard those first sermons, for Ward never achieved a felicitous style. That same reader will also note in Ward's longing "to know what my work in life is to be" a foreshadowing of his later psychology in which each mind must largely forge its own place in the world and create its own character as it interacts with the surrounding world.

In 1868, partly to prepare for the "higher work" of the ministry and partly to postpone further vocational decision, Ward sought and won the Dr. Williams' Scholarship of his denomination for study in Germany.[11] He had prepared doubly for this year. In addition to the Spring Hill course work, Ward had successfully read for a University of London B.A. and had begun preparing for a similar degree in science. Once in Germany he settled in Berlin to attend the lectures of Dorner and Trendenlenberg. Later he moved to Göttingen to study under Lotze, who proved a profound influence on his thought. In later life, Ward's effort to wring something spiritual from the universe described by science led to his being compared with Lotze.[12]

The term of 1869–1870 in Germany marked the peak of Ward's intellectual struggle with Christianity. His letters from this period record the loss of "the power to believe," and the evocation of a "sceptical spirit." He wrote of a longing for rest—"I am out in an ocean of darkness where neither sun nor stars have for many days appeared: the whole horizon round in turn seems at every point to be brightening for dawn, but all is cheating fancy." One of his teachers in Germany called him a Pantheist. A Unitarian student

10. Ibid., p. 19 (FMT's emphasis).

11. For requirements of the Dr. Williams' Scholarship, see *The Congregational Year Book 1869* (London: Hodder & Stoughton, 1869), p. 356.

12. G. Dawes Hicks, "James Ward and His Philosophical Approach to Theism," *Hibbert Journal* 24 (1925–26): 63.

asked him to preach for the English Unitarians. Ward's agony climaxed as he demanded, "Can I ever again compact my shattered self into a definite ego whose mind shall reflect the mind of Christ?" [13]

The shattering of his "self" and his relationship to Christ reverberated further into his vocational considerations. His reading for the science degree and the lectures of Lotze no doubt opened new perspectives on both science and philosophy. In August 1870 in a note for his own eyes alone, Ward posed his present quandary:

> I feel I have two impulses, one that springs from my individuality mentally and that is to pursue a certain line of study, and here my first love Natural Science would receive a large share of my regard and the question here would be how to resolve the present general laws of Physics into a higher—in short what might be called cosmology philosophically considered. But another question that has more recently put in its claim is to make good the position and claims of Christianity against all opposition of the day, and to work out the lines of an apology for Christianity . . . that shall rest on first principles. . . . Shall I after all turn to science and revel in its delights and try to unfold something more of the glories of nature, and unlike other inquirers proclaim Nature as a Revelation of God, and by living a Christian life though retired shew that Science and Faith can go together?

The same month he wrote of possibly yielding "to a temptation which has long been strong and to which perhaps I have listened more of late, the temptation I mean to seek the walks of Science and Natur-philosophie." [14] At this point in his groping there can be little doubt that Ward viewed his vocational and intellectual alternatives as a life of science or a life of religion. Philosophy would eventually permit him to achieve a viable intellectual synthesis of both though not in the Christian manner he contemplated at this time.

It was this "shattered self," unsure of either vocation or faith, who fought the devil in 1870. Ward had received a call to minister to the Downing Place Chapel in Cambridge. With much trepidation he accepted the call and in so doing entered upon a year that more

13. Campbell, "Memoir," pp. 25, 26, 30.
14. Ibid., pp. 32, 38.

than half a century later he recalled as "the darkest and the saddest of a long and eventful life." [15] Save for personal scandal everything went wrong with his congregation that could go wrong for a young minister. They were suspicious about his theology. One section of the congregation, doubting Ward's salvation, began to pray for him. His liberal reputation spread beyond Cambridge and throughout the entire Congregational denomination. The chapel itself became divided over the question of constructing a new house of worship.[16] Ward also discovered that his situation allowed him to enjoy little advantage from being near a great university. He complained to his sister, "I am a minister among strangers, and not perhaps strangers merely but suspectors too in many cases. . . . Incomparably the most wretched men on Earth now are Christian ministers." [17] Just after a year had passed, Ward resigned, but the congregation refused to accept his decision. Shortly thereafter, he resubmitted the resignation and held firm. That same month, March 1872, at the age of twenty–nine, James Ward enrolled at Cambridge, hoping to pass from the rigors of Hebraism into the solace of sweetness and light.

University life did not immediately grant peace of soul, but it did afford rest and time for reflection. Like so many others who ventured from the orthodox fold, Ward distrusted his own motives. Nonconformist introspection was not easily escaped. Just after entering Cambridge he wrote in a letter, "In all this, in the practical, what I want is not light but grace, to be taken up into a higher life and delivered from the treacherous self. I tell you, Wolstenholme, I have no dread of God, no fear of the Devil, no fear of man, but my head swims as I write it—*I fear myself.*" A year later he spoke of himself as a "moral desperado, ready for any wild scheme, social, political, or ecclesiastical, that would absorb [him] wholly." [18]

Fortunately, there was at Cambridge one man and perhaps only one man who could aid this "moral desperado" with understanding and empathy—Henry Sidgwick. Ward once told an audience, "If I

15. Ibid., p. 52. JW made this statement in a letter of 10 May 1924, in which he declined to attend the Jubilee Celebration of his former congregation.

16. Clyde Binfield, "Chapels in Crisis," *Transactions of the Congregational Historical Society* 20 (1968) : 237–54.

17. Campbell, "Memoir," p. 43.

18. Ibid., pp. 47, 62.

am anything at all, I owe it to two men, Hermann Lotze and Henry Sidgwick." [19] Sidgwick persuaded Ward that the latter's shattered ego could be restored and that there were indeed schemes to which a "moral desperado" could devote himself. Sidgwick undoubtedly argued that in the study of philosophy and psychology, Ward might put to use his interests and training in theology and science. He probably convinced Ward that in writing and university teaching he could perform service as high, if not higher, than in the ministry. Sidgwick also recruited him to his favorite project of furthering women's education—an effort Sidgwick himself viewed as a positive compensation for his own retreat from orthodoxy. Ward's classes in the late 1870s were among the first to admit women.[20] One of his earliest and brightest female students became his wife in 1884.

Needless to say, this restoration of his personality did not occur in a day. For a time it appeared that Ward might become a physiologist. In 1876 his senior essay, *The Relation of Physiology to Psychology,* which foreshadowed his later thought, was awarded a prize.[21] The author was hustled off to Germany to study at Leipzig, where a laboratory for experimental psychology had been established. This second year in Germany proved less rewarding than his earlier experience, but Ward profited from the further exposure and training in experimental science. With the possible exception of William James, Ward received more scientific training and experience than any other philosopher of the day. However, he made clear to a friend that "there is not the least chance of my forsaking Psychology for Physiology: I simply wish to know all I can of what Sidgwick calls 'the margin of psychology'—the physical aspects of the psychical." [22]

After returning to Cambridge, he wrote an article outlining his Leipzig experiment for the *Archive für Physiologie* published in 1880.[23] He spent considerable time working with Michael Foster, also a nonconformist, in the latter's physiology laboratory. Ward's article on the nervous system of the freshwater crayfish appeared in

19. Ibid., p. 92.

20. W. R. Sorley, "James Ward," *Mind* 34 (1925) : 274.

21. JW, *The Relation of Physiology to Psychology* (London: R. Clay, Sons, & Taylor, 1875). Part of this essay later appeared in *Mind* as "An Attempt to Interpret Fechner's Law," *Mind* 1 (1876) : 452–66.

22. Campbell, "Memoir," pp. 67–68.

23. JW, "Ueber die Auslösung von Reflexbewegungen durch eine Summe schwachen Reize," *Archive für Physiologie,* Jahrgang 4 (1880) : 72–91.

the *Journal of Physiology* and received Huxley's praise.[24] Foster entertained high hopes for Ward's future physiological investigations. When his student turned to psychology and philosophy, Foster described him as "a physiologist spoiled." Ward remained sensitive to the influence of this scientific training. Years later when criticizing physiological psychology, he recalled Foster's remark in noting that opposition to such psychology "is an odd position for me, who has worked for two years in physiological laboratories and of whom it has been said that he is a 'physiologist spoiled.' " [25]

In 1881 Sidgwick used his influence to secure Ward as a Trinity College lecturer. Finally, at age thirty-eight, Ward's vocation was settled upon. However, the questions that had prolonged his vocational decision persisted though in a less pressing manner. He was still ready to do battle with the devil. In 1879 he wrote:

> What the world is going to come to without religious aspirations and the old feelings of awe and mystery that Nature inspired in the best minds, is more than I can tell or care to guess. These springs of higher life must revive again or the beggarly elements will starve us back into savages.

The rest of Ward's life, which constituted his entire productive intellectual career, consisted of an attempt to forestall those "beggarly elements" and to revive those "springs of higher life" which the devil of naturalism no less than the devil of Spring Hill threatened. As he wrote in 1889, "If we cannot have omniscience then, what we want is a philosophy that shall justify faith—justify it in the only way in which it can be justified by giving it room. . . . Knowledge that we could never attain, remaining what we are, may be attainable in consequence of higher powers and a higher life, which we may morally achieve." [26]

In forging room in life for faith, Ward articulated a philosophy

24. JW, "Some Notes on the Physiology of the Nervous System of the Freshwater Crayfish," *Journal of Physiology* 2 (1879) : 214–27. For an abstract of the article, see JW, "Observations on the Physiology of the Nervous System of the Crayfish," *Proceedings of the Royal Society of London*, no. 194 (6 March 1879) : 379–83. T. H. Huxley, *The Crayfish* (New York: D. Appleton & Co., 1880), p. 354.

25. Campbell, "Memoir," p. 72; JW to W. James, 10 November 1892, in R. B. Perry, *The Thought and Character of William James* (Boston: Little, Brown & Co., 1935), 2 : 100.

26. Campbell, "Memoir," p. 64; JW, *Essays in Philosophy*, pp. 139–40.

that incorporated most of the problems, ideas, contradictions, and directions of thought already seen in Wallace, Butler, Sidgwick, Myers, and Romanes. He succeeded more nearly than any other contemporary English philosopher in setting forth a system of philosophy that recognized the role and value of science while retaining a spiritual and nonmechanistic interpretation of man and nature. In attempting to carve out a niche for subjective human experience, he came to occupy a position in English philosophy that might be considered equivalent to that of William James in America, Henri Bergson in France, and Edmund Husserl in Germany.

A New Departure for British Psychology

James Ward is one of those figures who intrigues the historian. While well known and highly regarded during his lifetime and the author of a volume that the theologian Frederick Tennant once proclaimed "the greatest single work, of any age, on the human mind," Ward was almost forgotten soon after his death.[27] His thought attracted few followers. Only an occasional footnote or the dutiful and often grudgingly pedantic mentions in histories of late nineteenth- and early twentieth-century philosophy recall him and his books.

Within Ward's lifetime the case had been different. His was a voice to be contended with in English thought. Edinburgh awarded him an honorary degree. He was one of the original members of the British Academy and participated in the discussions of the Aristotelian and Synthetic societies. He was accorded the rare privilege of being twice selected to deliver Gifford Lectures. Writers from varied schools of psychological thought such as John Dewey, Bernard Bosanquet, and G. F. Stout referred to Ward's work with respect. On the publication of *Psychological Principles* in 1918, the *Times* reviewer unhesitatingly pronounced Ward to be "the Father of Modern British Psychology." A few months after his death in 1926, *Monist* devoted an entire issue to his work.[28]

27. F. R. Tennant, *Philosophical Theology* (Cambridge: Cambridge University Press, 1956), 1 : vii.
28. John Dewey, *Psychology*, 3rd ed. (New York: Harper & Bros., 1891), p. vi; Bernard Bosanquet, *Psychology of the Moral Self* (London: Macmillan & Co., 1897), p. 129; G. F. Stout, *Analytic Psychology* (London: Macmillan & Co., 1902), 1 : xi. *Times Literary Supplement*, 2 January 1919, p. 4. James Ward Commemorative Issue, *Monist* 36 (1926): 1–176.

Two factors explain the demise of Ward's reputation. The rapid strides of behaviorism and psychoanalysis brought the day of the general philosophical psychologist to its close.[29] Second, his metaphysics became a "period piece." Ward's criticism and that of others so undermined reductionist naturalism that the naturalistic philosophy of the twentieth century bore small resemblance to that of the nineteenth. Criticism, such as that embodied in his metaphysics, stirred a ferment of discontent with Victorian scientific naturalism and raised issues with which the latter could not deal. However, few of Ward's constructive ideas replaced the naturalistic synthesis that his criticism had largely destroyed.[30]

After 1880 James Ward remained strictly an academic man. Having painfully discovered his niche in life, he stayed there. His personality as a teacher aroused differing reactions. C. D. Broad did not greatly profit from Ward's lectures and, sensing the ever-present vestiges of the nonconformist past, recalled Ward as possessing "all those virtues which have tended to make virtue so unpopular." At the other extreme was Bertrand Russell, who considered Ward "my chief teacher" and who remembered many personal kindnesses. Among them was Ward's protest against the dismissal of Russell from his Trinity lectureship during World War I.[31] Nonetheless, the significance of Ward's life did not lie in his university activities but rather in his books and paradoxically in a book that for over thirty years he postponed writing. The circumstances for this unlikely occurrence centered upon that monument of Victorian scholarship, the ninth edition of the *Encyclopaedia Britannica*.

The editors of *Britannica* decided their ninth edition should incorporate the very latest in sound and precise scientific knowledge.[32] Among several modifications recognizing the advance of science, the

29. C. A. Mace, "James Ward," *The Encyclopedia of Philosophy* (New York: Macmillan Co. and The Free Press, 1967), 8 : 278.

30. Sterling P. Lamprecht, "James Ward's Critique of Naturalism," *Monist* 36 (1926) : 136–37.

31. C. D. Broad, "The Local Historical Background of Contemporary Cambridge Philosophy," in *British Philosophy at Mid-Century*, ed. C. A. Mace (London: Allen & Unwin, 1957), p. 35; Bertrand Russell, *Portraits from Memory* (New York: Simon & Schuster, 1956), p. 64 and *The Autobiography of Bertrand Russell* (Boston: Little, Brown, & Co., 1968), 2 : 85; G. H. Hardy, *Bertrand Russell and Trinity* (Cambridge: Cambridge University Press, 1970), pp. 40–53.

32. Herman Kogan, *The Great EB: The Story of the Encyclopaedia Britannica* (Chicago: Chicago University Press, 1958), pp. 52–60.

staff introduced a separate article on "Psychology," a topic previously covered in the article on "Metaphysics" by H. L. Mansel. Originally T. Spencer Baynes, the chief editor, had engaged Croom Robertson, a founder of *Mind* and a respected philosopher at the University of London, to write the psychology article. In 1884, for reasons of health, Robertson relinquished the task. James Sully, an important psychologist of the associationist school, declined an invitation to replace Robertson. Then, in Ward's words, "Baynes, chancing to have made my acquaintance, offered it to me." Ward had lectured on psychology since 1878, had written several articles, and, under the encouragement of Sidgwick and Michael Foster, had planned to write a book on the subject. However, as he later wrote, "I rashly sacrificed my book to the offer and so, as it has turned out, destroyed one of the dreams of my life." [33]

Ironically, the destruction of Ward's dream constituted the making of his career. He began the article in 1884 and completed it in 1885. It was published in 1886.[34] Alexander Bain, whose views it attacked, praised the discussion.[35] From the United States William James wrote to Croom Robertson that Ward's article "makes the transition to a new era in English psychology." In 1912 Theodore Merz recalled the discussion as "a kind of manifesto, as a program for modern psychological work." C. D. Broad wrote of the long encyclopedia essay, "This at once created a revolution in English psychology. No serious student of the subject could neglect to read it, and it remained available only in this inconvenient form for thirty-two years." [36] Revolution is perhaps too strong a term. Ward owed much to his predecessors. However, his emphasis was such as to set off his

33. JW, *Psychological Principles*, 2nd ed. (Cambridge: Cambridge University Press, 1933), p. v.

34. JW had outlined much of his thought in a series of papers and articles written between 1875 and 1884. See JW, *The Relation of Physiology to Psychology* (1875); "A General Analysis of Mind," *Journal of Speculative Philosophy* 16 (1882): 366–85; "Psychological Principles," *Mind* 7 (1883): 153–69, 485–86; "Objects and Their Interaction," *Journal of Speculative Philosophy* 17 (1883): 169–79. He had also discussed several of his major ideas at private meetings of the Cambridge Moral Science Club about 1880.

35. A. Bain, "Mr. James Ward's Psychology," *Mind* 11 (1886): 457, 477.

36. W. James to C. Robertson, 29 August 1886, in Perry, *The Thought and Character of William James*, 1: 602; J. T. Merz, *History of European Thought in the Nineteenth Century* (Edinburgh and London: W. Blackwood & Sons, 1912), 3: 277–78; Broad, "Local Historical Background of Contemporary Cambridge Philosophy," in Mace, *British Philosophy at Mid-Century*, p. 35.

work from that of past writers and from his English contemporaries.

Why should an encyclopedia article have stirred such excitement and enjoyed continuing influence? The reason was simple. Ward rejected the proposition then dominant in English psychology that "the progress of Psychology in fundamental truth, and its more complete emancipation from Theology and Metaphysics, are to be measured by the degree in which physical methods, physical conceptions, and even physical metaphors have been applied to the interpretation of the facts of mind." [37] In 1886 the schools of associationist and physiological psychology embodied this viewpoint.

Associationism originated with Locke and was developed in the eighteenth century by Berkeley, Hume, and Hartley. The two Mills, Alexander Bain, and Herbert Spencer were its chief nineteenth-century advocates.[38] These writers denied the doctrine of innate ideas and contended that the human mind resembled a *tabula rasa*. Sensations impinged upon the mind and left impressions that then arranged themselves and interacted according to the laws of association. The early associationists considered the mind itself to be almost wholly passive. J. S. Mill, Bain, and Spencer had introduced significant modifications into this basic picture. Mill thought the mind might have certain native proclivities. Bain suggested that energy within the body and the brain might account for some internal physical activity and for some sensations of the mind. Spencer introduced the metaphors of evolution and argued that the mind was in part the product of organic heredity as well as of the experience of the individual. Though the concept of a *tabula rasa* had been rendered considerably more complex and some autonomous activity ascribed to the mind, associationists still regarded human beings as products of their environment which now included their physical bodies and their heredity as well as surrounding physical circumstances. As one historian of associationism has explained, these psychologists considered "each individual mind as consisting of many unit experiences, which are so firmly bound together in simultaneous groups and in one long train, that they constitute a unitary conscious-

37. "The Development of Psychology," *Westminster Review* 101 (1874) : 378.
38. For the best discussions of associationism see T. Ribot, *English Psychology* (New York: D. Appleton & Co., 1874); Howard C. Warren, *A History of the Associationist Psychology* (New York: Scribner's, 1921); Robert Young, *Mind, Brain and Adaptation in the Nineteenth Century* (Oxford: The Clarendon Press, 1970).

ness."[39] The self or personality was the accumulated product of these individual unitary experiences.

Associationism was Ward's chief bête noire. Its analysis neither described nor accounted for experience but rather intellectualized all experience into cognition. "Presentationism or Associationism seem better names for a doctrine the gist of which is that all the elements of psychical life are primarily and ultimately cognitive elements, and that all the laws of their combination are reducible to association." Associationism represented a wholly artificial interpretation of experience and of nature that as Ward once explained to William James is "everywhere zigzaggy, and the straightening out is artificial."[40] It ignored the spontaneous activity of the psychological subject, revealed by close analysis of experience, in order to reduce the activity of the mind to mechanical laws. By intellectualizing mental processes into the single act of rational cognition and by ignoring the mind's radically active and feeling nature, associationists had placed the cart before the horse. Their categories of analysis could include only such aspects of mental life as they had decided to include prior to examination of psychological experience.

After Bain, associationists had entered into a cooperative relationship with physiologists. Physiological psychology may be traced to Hobbes but more properly to Hartley. Its leading exponents in late nineteenth-century England were Alexander Bain, Herbert Spencer, Thomas Laycock, W. B. Carpenter, Henry Maudsley, and Hughlings Jackson.[41] According to the physiological psychologists most problems of the mind could be solved by studying the brain and the nervous system. The physical and psychical faculties of the body were believed to be parallel. Mind was an epiphenomenon of matter. The physiologists agreed with the associationists in asserting that a scientific psychology could be achieved through introducing the methods and metaphors of the established physical sciences into the study of the mind.

In Ward's eyes physiological psychology was doubly offensive. It

39. Warren, *History of Associationist Psychology*, p. 178.

40. JW, " 'Modern' Psychology: A Reflection," *Mind* 2 (1893) : 58–59; JW to W. James, 10 November 1892, in Perry, *The Thought and Character of William James*, 2 : 99–100.

41. Young, *Mind, Brain and Adaptation in the Nineteenth Century;* R. S. Peters, ed., *Brett's History of Psychology* (London: Allen & Unwin, 1953), pp. 584–642; L. S. Hearnshaw, *A Short History of British Psychology 1840–1940* (New York: Barnes & Noble, 1964), pp. 69–75.

subordinated psychology to biology in hope of rendering the former "scientific." Consequently, physiological psychologists equated "psychological fact and physiological interpretation." This procedure "entails a violation of scientific method; it confuses the stand-point from which the origin of the conception is *expounded* with the stand-point at which the conception is *acquired.*" William James later termed this slight of hand "the Psychologists' Fallacy," which consisted of the psychologist's investigating his own experience of the subject rather than the subject's own viewpoint or experience. Ward argued that the physiologist ignored the internal experience of the subject he examined in an endeavor "to escape the ontological assumptions of the conception of a subject." Ward had been trained in physiology and was determined that it should not be confused with psychology. As he wrote in 1893, "It is not so long since the world was shocked at Lange's *mot* about a psychology without a soul, but the 'modern' [i.e., physiological] psychology is a psychology without even consciousness." Second, Ward objected to physiological psychology because it marked another stage in associationism.

> It is the triumph of Associationism. Sensation, Retentiveness, Association by Contiguity—these are to be our ultimate and sufficient psychological conceptions: the facts of feeling and conation are resolved into facts of sensation; and all mind-processes held to be not merely conditioned but explained by brain-processes, which they accompany as epiphenomena or "Begleiterscheinungen." [42]

No such physiological explanation or description bore any resemblance to the lived and living experience of human beings.

That experience provided the touchstone for Ward's analysis. He sought to probe the prereflective experience that the associationists had intellectualized into sensation, retentiveness, and association and that the physiologists had reduced to nerve vibration. He sought to define the study of psychology so that it might include all the activities of the mind and not become confused with either physiology or

42. JW, "A General Analysis of Mind," *Journal of Speculative Philosophy* 16 (1882): 369–70; W. James, *The Principles of Psychology* (New York: Dover Publications, 1950), 1 : 196–97; JW, "A General Analysis of Mind," *Journal of Speculative Philosophy* 16 (1882) : 370; JW, " 'Modern' Psychology: A Reflection," *Mind,* n.s. 2 (1893) : 54–55.

epistemology. The peculiarly individualistic standpoint of psychological experience was the true subject matter of psychology and distinguished it from physiology.[43] That point of view was "the standpoint of conscious Life—or more fully the standpoint of the living subject in intercourse with his special environment." From that active intercourse, and not prior to it, human rationality emerged. Psychology must be understood as "the science of individual experience—understanding by experience not merely, not primarily, cognition, but also, and above all, conative activity or behaviour." [44] This activity could be neither perceived by the methods of physiology nor expressed through its categories. Ward believed that action preceded understanding, that emotion preceded reason, and that instinct stood prior to intellection. His thought thus bore a striking affinity to that of Samuel Butler as well as to the later existential analysis of man. Ward sought the roots of human existence from whence cognitive reason emerged.

Ward contended that Locke and more particularly his nineteenth-century epistemological and psychological successors had grounded their analysis in the erroneous supposition "that each man by himself is rational instead of recognizing that humanity has achieved rationality . . . [and they had] then proceeded to confound psychology with that division of philosophy which is now called epistemology, or the theory of knowledge." [45] The associationists had confounded psychology with or limited it to the process of knowing and had isolated the individual from his relationship with other men. Keenly aware of the role of social relationships in fostering human thought, Ward believed that humanity or society had preserved the achievement of man's individual and collective movement toward rationality.

Ward regarded this basic error of the associationists as leading to an incorrect use of the words *objective* and *subjective*.[46] *Subjective* had come to denote the private epistemological property of the individual but should refer to the viewpoint of the experiencing subject. *Objective* in associationist literature meant the common or shared

43. JW, "Psychology," *Encyclopaedia Britannica*, 9th ed. (Edinburgh: Adam and Charles Black, 1886), 20 : 37–38. Hereafter cited as JW, "Psychology."

44. JW, *Psychological Principles*, pp. 17, 28.

45. Ibid., p. 17.

46. Ibid., pp. 13–18.

epistemological property of individuals but should more properly refer to that which any individual subject observed. The definitions of subjective and objective that Ward opposed were fundamental to all the spokesmen for scientific naturalism. Scientific method could deal with the epistemologically objective. The epistemologically subjective (i.e., psychologically objective in Ward's analysis) was written off as invalid. The naturalistic writers had understood each human mind primarily as a cognitive agent in the process of coming to know common or shared objective truths. They considered only this common objective truth as real. Personal or subjective emotions or experiences were unreal because they could not become part of the common objective truth.

So far as Ward was concerned, psychology based on such erroneous concepts of subjective and objective was not psychology at all. Psychology proper must regard mental experience other than cognition and must study the mind as it internally experienced and coped with its objective circumstances. Ward regarded the mind not only as cognitive but also as feeling and conative.[47] Or in Samuel Butler's terminology, Ward viewed the mind as a "cunning" as well as a cognitive agent. Ward granted that associationism might account for as much as nine-tenths of mental experience, but it was the remaining tenth that fascinated him and the existence of which he demanded his rivals acknowledge.[48] In this manner, he "clearly challenged the Associationists to show cause why they should continue to exist." [49]

There can be little doubt that Ward's concept of psychology and his reaction against associationism and physiological psychology stemmed directly from his religious and vocational experiences. In 1870 just after returning from Germany, he had written to a friend:

> Now on the one hand it is as useless to refer the deductions of Science to the senses, as on the other it is impossible to deny that there are facts of the inner world quite as certain as, nay far more certain than, the facts of the outer world. . . . The most immediate knowledge we have is that of our own mental states—of ourselves: on the analogy of ourselves we build our

47. Ibid., p. 28.
48. Ibid., p. 411.
49. Peters, *Brett's History of Psychology*, p. 642.

knowledge of things without. . . . Is it not possible so to con-
nect knowledge with knowledge without a break as at last to
see in the Macrocosm such a resemblance to the Microcosm that
it shall be recognized as the expression of a Mind, whose image
we bear? [50]

Yet when Ward read the leading English psychologists, he found
little or no recognition of the validity of internal experience. Instead,
it was discarded as subjective illusion or hallucination. Moreover, the
microcosm was interpreted through the macrocosm. Yet he knew the
most vital elements of his own life had been the mental struggles of
his inner self. He also knew that his inner state largely determined
his perception of the outer world. In his psychology Ward set about
to describe this inner realm from the activities of which the outer
was organized.

Though often isolated in his efforts within England and ultimately
having few English disciples, Ward's psychology was part of the
broad late-century revolt against positivism and scientific reductionism. His development and many of his conclusions closely paralleled
those of Franz Brentano, another clergyman turned psychologist and
philosopher. Both men opposed associationism in favor of an active
conception of the mind. Considering Brentano's profound influence
on Husserl and then on Heidegger, it is significant that a recent
student of Brentano's thought has observed "that, as originally formulated, Ward's critique of associationism and his presentation of a
personalistic viewpoint in psychology were more articulate and
specific than those offered by Brentano in his *Psychology.*" [51] In
England Ward's ideas were interpreted within the context of English
psychology and the possibilities of existential development were
never considered.

WARD'S ANALYSIS OF MIND

The Psychological Subject

Ward's clearest departure from associationism lay in his positing
the existence of a psychological Subject, Self, or Ego. He asserted,

50. Campbell, "Memoir," pp. 36–37.

51. A. C. Rancurello, *A Study of Franz Brentano* (New York: Academic Press, 1968),
p. 86. JW presided as chairman at a lecture delivered by Husserl at the University of
London in 1923. See H. Spiegelberg, *The Phenomenological Movement: A Historical
Introduction* (The Hague: Nijhoff, 1965), 2 : 625.

"Whether seeking to analyze one's own consciousness or to infer that of a lobster, whether discussing the association of ideas or the expression of emotions, there is always an individual mind or self or subject in question." Alexander Bain termed this view the "aggrandizement of the Subject." [52] Unlike the Scottish school of Common Sense, Ward did not regard this Subject as a soul, nor did he conceive it as existing in several realms of being as did Myers's subliminal self.[53] Ward's Subject represented a logical and pragmatic ontological necessity. "By pure Ego or Subject it is proposed to denote the simple fact that everything mental is referred to a Self." [54] This subject, or Self, could never be directly perceived. The physiologist could not reveal it. In this regard, it closely resembled Kant's pure ego or Freud's unconscious.

For Ward, the Subject existed prior to experience; its *activity* rather than Kantian categories accounted for the unity of experience.

> For psychology the being of this subject means simply its actual knowing, feeling, and striving as an Ego or Self confronted by a counterpart non-Ego or not self: the two constituting a universe of experience, in which, as Leibniz held, activity is the fundamental fact,—*am Anfang war die That*.[55]

Only such a Subject, pragmatically posited, could account for the facts of lived and living experience. The active Subject, as well as the active environment, was an essential aspect of all psychological experience. Ward's employment of a Subject was parallel to Sidgwick's postulating the existence of God and to the scientists' assuming the uniformity of nature.

52. JW, "Psychology," p. 39 (*Psychological Principles*, p. 35). Wherever possible in this section, the references to quotations will be given for both the *Britannica* article and for *Psychological Principles*. This poses certain hazards since JW polished the article when he incorporated it into the book. In each case the reference outside parentheses will indicate the source of the direct quotation in the text. Bain, "Mr. James Ward's Psychology," *Mind* 11 (1886) : 459.

53. Merz, *A History of European Thought in the Nineteenth Century*, 3 : 279-80. In 1882 JW countered the claim that to posit a Self was to assert the existence of a soul. "It is not till reflection begins upon the question, What am I? that the notion of a soul or spiritual substance is formed, whereas the conception of a self not only obviously precedes such reflection, but remains distinct throughout it" (JW "A General Analysis of Mind," *Journal of Speculative Philosophy* 16 [1882] : 371).

54. JW, "Psychology," p. 39 (*Psychological Principles*, p. 35).

55. JW, "Present Problems of General Psychology," *Philosophical Review* 13 (1904) : 608.

General Analysis of Mental Activity

The concept of the Subject allowed Ward to interpret the mind and the experience of the mind differently from the associationists. He contended that all mental activity could be reduced to no less than three basal factors: "I feel somehow," "I know something," and "I do something." Consequently, mind included "the subject of these 'feelings' or phenomena *plus* the series of 'feelings' or phenomena themselves, the two being in that relation to each other in which alone the one is subject and the other a series of 'feelings' or phenomena, i.e. objects." [56] This subject–object relationship was basic to Ward's analysis and represented a unity of duality. Subject and object stood in mutual need of each other. Though conceptually distinct, they could not be separated. What, if anything, lay behind the Subject or the object was not a matter for psychology as psychology.

Within this subject–object relationship, the Subject granted attention to the presented object. The object, for its part, affected the Subject with varying degrees of intensity. The attenion of the Subject and the intensity of the object together accounted for the feelings occasioned by sensations. Feelings were not in themselves either sensations or presentations. A "flagrant psychological barbarism," was how Ward described the associationist contention that feelings of pleasure and pain were sensations. Feelings always followed presentations or sensations. Ward argued, "The simplest form of psychical life . . . involves not only a subject feeling but a subject having qualitatively distinguishable presentations which are the occasion of its feeling." [57] The feelings occasioned by the Subject's attention to and the intensity from presentations in turn provided occasions for conation or action that led to a change either in attention or in motor activity. Thus conative activity on the part of the Subject, whereby it changed its attention, as well as changes in external sensations, could arouse new feelings and subsequent action.

Ward employed the concept of an active mind with its three irreducible functions—cognition, feeling, and conation—to deny the idea of a *tabula rasa* and with it the laws of automatic association.

56. JW, *Psychological Principles*, pp. 34, 39 ("Psychology," p. 39).

57. JW, *Psychological Principles*, p. 45; JW, "Psychology," p. 41 (*Psychological Principles*, p. 45).

As far as the lived rather than the abstracted psychological experience of human beings was concerned, the individual mind had never
been blank nor did it ever receive individual sensations. Lived experience always commenced in *media res*.

> For we *cannot imagine the beginning of life but only life begun.*
> Psychology cannot start with a *tabula rasa.* The simplest picture,
> then, that we can form of a concrete state of mind is not one
> in which there are movements before there are any sensations
> or sensations before there are any movements, but one in which
> change of sensation is followed by change of movement, the
> link between the two being a change of feeling.[58]

Ward thus wrote and thought in the Leibnitzian tradition, which
in opposition to Locke held that prior to sensation there was nothing
in the intellect except the intellect itself.

In posing the questions of how the Subject related to, perceived,
and affected its environment, Ward found it necessary to differen-
tiate between the concepts or categories of psychology and those of
the other natural sciences.

> The concept of pure passivity or inertia is a convenient an-
> alytical fiction in physics, but we find no such reality in concrete
> experience. Even receptivity is activity, and though it is often
> non-voluntary, it is never indifferent. In other words, not mere
> receptivity but conative or selective activity is the essence of
> subjective reality; and to this, known or objective reality is the
> essential counterpart. Experience is just the interaction of these
> two factors, and *this duality is a real relation antecedent to, but
> never completely covered by, the reflective knowledge we come
> to attain concerning it.*[59]

Ward sought to discover the nature and activity of the mind in its
prereflective reality before deciding what categories would best
describe it. Naturalistic writers from the associationist and physiological schools of thought had selected only certain features of
mental reality, had abstracted or intellectualized them, and had
channeled them into preconceived passive categories of the physical

58. JW, *Psychological Principles,* p. 54 ("Psychology," p. 43).
59. JW, "Present Problems of General Psychology," *Philosophical Review* 13 (1904):
607 (FMT's emphasis).

sciences. Ward contended his analysis of prereflective mental phenomena revealed a set of active agents for which atoms, energy, and
evolution alone could not account. The scientific categories were, if
not invalid, at least very incomplete means of describing psychological experience.

Ward did more than challenge the naturalistic view of mind as an
automatic cognitive agent that discovered an existing and relatively
unchanging objective environment. He also questioned its logical
corollary that men come to perceive and understand the world or
nature by disinterested cognition and curiosity. Ward regarded the
primal function of the mind as practical self-conservation spurred by
feeling and conation. Cognition and theoretical interpretation resulted from feeling and conation and were conditioned by them.

> [T]he notion of an independent realm of truth existing *sub
> specie aeternitatis* has literally no place within the purview of
> a psychology that knows its business. Here we find no such thing
> as mere cognition: the uninteresting is not known but ignored,
> and the interesting leads at once to response, and sooner or later
> to adjustment—in the race, at all events. Success is then com-
> pleted experience or expertness, and in general prepares the
> way for a new advance. So far the true is the useful, and the
> criterion is not theoretical but practical. Looking broadly at
> the progress of life, as it ascends through the animal kingdom
> and onwards through the history of man, it seems safe to say
> that knowledge is always a means to ends, is never an end by
> itself—till at length it becomes interesting and satisfying in
> itself. Psychologically regarded, then, the sole function of per-
> ception and intellection is, it is contended, to guide action and
> subserve volition—more generally to promote self-conservation
> and betterment.[60]

Feeling and action thus in part determined cognition. Psychologically speaking, cognition was never disinterested activity supposedly
epitomized by the scientific investigator but rather was part of a
general instinct toward survival and betterment. As Ward com-

60. JW, *Psychological Principles*, p. 21. This idea was implicit in his original article,
but JW did not explicitly develop it as it would appear in *Psychological Principles*
until 1904. See JW, "On the Definition of Psychology," *British Journal of Psychology*
1 (1904): 3–25.

mented on another occasion, conation was the source of both scientific knowledge and the faith that led to such knowledge: "Both merge in that primitive credulity which leads us to trust our hopes and to try before we know." [61]

Samuel Butler would undoubtedly have applauded Ward's concept of the active mind whereby knowledge followed action. But he would also have claimed that Ward had failed to credit him with prior formulation. In 1883 Butler read one of Ward's early articles for *Mind* and thought he had copied the life-and-habit theory. In 1884 an *Athenaeum* reviewer noted a likeness between the two writers. Yet, despite many similarities in their psychology and metaphysics, it is impossible to discover fruitful links between the two men. Ward was an omnivorous reader and may well have read one or more of Butler's books in the late seventies. However, Ward's only two references to Butler occurred after 1912 and allude to the posthumously published notebooks. Nevertheless, like Butler, Ward did prefer not only an active concept of mind, but also a teleological interpretation of evolution.[62]

Ward interpreted the chance variations involved with natural selection as the external manifestation of the internally conscious aim of all living creatures to conserve themselves.[63] A Lamarckian will to survive underlay all psychical activity and existed in the mind as a primal urge prior to any reflective or abstract understanding of nature. Indeed, discursive understanding was but the result of the urge toward self-conservation. That which was regarded as cognitively true was true only because of its relationship to the conative and feeling Subject, which sought not to understand its objective environment but to preserve itself therein.[64] Progress toward self-

61. JW, "Faith and Science," in *Papers Read before the Synthetic Society 1896–1908,* ed. Arthur J. Balfour (London: Spottiswood & Co., 1909), p. 366.

62. SB, Manuscript Notebooks, Williams College, 2 : 7–8; *Athenaeum,* 22 March 1884, p. 379; JW, *Psychological Principles,* p. 420, and *Essays in Philosophy,* p. 257. Robert Rattray observed similarities between the two writers in "The Philosophy of Samuel Butler," *Mind* 23 (1914) : 383.

63. JW grew increasingly Lamarckian over the span of his career. His was, however, a highly sophisticated Lamarckianism. The seeking for self-preservation was not conscious but simply part of the general psychic movement to avoid pain. In some respects he went beyond Lamarck. For Lamarck, creatures simply reacted to the environment. JW pictured man as changing the environment. The instinctive aim to activity became for JW a means of self-conservation. See JW, *Psychological Principles,* pp. 246, 278; *Heredity and Memory* (Cambridge: Cambridge University Press, 1913).

64. JW often came very close to affirming an almost Kierkegaardian view of truth as being relational. See R. May, "The Origins and Significance of the Existential Move-

conservation, and in the case of man toward self-betterment as well, was the result of existential subjective interest rather than of effort to discover objective truth. As Ward explained to the Synthetic Society in 1902,

> Life is made up of impulses; self-maintenance is its main endeavour, and knowledge is obtained only as fast and as far as this paramount interest is concerned, and primarily as a means to this end. What is learnt here takes the form, not of theoretical propositions, but of practical maxims, which are thought of not as true but as useful. This difference is deeper than it seems. In the first place, such maxims are self-imposed imperatives rather than impersonal affirmations; in the next they imply always the notion of worth or value, a teleological category for which there is no purely objective counterpart; finally, maxims are true—or, as we say, sound—or the reverse, solely in view of their practical consequences; deduction from premises is usually impossible.[65]

The human mind was essentially pragmatic and instinctive. Reason did not lead to human improvement but was the product of primal human striving for self-conservation. Ward did not seek to delineate the features of subjective interest; it was both existential and contingent; it differed somewhat in all minds. No two minds reacted in quite the same fashion nor did they act exactly the same since a somewhat different interest or intensity of interest guided each.

Subjective Selection and Intersubjective Intercourse

At one point in his analysis, Ward posed the question: "How is this change of movement through feeling brought about?" He responded, "By a change of attention." The ability to change or redistribute attention was the sole power or capacity of the Subject. Assimilation, differentiation, reproduction, and association of ideas —the mental chemistry of the associationists—were to be explained by this subjective change of attention. Ward rejected any mechanistic explanation of the change of attention on the part of the Subject.

ment in Psychology," in *Existence*, ed. R. May, E. Angel, and H. F. Ellenberger (New York: Basic Books, 1958), pp. 25–28. Though JW was not discussed in this article, many of the topics probed suggest that he often trod near an existential position.

65. JW, "Faith and Science," *Papers Read before the Synthetic Society, 1896–1908*, pp. 365–66.

The inexplicable and existential interest of the Subject accounted for the subjective selection of the particular sensations that received more or less attention.

> [I]t is only what subjective interest has integrated that is afterwards automatically redintegrated. Were association a purely passive process so far as the experient is concerned, it would be difficult to account for the diversities which exist in the organized experiences of creatures with the same general environment; but subjective selection explains this at once.

Subjective selection lay at the core of the mental life of every individual as an absolute fact of all psychological experience. Yet it stood ignored and unexplained by the naturalistic psychologists, who in their analysis tended "to lose sight of the *Leben* implied in *Erlebnisse*." [66]

Ward considered subjective selection a process that had existed primevally but the influence of which had developed more fully in the course of human evolution.

> A sentient creature moves first of all . . . because it feels, not because it intends. A long process of trial and error must have been necessary to secure as much purposive movement as even a worm displays. In this process natural selection probably played the chief part at the outset, subjective selection becoming more prominent as the process advanced.

The evolution of subjective selection closely resembled the process of human evolution suggested by Alfred Wallace in his 1864 Anthropological Society paper. In both cases the human mind was subject to natural selection until physical survival had been stabilized. At that point a new factor latent during the earlier period came into play and qualitatively modified the human condition. Both Ward and Wallace saw men as having become "more than the creatures of circumstances." According to Ward,

> the representation of what interests us comes then to be associated with the representation of such movements as will secure its realization, so that—although no concentration of attention will secure the requisite intensity to a pleasurable object present

---

66. JW, *Psychological Principles*, p. 54 ("Psychology," p. 43); JW, "Present Problems of General Psychology," *Philosophical Review* 13 (1904): 618; JW, *Psychological Principles*, p. 59.

only in idea—we can, by what is strangely like a concentration of attention, convert the idea of a movement into the fact, and so, by means of movement, attain the coveted reality.[67]

By this means man had become a creature of intention who could strive and often succeed in affecting his environment. The subjective interest displaying itself in subjective selection rendered man a dynamic factor in that environment.

In time the individual mind had ascribed to other similar beings a nature like its own. Intersubjective intercourse resulted and expanded the area of individual human experience into the social realm. Here men could more fully enlarge their experience and learn from other men. Those individual practices of self-conservation that had been most successful would come to be shared as habits by the entire society. From this sharing emerged reason or the concept of a reasoned objective knowledge, which consisted of the shared individual successes originally achieved subjectively and pragmatically.

Moreover, intersubjective intercourse led to the creation of values whereby men might collectively survive and better themselves. Through social experience the individual man learned that he could do more than simply preserve himself—he could morally improve himself. Ward stood at one with Wallace in the belief that self-betterment through social relations set man apart from the rest of nature.

> Life has been defined as the adjustment of internal relations to external relations; it tends directly, that is to say, only towards self-conservation. But character shows itself rather in a certain adjustment of external relations to internal relations; in other words, the end here is the self-conscious realization or betterment of self. *Simplex in vitalitate, duplex in humanitate:* the human individual is amenable to both principles, does not merely live from hand to mouth but lives also in the domain of values and is possessed of ideals which it strives to realize.[68]

The social situation by insuring self-preservation allowed this realization of values. It was a realm of ends or of freedom. Though Ward

---

67. JW, *Psychological Principles,* p. 140 ("Psychology," p. 52); JW, *Psychological Principles,* p. 51; ibid. ("Psychology," p. 42).
68. JW, *Psychological Principles,* p. 462.

was not a social or political philosopher, his psychology pointed toward the social interdependence of human beings and toward their betterment through society rather than to the socially atomistic individual postulated by liberal thinkers whose political thought stemmed from associationism.

Ward's was a psychology of freedom rather than of determinism. However, it was a freedom within the limits of physical environment and heredity.[69] It was the freedom to intend, the freedom to seek to achieve, and the freedom to become moral. Ward thought men were free to achieve a human nature psychologically regarded, in other words, to exercise subjective selection. This was not a human nature that existed prior to experience but one acquired through experience. "Every man shares with others the specific nature that we call human; but this nature is equally entitled to be called the character that our psychological individual in the course of experience has gradually acquired." Each man was free to exercise his subjective selection; save for the urge to self-conservation, he was subject to no inner entelechy determining his nature. The objective environment, or presentation continuum, limited what he selected but his selection from that continuum was at least in part free. The environment did not circumscribe man's "active, interested, and directive" nature but provided the field for its realization.[70]

Circumstances for such active human minds were not only limitations but also "occasions" that might be turned "into opportunities for progress or at the worst [the individual] may struggle and defy them." More important, from the individual's character environ-

---

69. JW's discussion of freedom occurred in the final section of *Psychological Principles* and reflected his thought as developed in *The Realm of Ends or Pluralism and Theism* (Cambridge: Cambridge University Press, 1911). In this final section of *Psychological Principles* JW took leave of the abstract psychological individual that had served as his model. He turned to the concrete human being. The psychic character of that human being was the result of his physical environment, heredity, and subjective selection. JW here developed his concept of *Anlage*, which were inherited propensities, a concept less rigid than inherited characteristics. The *Anlage* somewhat determined a person's viewpoint toward the world. However, the influence of the *Anlage* could be overcome through subjective selection. The point of the entire section was that even with all of these determining factors, human beings possessed a considerable degree of freedom and were by no means totally determined (JW, *Psychological Principles*, pp. 452–70).

70. JW, *Psychological Principles*, p. 406. The "presentation continuum" was JW's term for the realm of objects which the Subject attends with its interest and over which it modifies its attention. See *Psychological Principles*, pp. 49–50.

mental circumstances received their character. "To him pertains the standard by which their values are appraised; and to him the motives they may occasion owe their strength." [71]

Finally, through intersubjective intercourse men could behold themselves and receive the gift of conscience. They could thus freely add to their mental and moral stature. A man "may have an ideal and he can determine *proprio motu* to strive to realize it." Ward believed his empirical analysis of mind provided grounds for belief in the human "freedom to initiate, to turn circumstances to account, even . . . so to deal with oneself." In this respect his concept of freedom very closely resembled the freedom described by the French philosopher Emile Boutroux, who argued, "The individual is not only the creator of his character, he can also intervene in the events of his life and change their course; every moment he can strengthen his acquired tendencies or endeavor to modify them." [72] In Ward as in Butler the continental affinities are clear and certain.

Shades of later existentialism appear throughout Ward's psychology. He sought to understand man's mental existence prior to and outside of scientific abstractions. He was suspicious of reason or intellectualization that might be confused with existing psychological activities themselves. He saw man in large measure creating his own nature and the nature of the world. For Ward, like the later existentialists, man was free. But unlike the existentialists, Ward considered man's freedom a privilege rather than a condemnation. It was the privilege to create freely without hindrance to ideals and aspirations erected by the doctrines of both sin and mechanism. One might almost say that James Ward was an existentialist without *angst*. His metaphysics rather than his psychology, however, accounted for his general optimism.

Henry Sidgwick once noted, "Though the study of the human mind is not itself philosophy . . . it is at least a sort of vestibule of philosophy, from which one passes directly to the *locus principiorum*." [73] In the decade of the nineties Ward moved through that vestibule to combat not only the psychology of scientific naturalism

---

71. Ibid., p. 407.

72. Ibid., p. 407; Emile Boutroux, *The Contingency of the Laws of Nature*, trans. Fred Rothwell (Chicago and London: The Open Court Publishing Company, 1916), p. 172.

73. HS, "Review of Spencer's *The Principles of Psychology*," *Academy* 4 (1873): 131.

but also the entire philosophy that supported the naturalistic interpretation of man and nature.

NATURALISM VANQUISHED: THE GIFFORD LECTURES OF 1896–1898

During the 1890s and the early decades of the twentieth century
the adequacy and the validity of the nineteenth-century mechanistic
and positivistic analysis of nature came under heavy attack from a
number of internationally distinguished thinkers. Among others,
these writers included William James in the United States, Henri
Bergson and Henri Poincaré in France, Edmund Husserl in Germany, and James Ward in England. Each worked independently.
While rarely in accord as to the new alternative to mechanism, they
were fully agreed as to the inadequacy and inappropriateness of the
existing naturalistic model. The fact that the figures mentioned had
received extensive scientific or mathematical training rendered their
attack all the more significant. Developments within experimental
physics, such as energetics and relativity, added impetus to their
critique of the mechanical model.[74]

In 1896 when James Ward rose before his audience at Aberdeen
University to deliver his Gifford Lectures, he knew his was but one
of many voices then being raised against the philosophical pretensions of scientific naturalism. Indeed, he saw the rejection of mechanism about to triumph. "Perhaps," he told the assembly, "some of
you may live to see a second intellectual reformation in which the
mechanical ideal of modern science will be proved in its turn to be
defective and chimerical." [75] Mechanism had been the bronze serpent
that Huxley, Tyndall, Spencer, and lesser naturalistic authors had
held aloft to cure men of metaphysical confusion and religious superstition so they might enter the promised land of the New Nature.
Now James Ward, Michael Foster's "physiologist spoiled," the one-
time experimenter in Leipzig's psychological laboratories and the

74. JW recommended the following books as correcting excessive realism in science:
E. Mach, *Mechanism* and *Popular Science Lectures*; K. Pearson, *The Grammar of
Science*; and J. Stallo's *Concepts of Modern Physics*. (JW to ?? Thomson, 27 September
1917, Cambridge University Library, add. MSS. 7654/W10.) For the general reaction
against nineteenth-century science, see Antonio Aliotta, *The Idealistic Reaction against
Science* (London: Macmillan & Co., 1914); Spiegelberg, *The Phenomenological Move-
ment*, 1 : 25–268; H. Stuart Hughes, *Consciousness and Society* (New York: Random
House, Vintage Books, 1958), pp. 33–66.

75. JW, *Naturalism and Agnosticism* (London: A. & C. Black, 1899), 1 : 166 (hereafter
cited in text of this chapter as *NA*). See JW's discussion of the meaning and definition
of naturalism previously considered in chapter 2, pp. 14–17.

advocate of constructing such a laboratory at Cambridge, turned his intellectual prowess against the mechanical ideal and its late Victorian advocates.

For Ward, more than the philosophical concept of mechanism was at stake. The concept and the ideas derived from it represented a denial of life and a fragmentation of human experience. "Rigorously carried out as a theory of the real world," he declared "that [mechanical] ideal lands us in nihilism" (*NA,* 1 : 166).[76] In their descriptions of man and nature, the exponents of scientific naturalism had excluded vast tracts of human experience (*NA* 1 : 5–9, 27). The fertile islands of freedom, spontaneity, faith, value, and subjective reflection did not appear on the maps of the New Nature. Ward demanded that those areas of ideal and internal human experience left uncharted by naturalistic thinkers be acknowledged to exist and that the cartographers of the New Nature be confronted with the futility of their efforts at exclusion and the fraudulence of their interpretation of experience.

The mechanical ideal and the philosophy of nature linked to it were little more than associationism writ large. They illustrated on a cosmic scale all the faults of the current naturalistic psychologies. In these lectures and in later essays, Ward often contrasted the world of science with the world of history or the realm of symbol with the realm of reality (*NA,* 2 : 169–70, 280–83).[77] To follow scientific naturalism was to detach oneself from concrete life and historical experience. The theories of the scientific publicists—mechanism, evolution, psychophysical parallelism—were abstract and symbolic. However,

> the real is always concrete, the symbolic is always abstract. The real implies individuality more or less; the symbolic is always a logical universal. Within the range of our experience the real implies always a history, that is, places and dates, converse with concrete environment. The symbolic is the creature of logic (*NA,* 1 : 179–80).

No less than Samuel Butler, Ward believed men must begin by flying in the faces of the professors of logic. In his psychology Ward

76. See also Viktor E. Frankl, "Reductionism and Nihilism," in *Beyond Reductionism: New Perspectives in the Life Sciences,* ed. Arthur Koestler and J. R. Smythies (London: Hutchinson & Co., 1969), pp. 309–33.

77. JW, *Essays in Philosophy,* pp. 229–52.

had demonstrated that logical analysis postdated the lived and living experience of men. Human beings did not dwell in the realm of symbol and abstraction. Theirs was the realm of history where all events were marked by time and place. If the experiences of men dwelling in a particular time and place were not to appear meaningless and absurd, the ideas guiding them must be rooted in that concrete, unique historical and psychological experience rather than in some abstracted version of it. Ward did not deny that abstractions were necessary for the pursuit of science and even for expedient living, but he protested the confusion of science with history, symbol with experience, and mechanism with life. Like Butler, Ward sought to clarify the conventional nature of abstractions and by so clarifying to end the confusion of "abstraction with analysis" (NA, 1 : 255). Scientific naturalism need not be the necessary outcome of scientific research or scientific thought. It was rather a mode of thought into which some scientists and scientifically oriented men fell when they confused analytical abstractions with reality.

Ward criticized the ascribing of a mechanical nature to reality on two grounds.[78] Mechanism was the product of a careful selection of details and was thus a mental construct that did not encompass all experienced reality. The ideas of mass, atoms, and molecules were abstract concepts that stood several stages removed from the reality which they were employed to describe.[79] Quoting Mach on the descriptive nature of these concepts and the invalidity of hypostatizing their ontological existence, Ward concluded, "The mechanical theory of the universe, then, begins with abstractions, and in the end has only abstractions left; it begins with phenomenal movement and ends by resolving all phenomena into motion" (NA, 1 : 152–53). He then pointed to the fact that the laws of science were actually statistical probabilities which again had no special correspondence with reality. Ward's entire analysis of mechanism foreshadowed the radical critique of classical physics that would later be enunciated by men such as Heisenberg.

78. S. P. Lamprecht, "James Ward's Critique of Naturalism," Monist 36 (1926) : 136–52; A. H. Murray, The Philosophy of James Ward (Cambridge: Cambridge University Press, 1937), pp. 48–70.

79. "Science cannot originate experience; for experience is the source of science, yet always more than its product, so surely as the workman is more than his tools. Science is but the skeleton, while experience is the life; science but a means, and experience the end itself" (NA, 2 : 282–83).

Second, because mechanism dealt only with abstractions, it was inadequate to describe or interpret the reality of life experienced by concrete human beings.

> [D]angerous as teleological arguments in general may be, we may at least safely say the world was not designed to make science easy. Struggling men and women, like the soldier on the march when his machine-made shoe pinches, might reasonably complain if science should succeed in persuading them that Nature's doles and Nature's dealings from first to last are ruthlessly and rigidly mechanical (*NA*, 1 : 108).

Living human beings knew the zigzaggy turns of nature as well as its regularities. They knew that their responses to nature were not mechanical but subject to their own purposeful subjective selection. Indeed, the entire mechanical ideal stood as a witness to the teleological nature of conceptual reasoning and to the creativity of the mind unrecognized by the exponents of mechanism.

Ward continued his assault on the naturalistic synthesis by explaining that just as the mechanical ideal did not reflect human experience, so the concept of mechanical evolution, as advocated by Spencer, was untrue to the development of human history. Assuming the law of the conservation of energy, evolution must occur in a finite universe. However, if evolution were strictly mechanical,

> the entire history of things would thus be nothing better than the monotonous uniformity of a long series of gigantic Nautical Almanacs. Change there would be certainly, but only change of motion, change of grouping of unchangeable elements, unchangeable because utterly devoid of qualitative diversity or internal character. Progress, development, history, meaning— of these there would be nothing (*NA*, 1 : 246).

Yet human experience revealed progress, development, history, and meaning. Spencerian evolution portrayed change but did not explain the quality and direction of that change. Such a version of evolution dissatisfied Ward for exactly the same reason that natural selection applied to man dissatisfied Alfred Wallace. Neither version of evolution accounted for human beings as creatures of value.

Ward was convinced that no mechanistic evolution could "convert the dead letters of the mechanical alphabet into the living sense of

things" (*NA*, 1 : 261). He believed in natural selection, but he perceived a microteleological impulse behind the variations in organisms
that permitted some to survive the struggle for existence. The impulse displayed itself in the striving of all creatures for self-conservation and in some cases for self-betterment.

> Here we have a teleological factor, and one suggesting not so
> much a nondescript force called vital, as a psychical something
> endowed with feeling and will. Feeling and will answer to the
> psychological principle of self-conservation; when to these we
> add knowledge, we reach a principle to which I have ventured
> to give the name of subjective selection, the counterpart and
> supplement of natural selection and the source of a different
> order of species; to wit, species of environments (*NA*, 2 : 92).

The subjective selection that rendered psychological development
purposeful also allowed Ward to see all evolution as immanently
teleological rather than mechanistic.

Ward reserved his most devastating critique for the fallacies of
psychophysical parallelism, the mechanistic basis for physiological
psychology. This theory held that thought could not influence matter
but changed in a manner parallel to modifications in matter. Ward
argued that the dualism of psychophysical parallelism resulted from
confusing the two different kinds of experience that he had outlined
in his psychology. The first and primary form of experience was that
of the individual mind seeking its own self-conservation. The second
form of experience was the general experience of the race, which
presupposed the first and which arose through intersubjective intercourse. Dualism was the fallacy of ascribing reality to the pragmatic
abstractions of language achieved through intersubjective intercourse.

> Experience in the first sense being relegated to psychology,
> experience in the second remained as the sole business of natu-
> ral science; and the one experience coming then to be regarded
> as exclusively subjective and the other as altogether objective, a
> clear line emerges between the two and the dualism of Mind
> and Nature is the result (*NA*, 2 : 153).

However, experience revealed duality not dualism. Nature received
its particular conceptual arrangement only after subjective percep-

tions achieved pragmatically had been shared through intersubjective intercourse. A model of nature represented a collective, pragmatic convention which possessed no claim to reflect reality. Dualism thus represented a faulty understanding of the role of intersubjective intercourse.

Ward did not seek to deprecate what intersubjective intercourse had achieved for mankind. Without it, "mankind would remain a herd; with it they became a society" (*NA*, 2 : 168). Dwelling together in a society greatly expanded the realm of individual human experience and the area of man's control over his environment. However, to misrepresent these pragmatic abstractions as reality or to regard them as the basis for a self-sufficient environment, such as the New Nature, was to separate man from the real subjective source of all his achievements.

Having criticized mechanism as a basis for philosophy, Ward turned to agnosticism, which he regarded as a not wholly sound ally of the mechanical theories. Nevertheless, naturalism, in the form of mechanism, and agnosticism had become "the complementary halves of the dominant philosophy of our scientific teachers" (*NA*, 1 : 20). The two doctrines had mutually influenced each other so as to exaggerate the worst features of each.

> Agnosticism . . . has reacted upon naturalism, inducing in it a more uncompromising application of scientific method to all the phenomena of experience. . . . [N]aturalism in its turn has reacted upon agnosticism, inducing in that a more pronounced scepticism, or even the renunciation of higher knowledge as a duty, in place of the bare confession of ignorance as a fact (*NA*, 1 : 20–21).

It will be recalled that this tension between popular and pure agnosticism had turned George Romanes back toward faith. Ward argued, as had Romanes, that agnosticism simply amounted to a neutral monism replacing the untenable monism of materialism. However, in the hands of its naturalistic advocates, this neutral monism became highly unstable and oscillated between materialism and dualism. Ward suggested that agnostic monism, as well as materialism, was incommensurate with human experience which required an idealistic or, as he preferred to call it, a "spiritualistic monism" that encompassed active mind as well as matter (*NA*, 2 : 202).

Ward believed that man's experience with physical nature proved the latter to be teleological and spiritual in two regards. First, nature was conformable to human intelligence (NA, 2 : 253–55). Second, physical nature was amenable to human ends.

> A rude anthropomorphism gives us our first bearings, and every advance in knowledge of the Not-self is a further self-revealing. With this clearer self-consciousness we judge the world more adequately, employ truer and more perfect categories. But all through it is a process of assimilating the non-Ego to the Ego, not the Ego to the non-Ego; and therefore self-realization is the sole way to advance (NA, 2 : 256).

This process, fully described in his psychology, revealed to "an unbiassed and reflective mind that Nature and Man are one in being rational" (NA, 2 : 257).

Through these arguments Ward believed he had begun to dispel the "chaos" of naturalism. "Chaos I call it, for the world described strictly in mechanical terms can have not a vestige of meaning. There is exactness, there is precision, but there is no true unity and no sense (NA, 2 : 89) . Naturalism carried men further and further away from the subjective source of their experience and placed them under the sway of necessity rather than of the reality of freedom. Naturalism ignored the psychological experience that revealed a contingency that is "not that of chance, but that of freedom; so far as everything that is is a law in itself, has an end for itself, and seeks the good" (NA, 2 : 281). Such freedom the dualism of naturalism denied, but human experience confirmed.

Just as the naturalistic cartographers had swept away purpose and freedom from the map of human experience, they had also attempted to banish interest in the problem of theism and, by implication, interest in moral values. "Naturalism, speaking in the name of science, declares the problem superfluous, and agnosticism, professing to represent reason, declares it to be insoluble" (NA, 1 : 37). During the next two decades of his life, Ward sought to correct the misdrawn map and to shade in the islands of human experience omitted by so many of his contemporaries. In doing so he hoped to keep alive interest in theism and in the possible relationship of man and the divine. When he drew his own map of the macrocosm, he did not include the lands of the divine, but he did remove those signs that had discouraged such adventuresome intellectual exploration.

The New Cartography—The Realm of Ends

In his second set of Gifford Lectures, delivered between 1907 and 1910, James Ward sought to portray the macrocosm as it appeared to and was experienced by the cognitive, feeling, and conative minds of his psychology. He set about to draw a map of the macrocosm that would chart the world of life, history, and faith. Ward hoped to "ascertain what we can know, or reasonably believe, concerning the constitution of the world, *interpreted throughout and strictly in terms of Mind.*" [80] This world was pluralistic, spontaneous, evolving, contingent, and theistic. It was rooted in the prereflective reality of psychological experience rather than in the abstractions of the New Nature. The lectures were one part of the broader intellectual movement emerging after the turn of the century "to bring philosophy into contact with life, to invest it with the charm of personality, and to breathe life into the 'dead bones of metaphysics'." [81] Ward was asserting the right and more significantly the necessity of constructive speculation about the nature and mode of existing things.

"No doubt," Ward once confessed to Henry Barker of the University of Edinburgh, "my view leads to certain metaphysical positions—approximately pluralistic; but I did not reach my psychological views by way of metaphysics, for they came to me first & independently." [82] Pluralism represented the point of departure for Ward's thought but not his conclusion. While not a pluralist, he believed that the human standpoint in the world was pluralistic. The "basal fact" of every finite experience was the duality of subject and object (*RE,* p. 10). That duality placed men at "the historical standpoint, the standpoint of the concrete and individual" (*RE,* p. 10). It was a prereflective standpoint of subjective synthesis prior to abstract analysis. Ward felt that by commencing with the individual mind in *media res,* he could account for mechanical appearances, but that

80. JW, *The Realm of Ends or Pluralism and Theism,* 2nd ed. (Cambridge: Cambridge University Press, 1912), p. v (hereafter cited in text of this chapter as *RE*).
81. L. Susan Stebbing, *Pragmatism and French Voluntarism* (Cambridge: Cambridge University Press, 1914), p. 3.
82. JW to Henry Barker, 17 March 1918, The Henry Barker Correspondence, University of Edinburgh Library, Dc.6. 1184.

beginning from abstract mechanism he could never explain a living mind.

From this pluralistic starting point, Ward worked his way out to the rest of reality. "The self of which we are conscious . . . furnishes us with our first paradigm of what we are to understand by the individuals of our plurality (*RE*, p. 52).[83] Each of these subjectively selecting selves provided an occasion for activity upon the part of another similar self. Each self spontaneously acted and reacted in response to the spontaneous activity of other selves. In terms of Ward's psychology this pluralism meant that the presentation continuum of objects toward which the Subject directed its attention through subjective selection possessed an active nature.

Through intersubjective intercourse these individually active minds had formed a community and achieved values whereby each agent could rise above striving only for self-conservation. Spontaneous practices communally adopted and converted into habits accounted for an appearance of uniformity that was "compatible with the spontaneity of living agents" (*RE*, pp. 66–67, also 52–56). The basis of mechanical regularity was the shared experience of independently active subjects. To explain this situation, Ward revived the scholastic distinction between *natura naturans* and *natura naturata* (*RE*, pp. 72–75, 357–58).

> What is done, *natura naturata*—the decisions made, the habits formed, the customs fixed—constitutes at any stage the routine, the general trend of things, within which future possibilities lie. What is still to do, *natura naturans,* implies further spontaneity and growth; new decisions to be taken, fresh experiments to be made, with their usual sequel of trial and error and possible eventual success; happy thoughts or inspirations occurring to the individual; and the rise of great men inaugurating new epochs for their race or for the world (*RE*, pp. 72–73).[84]

Via intersubjective intercourse, minds had discovered certain routines as expedient ways of sustaining themselves. These routines relearned by each generation now appeared to be mechanical. It should be noted that the education of new minds through this

83. Murray, *The Philosophy of James Ward*, pp. 123–48.
84. Cf. Boutroux, *The Contingency of the Laws of Nature,* pp. vi, 185–86.

process achieved for Ward's world view what organic memory did for Samuel Butler's.

This world was in its very essence active: "all changes in the environment will be the result of conative impulses somewhere" (*RE*, p. 68). Every part of the universe was alive. Like Romanes and Butler, Ward adopted a panpsychist view of nature. He argued there was no reason to believe that men had yet reached the limits of their knowledge of where life extended. He rejected the division of matter into organic and inorganic. Employing the paradigm of his psychological Subject, he posited the existence of lower and unknown living things that also were active and not subject to mechanism. All motions and activities in nature that appeared either mechanical or automatic were spontaneous acts of animal faith routinized through intersubjective intercourse (*RE*, pp. 52–59, 74–81).[85] No natural laws were prior to the action of "the active individuals who compose the world, no laws . . . [determine] *them*, unless we call their own nature a law; and then indeed the world would start with as many laws as there are individuals" (*RE*, pp. 75–76). Every physical law stood as a monument to an original spontaneous teleological act of faith whereby active minds determined their own natures through the striving for self-preservation and then for self-realization.[86]

The activity of these free agents created the uniformity of natural law and imbued the universe with its purposeful character. They were determining as well as determined entities. "The world limits me in manifold ways, but it is also dependent upon me. For I am not wholly passive and inert: I am able to react upon it and do in fact in some measure modify it: apart from me it would not be all in all just what it is" (*RE*, pp. 191–92). Contingency and spontaneity

85. Murray, *The Philosophy of James Ward*, pp. 104–11.

86. "There will be no laws, prior to these agents, making them what they are; but they, being what they are, their action and interaction, will result in uniformity and order. Habit, dexterity, and familiarity do not precede experience, but arise in the course of it: language and custom, social status and obligation, originate and consolidate with the progress of society and are nothing apart from it. On the spiritualistic view then—whether panpsychist or idealist—the agents are first: and law in every sense and evolution are but second. And surely this is the only tenable position. Laws without a lawgiver, intelligible order and no intelligible agents, meaning and purpose before there is aught that feels or strives—a phantom skeleton first which then quickens itself to life and power—is not this unthinkable?" (JW, "Mechanism and Morals" (1905), in *Essays in Philosophy*, pp. 247–48).

were part of the nature of things. Yet they were never the contingency and spontaneity of chance: "The purposive act or deliberate intention of one agent may for the experience of a second be a mere happening or accident. . . . Though contingent to others it was not in itself a case either of chance or necessity" (*RE,* p. 78). The very spontaneity of the world pointed to its being a realm of ends and purpose.

Ward insisted that "the more completely we can interpret the world as a realm of ends the more completely the tables are turned upon naturalism" (*RE,* p. 14). Ends, purpose, worth, values presented living realities that could not be reduced to evolving atoms and energy. The realm of ends was an evolving or emerging world. Its free agents via intersubjective intercourse created a synthesis entailing "new properties which its component factors in their previous isolation did not possess" (*RE,* pp. 102, also 103–07). Consequently, the present was qualitatively different from the past.

Such a creatively emerging world was a realm of history and morality, bearing little resemblance to the mechanical world of the New Nature. As Ward explained in 1905,

> [I]n the world of history we distinguish between what is and what ought to be; whereas in the world of science what is and what must be are one and the same. This, the supreme contrast between mechanism and morals, discloses in the historical world a far more complex and intimate unity than the merely quantitative continuity of the mechanical world, with its abstract categories of space, time, and mass, can possibly shew. For the ideal of moral order supposes a community of free persons, severally distinct and peculiar, but all cooperating for a supreme end.[87]

History was a far more complex world than that of science for it was the world of subjectively selecting participants. History resulted from the inward experiences and reflection of its participants. Consequently, spontaneity, purpose, and worth were to be found at every turn.

For James Ward, however, even this spontaneous, free, creatively evolving plurality was not a complete or a spiritually satisfying

87. JW, *Essays in Philosophy,* p. 233.

world. His map still did not assure the traveler certain bearings or probable arrival.

> It seems obvious that unless some supreme spiritual unity is found the universe will remain in the highest sense an absolute plurality, if such a term is allowable. Such a universe would be a merely sporadic manifold of realms of ends having a common physical basis but devoid of all teleological continuity; like so many village communities without a supreme federation, geographically neighbors but strangers politically. As society lifts the individual to a higher level, so we feel that a supreme unity would increase the worth of this universe both intellectually and morally (*RE,* p. 185).

In pursuit of unity through theism, Ward moved, and acknowledged the move as such, from empiricism to faith.[88] He believed the shift was justified by his psychology, which held that all knowledge, scientific or otherwise, originated in faith.

By quoting Alfred Wallace, Ward suggested in a manner reminiscent of Myers, Romanes, and Butler that the principle of continuity permitted and might even demand the positing of intelligences higher than man (*RE,* pp. 185–201). Ward thus extended his panpsychism into realms of higher spiritual being. The probable existence of these realms seemed to promise that the individuals in the plurality were not condemned to the "Sisyphean task" of realizing impossible goals or ideals (*RE,* p. 215). Ward's projection of spiritual continuity was analogous to Wallace's somewhat cruder appeal to the presence of spirits to guarantee further moral evolution. The positing of the theistic ideal not only gave unity to the plurality but also assured that the ideal goals of humanity were capable of achievement. Unlike Henry Sidgwick, Ward did not posit his deity as the guarantor of final ethical sanctions. Beyond assuring that ideal goals were indeed achievable, theism enhanced the character of those ideals "by all the ineffable blessedness that the presence of God must yield" (*RE,* p. 230).

Ward would have been the first to admit the absence of any

---

88. For discussions of JW's theism, see P. A. Bertocci, *The Empirical Argument for God in Late British Thought* (Cambridge: Harvard University Press, 1938), pp. 92–133; R. F. A. Hoernle, *Idealism as a Philosophy* (New York: Doran, 1927), pp. 140–46; Murray, *The Philosophy of James Ward,* pp. 143–48; G. Dawes Hicks, "James Ward's Philosophical Approach to Theism," *Hibbert Journal* 24 (1925–26): 49–63.

empirical proof for the existence of God or other lesser spiritual
beings. Yet like Kant, Ward contended the absence of proof did not
in itself constitute a disproof. In a spirit similar to George Romanes's
pure agnostic experiment of belief, Ward advocated only the possibility of a fruitful and reasonable *faith* in the presence of God.
He had long considered this faith better than the traditional
theistic proofs drawn in the natural theology of Paley, the *Bridge-
water Treatises,* and other similar works. The latter were subversive
to their own ends since the next scientific discovery might undermine them. In his approach to this reasonable theism, Ward confronted two principle difficulties—the idea of creation and the
presence of evil. His treatment of these two problems would not
have satisfied adherents of either Christianity or naturalism or many
other philosophers.

If the presence of a deity were to mean anything, God must be
more than just another mind in the plurality. Since His presence in
the world made Him a blessing to the world, He must be immanent
in all existing things. On the other hand, this immanence must not
be pantheistic since each existing entity was partially free. Consequently, Ward's God was also transcendent since He had created the
world. Yet Ward rejected both creation ex nihilo and creation in
time (*RE,* pp. 231–46). In place of these he appealed to a mystical
view of creation.

> If creation means anything, it means something so far involved
> in the divine essence, that we are entitled to say, as Hegel was
> fond of saying, that "without the world God is not God." In
> calling God the creator then it is simply the world's dependence
> on Him that we mean to express. . . . In other words God is
> the ground of the world's being, its *ratio essendi.* The notion of
> "ground," it will, I assume, be conceded, is wider than that of
> cause, which is only one of its special forms (*RE,* pp. 233–34).

Clearly Ward could express the relationship he wished God to maintain in regard to the world better than he could explain how it was
achieved. His God was immanent by presence and interest in the
world. He was transcendent in His granting freedom to His
creatures. God had limited His power in relation to this world to
permit His creatures to use freely their God-given talents to work

toward the realization of values. Ward admitted that such a relation-ship defied human understanding. He argued, however, in a mark-edly self-serving manner, that if the idea of a creating God were to be genuinely transcendent, men must not be able to understand it completely (*RE,* pp. 241–46).

The presence of physical and moral evil posed considerable diffi-culty for Ward. He admitted that even the world blessed by the presence of God was far from perfect. He then tried to regard im-perfection in an optimistic light. Like Wallace, he sought to prove that the possibility of physical evil might be essential to the ultimate perfection of the world. If the world were perfect, it would simply not be the world as we know it. A perfect world would of necessity be static, nonprogressive, and nonevolving. It would preclude the basic psychological activities, for there would be neither reason for nor possibility of subjective selection. It would render useless the social intercourse from which moral values had emerged (*RE,* pp. 349–53).

Second, Ward contended that the presence of physical evil and suffering worked toward good by prodding men to overcome them. Such evil was only relative and might ultimately benefit mankind: "This relativity of many so-called evils is apparent; in relation to the past, as marking progress, they are really good; only in view of future progress which they may delay do they become evil" (*RE,* p. 350). Suffering and relative evil were natural to a pluralistic and contingent world because the basis of that world was the initiative of the many. Yet the many learned as they overcame evil and were morally improved for having done so.

> Even if there be a God he certainly has not made the world what it is to be, but rather endowed it with talents to enable it to work out its own perfection in conjunction with himself. This working out is what we call experience, and experience can never pre-suppose the knowledge or the skill that is only gained by means of it. Where several possibilities are open a creature acting on its own initiative can only find out the right one by way of trial and often of error. Such error we may say is an evil; but we cannot straightway call it a superfluous, still less an absolute, evil, if it is an inevitable incident of experience

as such, and if in general the experience is worth what it costs (*RE,* p. 356).

By overcoming evil men attained a higher intellectual and moral existence; thus suffering worked toward good. Like Wallace, Ward seems to have considered the universe as a theodicy of emerging harmonies. Like Butler, he saw man moving toward that harmony through the trial and error of cunning.

Having thus dealt with physical evil and suffering, Ward proceeded to deny the presence of any principle of moral evil in the world (*RE,* pp. 376–77). He thus vanquished his old enemy, the devil of Spring Hill, and emancipated himself from another link with his nonconformist heritage. Ward believed the concept of moral evil postdated the emergence of moral consciousness via intersubjective intercourse. Sin was a social rather than an individual concept. What had been termed sin or moral evil were occasions for selfishness within society. Such selfish lapses formed part of the nature of a plurality in which the individuals were something more than puppets of the deity (*RE,* pp. 374–75). Ward no more wanted men condemned to perfection than to evil. The world was not perfect but perfectable. Such was the price and condition of freedom.

> This actual world of ours can lay no claim to such perfection; it has still to work out its own salvation. But it is certainly a moral world, for it acknowledges the authority of conscience even when it disobeys: conscience is ever a power in it working for the righteousness, in which alone the world finds its own meaning and its supreme ideal (*RE,* p. 373).

If this were not the case and immediate moral perfection were assured, man should be "an immaculate puppet rather than a man with all his shortcomings but also with all his capabilities (*RE,* p. 374). Ward would not rest content with any view of the world which seemed to rob men of their own native capacity to become creatures of value.

More than any other facet of his thought Ward's discussion of evil marked him as a man of the nineteenth century. He relished the idea of moral and social progress and never seems to have seriously doubted its validity. His denial of moral evil and his faith in the ultimate triumph of good from the experience of physical evil would not attract many thinkers after the trauma of World War I. This fact, among others, may explain why his metaphysics gained few followers during the next generation. Where he stood more in harmony with later intellectuals was in his concern for freedom from determinism and in his view of faith. His thoughts on the latter topic link him with pragmatists and possibly with later existentialists. On this issue, he stood in close agreement with Samuel Butler and, of course, William James.

In a highly Lamarckian and Butlerian vein, Ward argued that throughout the natural world "almost every forward step in the progress of life could be formulated as an act of faith—an act not warranted by knowledge—on the part of the pioneer who first made it" (*RE*, p. 415). Ward regarded such faith as "a sort of unscientific trustfulness" (*RE*, p. 416). He compared it with Abraham's leaving Ur and concluded, "We trust and try first, not understanding till afterwards: our attitude in short is not unlike that of Anselm's famous *Credo ut intelligam*" (*RE*, p. 416). With all deference to Ward, this faith was very different from that of Abraham or Anselm. Ward's faith was perfectly blind and not based on theological or ontological certainties.[89] Indeed, what theological or ontological certainties existed were products of a faith that had led men from isolation to subjective selection and into society. Faith might again bear great moral fruit if it allowed men to believe in God and in immortality. This faith was not unique either "psychologically" or "historically" (*RE*, p. 46). It was the faith that had given man his present humanity and might lead him to a higher humanity. It was the faith that permitted him to discover what he might become.

According to Ward, to view the world without faith was to regard life as irrational and to conclude that men had developed high ideals only to find that they could not fulfill them. To admit such irrationality was not a valid alternative when the door of faith rendered life rational by postulating a God and a future life. Such faith was what Henry Sidgwick had attained in his mental crisis of 1887. Faith

89. See H. Barker, "Review of Ward's *Essays in Philosophy*," *Mind* 32 (1927): 382–83; W. R. Sorley, "Ward's Philosophy of Religion," *Monist* 36 (1926): 56–69; Murray, *The Philosophy of James Ward*, pp. 159–71. Murray argued that JW's use of faith was in support of Christian theism. However, JW's God was hardly the Christian God. JW's view of faith was more nearly existential than it was traditionally Christian. Even in essays where JW was most eloquent about faith and friendly to Christianity, he spoke of himself as an outsider to the Christian faith.

saved the world from absurdity and by doing so proved itself to be not absurd (*RE*, pp. 420–22, 440–42). The existence of man's moral ideals and yearnings rendered such faith reasonable. "Humanity already has yearnings and aspirations that the flesh-pots of Egypt— material and temporal well-being—can never content; is it, impelled by these longings for higher things, destined to wander aimlessly in the wilderness forever unsatisfied?" (*RE*, pp. 425–26). Humanity would not so wander if it could live by faith. For by faith men had created new values that were not comprehended within the New Nature. Those values had begun to carry men beyond the strivings for self-conservation to a point within sight of "not a pre-established harmony but the eventual consummation of a perfect common-wealth, wherein all cooperate and none conflict, wherein the many have become one, one realm of ends" (*RE*, p. 435). The faith that had led men to that point of departure was essentially existential. It was not logical. It was founded on nothing other than the futurity that man carried within himself as his existence was grounded in the power of God (*RE*, pp. 447–48). It was the faith of "hopeful adventure." [90]

Thus Ward, like the other men in this study, came to affirm the world as good and as meaningful for the lives of human beings. He did so by interpreting the macrocosm through the microcosm. He stood equally far from the rigid dogmas of his Congregational youth and from the physiology of Michael Foster's laboratory. He had succeeded in fulfilling the yearnings he had voiced at the height of his religious turmoil.

> There are laws of evidence on which men agree and not a few valid ideas, let us work scientifically in sorting the material before us and building up the Sciences, then critically in the discussing of their principles, ground ideas and results. Who says that such a notion as purpose has not helped to explain much in the world? Grant that it be subjective. Still it helps us on. Does not the like hold of worth, a far more difficult idea, and many others? . . . Let all be provisional, yet if a whole, a perfect cosmos results at last who shall say then that these ideas are mere tools. . . . It is because our savants work with one eye, without perspective and chiaroscuro that they present us

90. JW, *Essays in Philosophy*, p. 139.

with those flat Egyptian pictures of the world with which no soul can rest content. But get both eyes at it, let the notions of worth and end play their part, and you may have a stereoscopic photograph of the whole, united and complete.[91]

By using both the eye of faith and the eye of experience, the one-time student of architecture had charted the map of the realm of ends between religion and science. It could perhaps only have been so charted by a man who felt drawn toward each but content with neither.

91. Campbell, "Memoir," p. 37.

9

Some Closing Considerations

H. Stuart Hughes once noted that the intellectual historian must deal "with reasoned argument and with passionate outburst alike." [1] There are also occasions when he must deal with both in the context of a single man's thought. This has been the case with Henry Sidgwick, Alfred Russel Wallace, Frederic Myers, George Romanes, Samuel Butler, and James Ward, who transformed passionate outbursts of contempt for scientific naturalism into reasoned or at least plausible arguments. Theirs was the protest of non-Christians against a world view that menaced ideals, hopes, and aspirations which gave their lives meaning and purpose.

Their intellectual stance must be distinguished from both the nineteenth-century Christian reaction to new scientific theory and the later twentieth-century disillusionment with scientific progress. Christians objected to the naturalistic contention that men could live honest, righteous, and meaningful lives without God, without faith in Christ's atonement, without the Bible, and without the church and clergy. Secular humanists of the twentieth century, such as Aldous Huxley, George Orwell, and C. P. Snow, questioned the cultural and ethical adequacy of the New Nature only after World War I, the scientism of totalitarianism, and the image of nuclear holocaust had revealed the destructive potential of science and technology. Sidgwick, Wallace, Myers, Romanes, Butler, and Ward criticized scientific naturalism before the demonic elements of the New Nature had emerged and without defending either Christianity or an ecclesiastical structure.

They shared with more liberal Christian spokesmen a belief in the validity and inevitability of questions ignored or unresolved by the advocates of naturalism. With the later secular humanists they shared the conviction of the intellectual centrality of man and

1. H. Stuart Hughes, *Consciousness and Society: The Reorientation of European Social Thought, 1890–1930* (New York: Random House, Vintage Books, 1958), p. 3.

human values. Yet their protest was neither sectarian nor secular. Rather it epitomized the cultural dilemma of certain late nineteenth- and early twentieth-century men and women once portrayed as knowing

> that they have outgrown the church as exemplified in Christianity, but who have not therefore been brought to deny the fact that a religious attitude to life is as essential to them as a belief in the authenticity of science. These people have experienced the soul as vividly as the body, the body as vividly as the soul. And the soul has manifested itself to them in ways not to be explained in terms either of traditional theology or of materialism.

While intended to depict the admirers of Jung during the interwar period, this statement precisely characterizes the intellectual situation of Sidgwick, Romanes, Butler, and the rest. They were nineteenth-century paradigms of the "modern man of culture" whom Routh associated with the twentieth century and described as seeking "a new spirituality which must be authorized by science and yet contain a religious value." [2] However, the religion they had known and the scientific naturalism they had encountered in the third quarter of the nineteenth century permitted no such spiritual synthesis. Therefore, they reached outward to discover evidence of a spiritual dimension in nature or searched inwardly to perceive a reality qualitatively different from that described by science.

The pursuit by these six men for an intellectual alternative to both Christianity and naturalism constituted an English facet of "the revolt against positivism," which Professor Hughes so carefully examined in regard to continental social thought.[3] Hughes was probably correct in excluding Britain from the purview of a study concerned largely with criticism of Marxism, since that ideology made practically no headway in Britain. Nevertheless, Marxism and scientific naturalism were cut from the same cloth, a fact not lost on Marx, who wrote of *Origin of Species*, "Although it is developed in the crude English style, this is the book which contains the basis in

2. Cary F. Baynes, Translators' Preface, in C. G. Jung, *Modern Man in Search of a Soul*, trans. W. S. Dell and Cary F. Baynes (London: Kegan Paul, Trench, Trubner & Co., 1933), p. viii; H. V. Routh, *Towards the Twentieth Century: Essays in the Spiritual History of the Nineteenth* (New York: Macmillan Co., 1937), p. 369.

3. Hughes, *Consciousness and Society*, p. 33.

natural history for our view." [4] Sidgwick's critique of contemporary evolutionary ethics and sociology was similar to later rejections of Marxism on the grounds of inadequate social guidance. Wallace perceived the implicit absence of human values in a purely material or technological culture. Ward pointed to the impossibility of explaining either material or moral progress without reference to nonmaterial and nonmechanical factors. All of them believed that something other than categories and theories from the physical sciences was required to explain the behavior and experience of human beings.

A more significant affinity of these writers with the general European reaction against positivism lay in their attempts to integrate nonrational elements of human nature into a rational synthesis wherein those elements might constitute meaningful or functional entities rather than symptoms of organic mental disorder or survivals of earlier stages of social evolution.[5] Sidgwick, Wallace, and Myers regarded the nonrational as normal to human experience. The psychical phenomena they investigated and considered significant for their own lives were often the same phenomena that Durkheim, Weber, Janet, Flournoy, Freud, and Jung were beginning to ponder. That the English explanations of such matters were generally unacceptable to social scientists and psychologists should not detract from the fact that British writers were deeply concerned with these problems.

Romanes, Butler, and Ward, in the manner of contemporary continental and American writers, stood prepared to assert that nonrational or nondiscursive impulses might guide human thought and undergird rational order. Like Bergson they saw intuitive factors contributing to human understanding, and like William James they regarded human knowledge as pragmatic in nature. For Butler and Ward, nature and human perception and interpretation of nature resulted from man's interaction with his environment. They and Romanes recognized that scientific theories were "at bottom a human construction, variable and relative, and that they suppose an

4. Quoted by Robert Young, "The Impact of Darwin on Conventional Thought," in *The Victorian Crisis of Faith*, ed. Anthony Symondson (London: Society for Promoting Christian Knowledge, 1970), p. 31.

5. J. W. Burrow, *Evolution and Society: A Study of Victorian Social Theory* (Cambridge: Cambridge University Press, 1966), p. 234–59.

act of faith at their roots." [6] By the turn of the century this viewpoint had become widespread throughout Europe and contributed to a new philosophical modesty on the part of many scientifically oriented writers.

Other resemblances with the thought of the continent are also evident. Certain ideas set forth by Butler, Ward, Wallace, and Myers suggest that some British intellectuals embraced theories similar to those of "the philosophy of life" associated with Schelling, Fechner, Schopenhauer, Bergson, and the French spiritual writers.[7] These philosophers pointed to an inner life force manifest in man or also in physical nature but insusceptible to scientific or mathematical analysis. This biophilosophical thought tending toward animism, vitalism, or panpsychism maintained considerable strength and displayed more persistence in Britain than has been generally recognized. Emerging during the romantic period, it received a new lease on life at midcentury from obscure writers such as James Hinton and J. A. Picton. Later it was embraced by Butler and implied in Myers's World Soul. By the twentieth century this vitalist or panpsychist tendency attained intellectual respectability, if not widespread acceptance, through the works of James Ward, Lloyd Morgan, Samuel Alexander, William McDougall, and C. H. Waddington.[8] These writers propounded some mode of creative or emergent evolution whereby life could not be reduced simply to mechanical arrangements of matter and energy. Their general outlook was expressed by Whitehead: "The only way of mitigating mechanism is by the discovery that it is not mechanism." [9]

Finally, as has been implied in earlier sections of this study, some of these figures bordered on an existential view of man and of man's

6. Antonio Aliotta, "Science and Religion in the Nineteenth Century," in *Science, Religion and Reality*, ed. Joseph Needham (New York: Macmillan Co., 1928), p. 166.

7. Paul Tillich, *Theology of Culture* (New York: Oxford University Press, 1968), p. 79.

8. Thomas McFarland, *Coleridge and the Pantheist Tradition* (New York: Oxford University Press, 1969); H. W. Piper, *The Active Universe* (London: The Athlone Press, 1962); James Hinton, *Life in Nature* (London: Smith, Elder, & Co., 1862); C. Lloyd Morgan, *Emergent Evolution* (London: Williams & Norgate, 1923); William McDougall, *Body and Mind: A History and a Defence of Animism* (London: Methuen & Co., 1911); Samuel Alexander, *Space, Time, and Deity* (London: Macmillan & Co., 1920); C. H. Waddington, *The Nature of Life* (New York: Atheneum, 1962).

9. A. N. Whitehead, *Science and the Modern World* (New York: Mentor Books, 1956), p. 77.

relationship to the surrounding world. Sidgwick's mental crisis of 1887, Myers's and Romanes's pondering of death, Butler's conviction of the illusory nature of discursive knowledge, and Ward's concept of subjective selection partook of an existential awareness. None was an existentialist, but each was considering the possibility or probability of a world in which existence stood prior to essence. They perceived both the inadequacy of scientific abstraction for expression of authentic human feelings or for complete guidance to life and the limitations of discursive reason for exploration of the world and direction of human action. They objected to the fragmentation of human experience for the convenience of abstract scientific analysis. However tenuous this suggestion may be, there can be little doubt that Paul Tillich overstated his case when he argued, "England is the only European country in which the Existential problem of finding a new meaning for life had no significance, because there positivism and the religious tradition lived on side by side, united by a social conformism which prevented radical questions about the meaning of human 'Existence.'" [10] There may have been no British existential movement, but there were men who found themselves thrust into existential situations and compelled to ponder existential questions because they could accommodate themselves to neither Christianity nor scientific naturalism.

The remonstrance lodged by Sidgwick, Wallace, Myers, Romanes, Butler, and Ward first against Christianity, then later and more pointedly against scientific naturalism, stemmed from what is perhaps most appropriately termed an intellectual hatred. And as Yeats wrote, "An intellectual hatred is the worst." [11] They rejected Christianity and scientific naturalism because both creeds offended what had become the most unquestionable convictions of their intellects —belief in the possibility of rational life and moral progress, hope of immortality, concern for intellectual integrity, and faith in the value of speculation and in the validity of subjective sources of knowledge. Both Christianity and scientific naturalism challenged these ideals and failed to provide an adequate framework for their realization.[12]

10. Tillich, *Theology of Culture*, p. 108.

11. W. B. Yeats, *The Collected Poems of W. B. Yeats* (New York: Macmillan Co., 1961), p. 187.

12. Howard R. Murphy, "The Ethical Revolt against Christian Orthodoxy in Early Victorian England," *American Historical Review* 60 (1955): 800–17.

Paradoxically, the intellectual hatred of scientific naturalism was intimately related to the initial rejection of Christianity. What each man had hated most about the Christian faith reappeared in secular guise within the context of scientific naturalism. Only by rejecting naturalism could each preserve the integrity of those principles for which he had initially left Christianity often at considerable social and personal cost. Sidgwick, unable to reconcile himself to the irrationality of the Virgin Birth or to the orthodoxy of the Anglican church, could not accept a new set of ideas that provided no basis for rational ethical decision and permitted only a restricted pursuit of philosophy. Wallace, having rebelled against the doctrine of arbitrary predestination, refused to leave moral progress to chance or to consider men as less than responsible for moral actions. From neither Christianity nor scientific naturalism could Myers receive assurance that his personality and those of persons he loved would escape annihilation. Romanes eventually found the doctrines of both the church and the scientists unsatisfactory as explanations of nature or as affirmations of life. Butler discovered that the advocates of science denied free will and spurned intellectual freedom and honesty no less than did the orthodox clergy. James Ward, for whom the nonconformist verities no longer dealt with the beggarly elements of life, could hardly place new trust in a scientific synthesis that also failed to deal with them; nor could he exchange the determinism of God for that of matter and energy.

Theirs was an intellectual hatred also because they perceived that scientific naturalism in the hands of its leading spokesmen could prove incompatible with the life of the mind. If the freethinkers of naturalism triumphed, freedom of thought, liberal pursuit of truth, and unhampered examination of human experience would perish. An intellectual movement that began by dismissing the validity of certain experiences and questions could end by denouncing alternative explanations of experiences and questions it did consider valid. A culture dominated by scientific experts would not necessarily be more emancipated than one dominated by the clergy. The discovery and dispersal of knowledge required a plurality of intellectuals cooperating with one another, tolerating one another, criticizing one another, and recognizing their own limitations.

None of the figures in this study, not even Butler, desired to discredit the expertise of the scientific profession. What they held in contempt was "philosophy which claimed that science was the only kind of knowledge that existed or ever could exist" and theories "which limited the intellect to the kind of thinking characteristic of natural science." [13] Their critique was not merely philosophical. From personal experience, they knew that scientific thinking and theories did not exist in a vacuum, but rather, as Toulmin, Kuhn, Gillispie, and Barber have since argued, are conditioned by scientific and sometimes nonscientific presuppositions and by professional practices.[14] This perception made them wary of the claims for objective disinterest on the part of scientific thinkers.

In addition to recognizing the professional nature of scientific thinking, many early and mid-twentieth-century intellectuals came to agree with Sidgwick, Wallace, Myers, Romanes, Butler, and Ward in regard to other objections to the pretensions of scientific naturalism. Later naturalistic writers often abandoned the reductionism of the nineteenth century for what Randall termed the antireductionist thesis that "intellectual analysis may discriminate hitherto unknown factors and structures in a subject-matter, but it can never validly take away from or destroy the subject-matter which it sets out to explore." Consequently, subjective perception, psychical phenomena, religious experience, and death have attracted considerable attention from intellectuals who have had no desire to explain them away. The demise of the specter of ecclesiasticism permitted a consideration of religion that concentrated on understanding rather than on criticism. Among sociologists and anthropologists, the profoundly antireligious bias of Tylor gave way to a new sensitivity voiced by Malinowski: "The substance of all religion . . . is deeply rooted in human life; it grows out of the necessities of life." More than one rationalist recognized with Bertrand Russell that "when the dogmas have been rejected, the question of the place of religion in life is by

13. R. G. Collingwood, *The Idea of History* (New York: Oxford University Press, 1956), p. 134.

14. Bernard Barber, "Resistance by Scientists to Scientific Discovery," *Science* 134 (1961): 596–602; C. C. Gillispie, *Genesis and Geology: The Impact of Scientific Discoveries upon Religious Beliefs in the Decades before Darwin* (New York: Harper Torchbooks, 1959); T. S. Kuhn, *The Copernican Revolution* (Cambridge: Harvard University Press, 1957); Stephen Toulmin, *Human Understanding* (Princeton: Princeton University Press, 1972). Victorian men of science certainly recognized the problems of professional orthodoxy, but they did not extend that understanding to the general role of science in society. See Leonard Huxley, *The Life and Letters of Thomas Henry Huxley* (New York: D. Appleton & Co., 1900), 2 : 335–36.

no means decided." [15] Psychical research has continued to perplex serious psychologists and philosophers such as C. D. Broad, H. H. Price, Gardner Murphy, and J. R. Smythies. The impotence of liberal theology and scientific thought in confronting the personal and social consequences of death have increasingly imposed themselves on the public mind. Psychologists and political scientists in this century have embraced the presence of the irrational in man with a passion equaled only by that of their nineteenth-century forebear's determination to banish it.

Since the late nineteenth century the framework and categories of scientific thought have so shifted that few scientific commentators still believe or wish to believe that physical science is so perfect a paradigm of knowledge or so near completion that all other human questions must be referred to it. In 1914 Russell advised "caution as regards all use in philosophy of general *results* that science is supposed to have achieved." Those results had been the foundation of philosophical confidence for Spencer, Huxley, and Tyndall, but they had proved to be ephemeral. In the wake of what Derek Price termed "the first atomic explosion in history," the billard-ball atom of the nineteenth century was replaced by the "atom" of electrons and nuclear and, later, subnuclear particles.[16] Relativity undermined the idea that men are or could be passive observers of an unchanging natural order. Heisenberg's uncertainty principle fundamentally challenged traditional assumptions about strict causal necessity.

Just as the physical certainties of the Victorian scientific publicists faded, so also was their concept of a law of nature or of science considerably modified. In popular lectures they often retained (perhaps in spite of themselves) a juridicial concept of laws of nature. For example, Huxley once termed them "the rules of the game," and Tyndall wrote of "the methods by which the physical universe is

15. J. H. Randall, Jr., "Epilogue: The Nature of Naturalism," in *Naturalism and the Human Spirit,* ed. Yervant H. Krikorian (New York: Columbia University Press, 1944), p. 362; Bronislaw Malinowski, *The Foundations of Faith and Morals* (London: Oxford University Press, 1936), p. 59 (this lecture provides an excellent example of a onetime rationalist reexamining his original intellectual presuppositions); Bertrand Russell, "The Essence of Religion," *Hibbert Journal* 11 (1912–13), p. 46.

16. Bertrand Russell, *Mysticism and Logic and Other Essays* (London: Longmans, Green, & Co., 1918), p. 102; Derek J. de Solla Price, *Science since Babylon* (New Haven: Yale University Press, 1961), p. 91.

ordered and ruled." [17] Others, such as G. H. Lewes, expressed themselves more guardedly:

> A Law of Nature is not an Agent nor an Agency by which substances are coerced, but an abstract expression of the series of positions which substances assume under given conditions. It is not a creator of phenomena, it is their formula. It does not precede and coerce them, it is evolved by them.[18]

Whether described carefully or carelessly, the laws of nature for nineteenth-century authors possessed two qualities. First, they applied to the entire physical universe regarded as a single vast system. Second, they were considered to be impersonal, empirical descriptions of the operation of the physical world or more precisely physical phenomena.

These assumptions are no longer operative. Juridical or anthropomorphic interpretations of the laws of science have been abandoned. Scientific laws are commonly considered to express regularities of phenomena within a particular system rather than throughout all nature, that is, "the form of a regularity whose scope is stated elsewhere." Moreover, today the predictive value rather than the purely descriptive function or empirical basis often determines whether a hypothesis is considered a scientific law. As Braithwaite has explained, "The most important fact about our acceptance of a scientific law is that of enabling us to make reliable predictions, and this predictive function of a scientific law would be ignored if the function of the law were taken as being purely descriptive." [19]

In this century laws of science have become means of explanation; they rarely serve as modes of exhortation as they did for nineteenth-century publicists. As Samuel Butler might have approved, they are generally regarded as conventional arrangements whose chief charac-

17. T. H. Huxley, *Lay Sermons, Addresses, and Reviews* (London: Macmillan & Co., 1870), p. 36. Huxley is perhaps the most inconsistent of the scientists on the nature of law. See also T. H. Huxley, *Collected Essays* (New York: D. Appleton & Co., 1894), 5 : 74–80, 108–15; Oma Stanley, "T. H. Huxley's Treatment of 'Nature,'" *Journal of the History of Ideas* 18 (1957) : 120–27; and J. Tyndall, *Fragments of Science,* 6th ed. (New York: D. Appleton & Co., 1892), 1 : 132.

18. G. H. Lewes, *Problems of Life and Mind, First Series* (London: Trubner & Co., 1874), 1 : 366.

19. Stephen Toulmin, *The Philosophy of Science: An Introduction* (London: Hutchinson University Library, 1953), p. 86; R. B. Braithwaite, *Scientific Explanation: A Study of the Function of Theory* (Cambridge: Cambridge University Press, 1953), p. 348.

teristic is that they are useful and helpful. Again to quote Braithwaite,

> A calculus [of scientific explanation] is an artefact, and the interpretation of a calculus is a resolution to employ this artificial tool to organize our experience in a particular way—in a way appropriate both to enable us to make predictions as to the future course of our experience and to yield us intellectual satisfaction by providing systematic explanation.

Such admissions of pragmatic selectivity on the part of scientific thinkers (and these date from the turn of the century) combined with the expectation of future refinement or correction in presently accepted scientific generalizations have tended to make twentieth-century naturalistic writers somewhat less dogmatic and less sanguine than many of their nineteenth-century predecessors in attempting to create an entire philosophy of man and nature based on existing knowledge and theory. As Stephen Toulmin has recently commented,

> The problem of human understanding in the twentieth century is no longer . . . to recognize the fixed Essences of Nature. . . . Rather it is a problem that requires us to come to terms with the developing relationship between Human Ideas and a Natural World, neither of which is invariant.[20]

So much that seemed forever certain and decided for the nineteenth-century champions of science has in the course of a rather brief period of time once again become problematic.

Had Henry Sidgwick, Alfred Wallace, Frederic Myers, George Romanes, Samuel Butler, and James Ward come of age about a generation later, they might very well have been able to accommodate themselves to much of the naturalistic thought of the twentieth century and might not necessarily have considered science a threat to their inner ideals and aspirations. In all probability they would have rejected behaviorism and like the secular humanists would have been appalled by the destructive side of twentieth-century technology. Yet a generation or so later they would have found more intellectuals, and some even in the naturalistic camp, who shared many of their concerns. For example, just after the turn of the century Bertrand Russell, in private letters, wrote of religion

20. Ibid., p. 367; Toulmin, *Human Understanding*, 1 : 21.

as "an achievement, a victory, an assurance, that although man may be powerless, his ideals are not so," and urged the necessity of preserving "the seriousness of the religious attitude and its habit of asking ultimate questions." [21] Several years later, he publicly admitted the value of mystical feeling and contended, "Instinct, intuition, or insight is what first leads to the beliefs which subsequent reason confirms or confutes; but the confirmation, where it is possible, consists, in the last analysis, of agreement with other beliefs no less instinctive." [22] Russell had perhaps imbibed more from his classes with Sidgwick and Ward than he ever admitted or perhaps realized. In his tempered naturalism, which took into account a world of possibilities outside the categories and perceptions of science, Russell displayed an intellectual stance that the men in this study would have found congenial even if they could not have fully agreed with other features of Russell's philosophy.

In that later climate they would probably have felt less necessity to fend off both Christianity and naturalism. However, because they did come of age at what Myers described as "the very flood-tide of materialism, agnosticism—the mechanical theory of the Universe, the reduction of spiritual facts to physiological phenomena," they could find no intellectual home in the naturalism of their day, just as they had found no home in contemporary Christianity. They confronted the unpalatable choice of "a premature naturalism" that claimed "a final and complete philosophy can be worked out in terms of physical atomism or of blind and unconscious forces," or of "an antiquated Religion," that was "identified with some particular set of beliefs, which arising in the context of some historic culture, are laid down as an authoritative orthodoxy to which men's thinking must conform." [23] In the face of such alternatives, the only place for men who raised the issues of subjectivity, open speculation, values, ends, faith, and death lay between science and religion.

21. Bertrand Russell to G. Lowes Dickinson, 26 August 1902 and 16 July 1903, in *The Autobiography of Bertrand Russell* (New York: Bantam Books, 1967), pp. 247, 250. For a stimulating discussion of Russell's religious outlook during this period, see Ronald Jager, *The Development of Bertrand Russell's Philosophy* (London: George Allen & Unwin, 1972), pp. 484–587.

22. Russell, *Mysticism and Logic*, p. 13.

23. FM, *Fragments of Inner Life* (Privately printed, 1893), p. 15; S. P. Lamprecht, "Naturalism and Religion," in *Naturalism and the Human Spirit*, ed. Krikorian, p. 17.

Bibliographical Essay

What follows is not intended as a complete list either of works cited or of works consulted in the preparation of this study. It is meant rather to provide a convenient guide to some of the literature on Victorian scientific naturalism and religion and on the specific individuals who have been discussed. Many of the following volumes include extensive bibliographies that will aid the reader in further research and study.

VICTORIAN SCIENCE, NATURALISM, AND RELIGION

Certain standard works remain both useful and essential for an understanding of nineteenth-century science and its relation to other fields of thought. Among the most helpful are William C. Dampier, *A History of Science and Its Relations with Philosophy and Religion*, 4th ed. (Cambridge: Cambridge University Press, 1961); Charles Singer, *A Short History of Science in the Nineteenth Century* (London: Oxford University Press, 1941); and, of course, J. T. Merz, *A History of European Thought in the Nineteenth Century*, 4 vols. (Edinburgh and London: W. Blackwood & Sons, 1896–1914). The modifications in scientific outlook since the mid-nineteenth century are outlined in Herbert Dingle, ed., *A Century of Science, 1851–1951* (New York: Roy Publishers, 1951). H. L. Sharlin points out the increasing interdependence and interrelationships of the several scientific disciplines in *The Convergent Century: The Unification of Science in the Nineteenth Century* (New York: Abelard–Schuman, 1966). As the study of Victorian science moves from general to more specific subjects, the difference between the scientific publicists and the laboratory scientists will loom larger.

No single work on the nineteenth-century philosophy of science has yet appeared, but two helpful articles are Curt J. Ducasse, "Whewell's Philosophy of Scientific Discovery," *Philosophical Review* 60 (1951): 59–69, 213–34, and Edward W. Strong, "William Whewell and John Stuart Mill: Their Controversy about Scientific Knowledge," *Journal of the History of Ideas* 16 (1955): 209–31. Less technical discussions of considerable importance are found in two articles by Walter F. Cannon, "The Normative Role of Science in Early Victorian Thought," *Journal of the History of Ideas* 25 (1964): 487–502, and "Scientists and Broad

Churchmen: An Early Victorian Intellectual Network," *Journal of British Studies* 4 (1964): 65–88. Charles C. Gillispie considers the modifications in scientific thought prior to Darwin in *Genesis and Geology: A Study in the Relations of Scientific Thought, Natural Theology, and Social Opinion in Great Britain, 1790–1850* (New York: Harper Torchbooks, 1959). Alvar Ellegard explores the problem of natural selection and contemporary philosophy of science in *Darwin and the General Reader: The Reception of Darwin's Theory of Evolution in the British Periodical Press, 1859–1872* (Göteborg, 1958). A veritable treasure chest of largely untapped information exists in the annual *Report of the British Association for the Advancement of Science,* (London: John Murray, 1833–1938).

Naturally, evolution has occupied the attention of numerous writers. One can only hope that the examination of Darwin will soon be supplemented by studies of contemporaries of lesser stature. On Darwin one should begin with Loren Eiseley, *Darwin's Century: Evolution and the Men Who Discovered It* (Garden City, N. Y.: Doubleday & Co., 1961) and immediately pass on to Gavin DeBeer's *Charles Darwin: Evolution by Natural Selection* (London: Nelson, 1963). Phillip Appleman's recently published anthology *Darwin* (New York: W. W. Norton & Co., 1970) gathers together documents which relate to the entire development of evolution both prior to and after Darwin. Robert Young has set evolution within the general context of midcentury thought in "The Impact of Darwin on Conventional Thought," in *The Victorian Crisis of Faith,* ed. Anthony Symondson (London: Society for Promoting Christian Knowledge, 1970), pp. 13–35. Young is incorrect, however, in his remarks on Alfred Wallace and perhaps overemphasizes the fact that many evolutionists were not antitheistic. Peter J. Vorzimmer's *Charles Darwin: The Years of Controversy, the Origin of Species and Its Critics, 1859–1882* (Philadelphia: Temple University Press, 1970) is an important addition to the neglected story of evolutionary theory after 1859.

All the naturalistic writers were as deeply involved with psychology as with other issues. There are few adequate histories. Robert Young's *Mind, Brain, and Adaptation in the Nineteenth Century: Cerebral Localization and Its Biological Context from Gall to Ferrier* (Oxford: The Clarendon Press, 1970) is a far more broad-ranging discussion than its title suggests. Young includes important information on phrenology. One should also consult the following standard works: T. Ribot, *English Psychology* (New York: D. Appleton & Co., 1874); Howard Warren, *A History of Associationist Psychology* (New York: C. Scribner's Sons, 1921); R. S. Peters, ed., *Brett's History of Psychology* (London: Allen & Unwin, 1953); and L. S. Hearnshaw, *A Short History of British Psychology*

1840–1940 (New York: Barnes & Noble, 1964). Henri Ellenberger's *The Discovery of the Unconscious* (New York: Basic Books, 1970) demonstrates the serious interest in that subject expressed by numerous writers throughout the nineteenth century.

The advocates of scientific naturalism remain their own best expositors. Their major works are T. H. Huxley, *Collected Essays,* 9 vols. (New York: D. Appleton & Co., 1893–1894); John Tyndall, *Fragments of Science,* 2 vols., 6th ed. (New York: D. Appleton & Co., 1892); Francis Galton, *English Men of Science: Their Nature and Nurture* (New York: D. Appleton & Co., 1875); W. K. Clifford, *Lectures and Essays,* ed. L. Stephen and F. Pollock, 2 vols. (London: Macmillan & Co., 1901); F. H. Collins, *Epitome of the Synthetic Philosophy* (New York: D. Appleton & Co., 1889). These men were also frequent contributors to the *Fortnightly Review* and the *Nineteenth Century.*

The secondary works on scientific naturalism are many and of varied quality. The two earliest, A. W. Benn, *A History of English Rationalism in the Nineteenth Century,* 2 vols. (London: Longmans, Green & Co., 1906) and J. M. Robertson, *A History of Freethought,* 2 vols. (New York: G. P. Putnam's Sons, 1930), are still valuable but highly polemical. For the larger context, see Franklin Le Van Baumer, *Religion and the Rise of Scepticism* (New York: Harcourt, Brace & Co., 1960) and H. G. Wood, *Belief and Unbelief since 1850* (Cambridge: Cambridge University Press, 1955). Alan Brown's *The Metaphysical Society: Victorian Minds in Conflict, 1869–1880* (New York: Columbia University Press, 1947) is a source of continuing stimulation. In *Evolution and Society: A Study in Victorian Social Theory* (Cambridge: Cambridge University Press, 1966), J. W. Burrow suggests that many thinkers turned to evolution for reasons that had little or nothing to do with scientific theory. Noel Annan's *Sir Leslie Stephen: His Thought and Character in Relation to His Time* (London: MacGibbon and Kee, 1951) remains essential reading, although agnosticism was a much more diffuse concept than he suggests. Sidney Eisen has contributed several very important articles on the English Positivists and their relationship to other freethinkers. These include "Frederic Harrison and the Religion of Humanity," *South Atlantic Quarterly* 66 (1967) : 574–90; "Huxley and the Positivists," *Victorian Studies* 7 (1964) : 337–58; and "Frederic Harrison and Herbert Spencer: Embattled Unbelievers," *Victorian Studies* 12 (1968) : 33–56. For a rather loosely organized treatment of free thought toward the end of the century, see Warren Sylvester Smith, *The London Heretics, 1870–1914* (New York: Dodd, Mead & Co., 1968).

For the history of the church and its relation to the new currents of thought, consult Owen Chadwick's *The Victorian Church,* 2 vols. (London: Oxford University Press, 1966, 1970); L. E. Elliott–Binns, *English Thought, 1860–1900: The Theological Aspect* (London: Longmans, Green, & Co., 1956); and Bernard M. G. Reardon, *From Coleridge to Gore: A Century of Religious Thought in Britain* (London: Longman, 1971). Of course, Basil Willey's *Nineteenth Century Studies* (New York: Harper Torchbooks, 1966) and *More Nineteenth Century Studies* (New York: Harper Torchbooks, 1966) remain important. However, the works on the church and those on the naturalistic thinkers rarely suggest that there were highly intelligent men who stood aloof from both Christianity and scientific naturalism.

HENRY SIDGWICK

Of that peculiarly Victorian genre, the life and letters of late distinguished men, one of the very finest is A. and E. Sidgwick's *Henry Sidgwick: A Memoir* (London: Macmillan & Co., 1906). This volume remains the single best source for Sidgwick's life and for the concerns that underlay his thought. It also contains a complete bibliography of his writings. His unpublished papers in the Trinity College Library, Cambridge, add some information but in no way change the portait drawn by his wife and brother. The only other scholar to make use of these papers is Alan Gauld, whose study *The Founders of Psychical Research* (New York: Schocken Books, 1968) examines Sidgwick's role in founding and aiding the Society for Psychical Research. Gauld does not probe deeply into the relationship of psychical research to Sidgwick's philosophy and personal life. The latter subjects are admirably and succinctly discussed by Professor C. D. Broad in *Ethics and the History of Philosophy* (New York: Humanities Press, 1952) and *Religion, Philosophy, and Psychical Research* (New York: Harcourt, Brace & Co., 1953). Broad's *Five Types of Ethical Theory* (London: Routledge & Kegan Paul, 1967) provides the clearest guide to Sidgwick's ethical thought. W. C. Havard examines Sidgwick's social ideas in *Henry Sidgwick and Later Utilitarian Political Philosophy* (Gainesville, Fla.: University of Florida Press, 1959). The late D. G. James delivered a series of thoughtful lectures entitled *Henry Sidgwick: Science and Faith in Victorian England* (London: Oxford University Press, 1970). He included a very perceptive essay on Sidgwick and Arthur Hugh Clough. Sidgwick's own essay on Clough is included in Henry Sidgwick, *Miscellaneous Essays and Addresses*, ed. A. and E. Sidgwick (London: Macmillan & Co., 1904). This collection is the best introduction to the problems that interested Sidgwick. These essays should be supplemented by Henry Sidgwick, *The Methods of Ethics*, 7th ed. (Chicago: University of Chicago Press, 1962); *Philosophy, Its Scope and Relations: An Introductory Course of Lectures*, ed. James Ward (London: Macmillan & Co., 1902); *Lectures on the Philosophy of Kant and Other Philosophical Lectures and Essays,* ed. James Ward (London: Macmillan & Co., 1905); and "The Theory of Evolution in Its Application and Practice," *Mind* 1 (1876) : 52–67.

ALFRED RUSSEL WALLACE

One must approach Alfred Russel Wallace primarily through his own work. His autobiography *My Life: A Record of Events and Opinions,* 2 vols. (New York: Dodd, Mead & Co., 1905) is long, rambling, and often unclear or inconsistent about dates. He polished and edited most of the letters he included. It should be supplemented by James Marchant's *Alfred Russel Wallace: Letters and Reminiscences,* 2 vols. (New York: Cassell & Co., 1916), a wholly uncritical biography but one that contains considerable primary material, including the entire Wallace–Darwin correspondence, and a bibliography of Wallace's works. There are three major collections of Wallace manuscripts. The largest is that in the British Museum, which consists primarily of his correspondence. The Linnean Society possesses his notebooks and a few letters. Several very important early letters remain in the possession of his grandson, Mr. John Wallace of Bournemouth.

The most significant of his scientific works, as far as the present study is concerned, are to be found in Alfred Russel Wallace, *Contributions to the Theory of Natural Selection* (London: Macmillan & Co., 1870), and *Darwinism* (London: Macmillan & Co., 1889). The original version of his 1864 Anthropological Society address should be consulted in the *Journal of the Anthropological Society* 2 (1864) : 108–70. Wallace also wrote widely on social issues. In addition to the closing passages of *The Malay Archipelago* (New York: Dover Publications, 1962) one should examine his essays in *Studies Scientific and Social,* 2 vols. (London: Macmillan & Co., 1900) and *The Wonderful Century* (New York: Dodd, Mead & Co., 1899).

Wallace's spiritualistic writings are extensive but not particularly original within the context of such literature. His works in this area include the following: "Review of R. D. Owen's *The Debatable Land between This World and the Next,*" *Quarterly Journal of Science* 9 (1872) : 237–47; "Review of Carpenter's *Mesmerism, Spiritualism, etc.,*" *Quarterly Journal of Science* 14 (1877) : 391–416; "Psychological Curiosities of Scepticism," *Fraser's* 16 (1877) : 694–706; "Are the Phenomena of Spiritualism in Harmony with Science?" and "The 'Journal of Science' on Spiritualism," *Light* 5 (1885) : 255–56, 327–28; *If a Man Die, Shall He Live Again?: A Lecture* (San Francisco, 1887); "Spiritualism," *Chamber's Encyclopedia* (Edinburgh: W. and R. Chambers, 1892), 9 : 645–49; "Why

Live a Moral Life?" (1895), "Justice Not Charity" (1899), and "True Individualism" (1899), in *Studies Scientific and Social* 2 : 375–83, 510–20, 521–28; *Miracles and Modern Spiritualism*, rev. and enl. ed. with chapters on Apparitions and Phantasms (London: Nichols, 1901); and *The World of Life: A Manifestation of Creative Power, Directive Mind and Ultimate Purpose* (London: Chapman and Hall, 1910). Wallace also contributed numerous letters to the editor in defense of spiritualism among which are those found in *The Spiritual Magazine* 2 (1867) : 51–52; *Report on Spiritualism of the Committee of the London Dialectical Society* (London: Longmans, Green, Read & Dyer, 1871), pp. 82–90; *Nature* 5 (1872) : 363–64; 17 (1877) : 101; *Times,* 4 January 1873, p. 10; and the *Journal of the Society for Psychical Research* 9 (1890): 22–30, 56–57.

Wallace has not fared so well among the historians of science as has Darwin. The only substantial biography is Wilma George's *Biologist Philosopher: A Study of the Life and Writings of Alfred Russel Wallace* (New York: Abelard–Schuman, 1964). Ms. George did not consult any of the manuscripts. Her discussion of Wallace is more of a general overview than a critical assessment. In *Darwin's Century* Eiseley contributes a sympathetic but erroneous chapter on Wallace. Another significant discussion is Barbara Beddall, "Wallace, Darwin, and the Theory of Natural Selection," *Journal of the History of Biology* 1 (1968) : 261–323. All previous studies must now take second place to H. Lewis McKinney's fine work on *Wallace and Natural Selection* (New Haven: Yale University Press, 1972). However, these books and articles take little account of the influence of phrenology on all of Wallace's thought.

FREDERIC W. H. MYERS

In 1893 Frederic Myers composed a very brief autobiography entitled *Fragments of Inner Life,* which was privately printed. Myers took exceptional precautions with this pamphlet because its central event was his affair with Annie Marshall, whom he called Phyllis in this work. Moreover, he related the incident through a number of poems calculated to conceal more than to reveal. In a prefatory note to the private edition of *Fragments of Inner Life,* which was limited to twenty-five copies, Myers wrote:

> I desire that the following sketch should someday be published in its entirety; but it may probably be well to reserve at least part of it until some years after my death. To avert accidents, therefore, I now propose to get these pages privately printed, and to send a sealed copy to each of the following intimate friends: Professor Henry

Sidgwick, Cambridge; Professor Oliver Lodge, Liverpool; Professor William James, Harvard; Dr. R. Hodgson, Boston; Sir R. H. Collins, K. C. B., Claremont; Mr. R. W. Raper, Oxford. I shall desire these friends to open the packet after my death, and I shall be grateful if any of them, in the order in which their names are mentioned, will act as my literary executor using their discretion as to the publication both of this privately printed matter and of matter already given to the world; but not publish in my wife's lifetime anything to whose publication she may object (p. 3).

Mrs. Myers understandably did object to the more intimate passages of the sketch. However, she published an abridged version which contained most of Myers's account of his intellectual development in F. W. H. Myers, *Fragments of Prose and Poetry*, ed. Eveleen Myers (London: Longmans, Green, & Co., 1904). Of the twenty-five original copies, all but the six distributed to trusted friends remained in the leather box where Myers had deposited them in 1893. (Most of them were still there in 1969 when the present author consulted them.) There the matter stood until 1961 when Myers's granddaughters permitted the Society for Psychical Research to publish the sketch as F. W. H. Myers, *Fragments of Inner Life* (London: The Society for Psychical Research, 1961).

Three collections contain the most important of the manuscript materials for Myers. The smallest is that of several letters to J. A. Symonds in the University of Bristol Library. The second consists of a large number of letters from Myers to Oliver Lodge preserved in the Sir Oliver Lodge Papers in the Archives of the Society for Psychical Research, London. The most significant collection of materials is that which until late in 1969 was in the possession of Mrs. E. Q. Nicholson, a granddaughter. The author consulted these manuscripts in Mrs. Nicholson's home, but since then they have been deposited in the Trinity College Library, Cambridge.

There is no biography of Myers. The most useful discussion is in Alan Gauld's *The Founders of Psychical Research*. Professor Gauld is a psychologist at the University of Nottingham and the present editor of the *Journal of the Society for Psychical Research*. He has been able to draw not only upon all relevant manuscript materials but also upon the oral tradition of the Society for Psychical Research. His study is quite excellent, but it does not take into account the broad interest in the unconscious that was manifest throughout the nineteenth century. The most perceptive discussions of Myers in regard to contemporary psychology are found in William James, *Memories and Studies* (New York and London: Longmans, Green & Co., 1911) and his review of *Human Person-*

ality in *The Proceedings of the Society for Psychical Research* (London: R. Brimley Johnson, 1904), 18 : 22–23. Also consult William McDougall, "Critical Notice of F. W. H. Myers' *Human Personality and Its Survival of Bodily Death,"* *Mind,* 12 (1903) : 513–26, and G. F. Stout, "Mr. Frederic Myers' *Human Personality and Its Survival of Bodily Death,"* *Hibbert Journal* 2 (1903–04) : 44–64.

Human Personality and Its Survival of Bodily Death, 2 vols. (New Impression, London: Longmans, Green, & Co., 1915) remains the most important work for an understanding of Myers. However, it must be read in the context of the essays he published in F. W. H. Myers, *Science and a Future Life with Other Essays* (London: Macmillan Co., 1893) and *Essays: Classical and Modern* (London: Macmillan & Co., 1921). A bibliography of his contributions to the *Journal* and the *Proceedings of the Society for Psychical Research* appears as an appendix to Oliver Lodge, *Conviction of Survival: Two Discourses* (London: 1930).

GEORGE JOHN ROMANES

Ethel Romanes's *The Life and Letters of George John Romanes* (London: Longmans, Green, & Co., 1896) stands as the chief source of information on his life. It should be immediately supplemented by the excellent article by C. Lloyd Morgan, "George John Romanes," *Dictionary of National Biography* (London: Oxford University Press, 1949–1950), 17 : 177–80. The essay "Through Scientific Doubt to Faith," *Quarterly Review* 183 (1896) : 285–309 is by far the most perceptive and sensible of contemporary accounts. However, the letters from Romanes to T. H. Huxley, which have not been previously published or consulted, cast important new light on the Romanes episode. These are in the Huxley Papers, Imperial College of Science and Technology, London. The most important of Romanes's own works in regard to the development of his religious thought are *Christian Prayer and General Laws being the Burney Prize Essay for the year 1873, with an Appendix, The Physical Efficiency of Prayer* (London: Macmillan & Co., 1874); *A Candid Examination of Theism* (Boston: Houghton, Osgood, & Co., 1878); *Thoughts on Religion,* ed. Charles Gore (Chicago: The Open Court Publishing Co., 1895); and *Mind and Motion and Monism,* ed. C. Lloyd Morgan (London: Longmans, Green, & Co., 1895).

SAMUEL BUTLER

The literature on Samuel Butler is immense. The major primary sources are *The Shrewsbury Edition of the Works of Samuel Butler,* ed. H. F. Jones and A. T. Bartholomew, 20 vols. (London: Jonathan Cape,

1923–1926); *The Note-Books of Samuel Butler,* ed. H. F. Jones (London: Fifield, 1913); *Further Extracts from the Note-Books of Samuel Butler,* ed. A. T. Bartholomew (London: Jonathan Cape, 1934); *Samuel Butler and E. M. A. Savage, Letters, 1871–1885,* ed. Geoffrey Keynes and Brian Hill (London: Jonathan Cape, 1935); *The Family Letters of Samuel Butler,* ed. Arnold Silver (Stanford, Calif.: Stanford University Press, 1962); and *The Correspondence of Samuel Butler and His Sister May,* ed. Daniel F. Howard (Berkeley, Calif.: University of California Press, 1962). Daniel F. Howard's edition of *The Way of All Flesh* (London: Methuen & Co., 1965) supplants all previous editions. There are two chief collections of Butler's papers. Twelve volumes of his self-annotated correspondence are in the British Museum. The four volumes of his notebooks are preserved in the Chapin Library, Williams College, Williamstown, Massachusetts.

So much has been written about Butler by both admirers and detractors that it is almost impossible to know if one has said anything original. One can only hope to have been sensible where others have often been silly. There are two bibliographies of writings by and about Butler. These are J. A. Hoppé, *A Bibliography of the Writings of Samuel Butler* (London: Bookmans, 1925) and Stanley B. Harkness, *The Career of Samuel Butler 1835–1902: A Bibliography* (New York: Macmillan Co., 1956). The latter is the definitive work.

Seven secondary volumes deserve special mention. Henry Festing Jones, *Samuel Butler, Author of Erewhon (1835–1902): A Memoir,* 2 vols. (London: Macmillan & Co., 1919) was written by his close friend and confidant. It is a mine of information but wholly uncritical. Most of the letters reprinted in this work were edited to conform to Butler's self-image. This is especially true in regard to his relationship with his family. C. E. M. Joad's *Samuel Butler 1835–1902* (London: Leonard Parsons, 1924) represents a discussion of Butler in the halcyon days of his postwar popularity. Joad attempts, rather unconvincingly, to demonstrate Butler's influence on later thought. He includes an excellent chapter on Butler's hatred of professionalism. Probably the best English biography is Clara Stillman's *Samuel Butler, a Mid-Victorian Modern* (New York: The Viking Press, 1932). Ms. Stillman's treatment is generally even-handed but quite weak on Butler's philosophy. Malcolm Muggeridge demonstrates the exasperation that Butler could still arouse thirty-four years after his death in *A Study of Samuel Butler, the Earnest Atheist* (London: G. P. Putnam, 1936). The single finest study of Butler is Joseph Fort, *Samuel Butler (1835–1902), Etude d'un Caractère et d'une Intelligence* (Bordeaux: J. Biere, 1934). The Butler–Darwin quarrel has been thoroughly set forth by Basil Willey in *Darwin and Butler: Two Versions of Evolution* (London: Chatto and Windus, 1960). Lee E. Holt contributes a suggestive analysis in *Samuel Butler* (New York: Grosset & Dunlap, 1964). Unfortunately, in his eagerness to give Butler's thought further stature, Holt associates his subject with almost every seminal mind who wrote after Butler. The major problem with all these works is that they pay both too much and too little attention to what Butler wrote about himself. His quarrel with his family and with Darwin receive considerable attention but not the underlying desire for a world of emancipating rather than constricting conventions. Moreover, too often Butler's comments about the purpose of his books have been ignored. Also, as suggested in the chapter on Butler, he has been regarded as a unique figure when in reality he was but the most successful of numerous minor figures who attempted to find a place for mind in the nature described by the scientific publicists.

James Ward

Virtually the only information on the life of James Ward is contained in the "Memoir" by his daughter Olwen Ward Campbell in James Ward, *Essays on Philosophy*, ed. W. R. Sorley and G. F. Stout (Cambridge: Cambridge University Press, 1927). Except for an occasional letter, there are no remaining manuscripts. A bibliography of Ward's works appears in *Monist* 36 (1926): 170–76. A. H. Murray, *The Philosophy of James Ward* (Cambridge: Cambridge University Press, 1937) is the only full treatment of his thought. Murray gives his subject no historic dimensions. Moreover, he incorrectly assesses Ward's religious thought as Christian theism.

Numerous articles on Ward's ideas appeared during his lifetime and immediately after his death. On his psychology consult A. Bain, "Mr. James Ward's Psychology," *Mind* 11 (1886): 457–77; G. Dawes Hicks, "Professor Ward's Psychological Principles," *Mind* 30 (1921): 1–24, and "The Philosophy of James Ward," *Mind* 34 (1925): 281–89; J. Laird, "James Ward's Account of the Ego," *Monist* 36 (1926): 90–110; Emmanuel Leroux, "James Ward's Doctrine of Experience," *Monist* 36 (1926): 70–89; G. F. Stout, "Ward as a Psychologist," *Monist* 36 (1926): 20–55; D. W. Hamlyn, "Bradley, Ward, and Stout," in *Historical Roots of Contemporary Psychology*, ed. Benjamin B. Wolman (New York: Harper & Row, 1968), pp. 297–311. His attack on naturalism is discussed in S. P. Lamprecht, "James Ward's Critique of Naturalism," *Monist* 36 (1926): 136–52. For considerations of his theism, see G. Dawes Hicks, "James Ward's Philosophical Approach to Theism," *Hibbert Journal* 24 (1925–1926): 49–63, and P. A. Bertocci, *The Empirical Argument for*

God in Late British Thought (Cambridge, Mass.: Harvard University Press, 1938), pp. 92–133. All these articles tend to be strictly philosophical and rarely relate Ward to intellectual developments outside of England or even to the strands of thought discussed in this study.

These relationships become quite evident in Ward's major works. See J. Ward, "Psychology," *Encyclopaedia Britannica*, 9th ed., 20 : 37–85; *Psychological Principles* (Cambridge: Cambridge University Press, 1918); *Naturalism and Agnosticism*, 2 vols. (London: A. and C. Black, 1899); *The Realm of Ends or Pluralism and Theism* (Cambridge University Press, 1911); and *Essays in Philosophy* (1927). The nature of the late nineteenth- and early twentieth-century revolt against positivism of which these books are a part is discussed in Antonio Aliotta, *The Idealistic Reaction Against Science* (London: Macmillan & Co., 1914); H. Stuart Hughes, *Consciousness and Society: The Reorientation of European Social Thought, 1890–1930* (New York: Vintage Books, 1958); and H. Spiegelberg, *The Phenomenological Movement: A Historical Introduction,* 2 vols. (The Hague: Nijhoff, 1965).

ADDENDUM, 1976

Mr. Lawrence F. Barmann has called to my attention a collection of over twenty letters from James Ward to Baron Friedrich von Hügel written between 1900 and 1922 which are deposited in the Saint Andrews University Library, Saint Andrews, Scotland. There are also a few letters from Ward to Croom Robertson in the library of University College, London.

Index